Super States

Puzzles, Games and Fascinating Trivia About the United States

by Cindy Barden

illustrated by Corbin Hillam

Teaching & Learning Company

1204 Buchanan St., P.O. Box 10
Carthage, IL 62321

This book belongs to

_____

 This book was developed for the Teaching & Learning Company
by The Good Neighbor Press, Inc., Grand Junction, CO.

Cover design by The Good Neighbor Press, Inc.

Cover illustrations by Corbin Hillam

Copyright © 1995, Teaching & Learning Company

ISBN No. 1-57310-029-3

Printing No. 98765432

Teaching & Learning Company
1204 Buchanan St., P.O. Box 10
Carthage, IL 62321

Table of Contents

Dear Teacher,

Why is Oklahoma called the Sooner State? What is the official state drink of Arkansas? Where would you find a city that elected a cat as its mayor? You and your students can learn the answers to these and many other questions as you travel together through the pages of Super States!

Super States! is arranged alphabetically by state but can be used in any order you prefer. For each state; you'll find a map and page of fun facts about the state including state firsts, biggest, smallest, highest and lowest. Two to three additional pages of material for each state give students a chance to learn as they play games like Alabama Bingo, Florida Tic-Tac-Toe and Louisiana Question Game. They can unscramble letters to find the names of animals in Alaska and solve a word search puzzle looking for cities in Michigan.

The majority of activities in this book are self-contained. Students can answer the questions, solve the puzzles and play the games without outside reference material. For each state, you'll also find two Challenge Questions which require students to reach out to other sources for the answers.

At the end of the book there's a master bingo game sheet, U.S. maps, suggestions for other activities and an answer key.

These activities are written for students in the third to sixth grades. Select the materials that are appropriate for your students' ages and abilities. You can use these activities in conjunction with other geography, history or social studies materials. Many are also appropriate for language arts. While the majority of these activities are written for individual student use, many would work well with small groups and some could be done by the entire class.

While this material has been created primarily to supplement your curriculum, you may find some items useful in proficiency and assessment programs, display materials for bulletin boards or parent conferences, take-home communiques with parents or care-givers and much, much more!

Sincerely,

Cindy

Cindy Barden

Alabama

Nickname: Yellowhammer State • State Bird: Yellowhammer • Capital: Montgomery

■ The world's largest cake was baked in honor of Fort Payne's 100th birthday in 1989. Shaped like the state of Alabama, this monster cake weighed 128,238.5 pounds.

■ Alabama was named for the Alibamu Indians whose name meant "thicket clearers" or "vegetation gatherers."

■ During the Civil War, soldiers from Alabama wore bright yellow patches on their uniforms. People said they looked like yellow-hammer woodpeckers. That's how Alabama got the nickname, the Yellowhammer State.

■ The first Confederate submarine, the *Huntley* was built in Mobile during the Civil War.

■ Opossums, the only marsupials (animals with pouches) found outside of Australia, live in the forests of Alabama.

■ In 1961, an Alabama farmer dug up a whale's skeleton 75 miles north of the Gulf of Mexico. Fossils of sea turtles and other marine animals have also been found in Alabama, far from the nearest water.

■ Did you know that Alabama is also known as the Heart of Dixie?

■ The only monument to an insect pest is in Enterprise, Alabama. On top of a fancy pedestal, a statue of a woman holds a giant boll weevil in her arms. The inscription reads: "In profound appreciation of the boll weevil and what it has done as the herald of prosperity." After weevils destroyed most of Alabama's cotton crop in the early 1900s, farmers learned to plant other crops.

Fort Payne

■ Russel Cave in northeastern Alabama was home to prehistoric people over 9,000 years ago.

Montgomery

■ Montgomery became the birthplace of the Civil Rights movement in 1955 when police arrested Rosa Parks for sitting in the "whites only" section of a city bus. Dr. Martin Luther King led protests against her arrest. A year later the Supreme Court decided that segregated buses were not legal.

Enterprise

Dothan

Mobile

■ Residents of Mobile claim that the first Mardi Gras festival in North America was held in their city in 1703.

■ The world's largest helicopter collection can be found at the United States Army Aviation Museum in Fort Rucker, Alabama.

■ Southern leaders met in Montgomery in 1861 to form the Confederate States of America. Nicknamed the "Cradle of the Confederacy," Montgomery became the Confederate capital for a short time until it was moved to Richmond, Virginia.

■ Before Montgomery became the capital of Alabama in 1846, the state had four other capitals: St. Stephens, Huntsville, Cahaba and Tuscaloosa.

■ The tarpon is Alabama's state saltwater fish. Marble is the state rock and the camellia ia the state flower.

■ Each year a contest is held in Dothan, Alabama, for the best peanut recipe.

Hooray for Peanuts!

A former slave, this man became famous for making over 300 new products from peanuts including ink, soap and shaving cream. Through his efforts, peanuts became a major crop in Alabama.

59 50 2 33 51 23   15 54 21 28 19 3 5 34 12 58   37 29 45 49 16 9

To find the answer, fill in the blanks below. Write the letter that corresponds with the number below each blank.

1. Where was the first capital of the Confederate States of America located?

1 2 3 4 5 6 7 8 9 10

2. Name the insects that destroyed most of Alabama's cotton crop in the early 1800s.

11 12 13 14   15 16 17 18 19 20 21

3. What nickname for Alabama came from a type of woodpecker?

The ___ ___ ___ ___ ___ ___ ___ ___ ___ ___ ___ ___ State
22 23 24 25 26 27 28 29 30 31 32 33

4. The word *Alabama* means:

"___ ___ ___ ___ ___ ___ ___   ___ ___ ___ ___ ___ ___ ___ ___" or
34 35 36 37 38 39 40   41 42 43 44 45 46 47 48

"___ ___ ___ ___ ___ ___ ___ ___ ___ ___   ___ ___ ___ ___ ___ ___ ___ ___ ___."
49 50 51 52 53 54 55 56 57 58   59 60 61 62 63 64 65 66 67

Challenge Questions

1. Describe some of Martin Luther King, Jr.'s accomplishments as a Civil Rights leader in Alabama.

2. How did the 1783 Treaty of Paris affect the area that later became Alabama?

Just for Fun

What did the Alabama scientist get when he crossed a turkey with an octopus?

Alabama Bingo

To the Teacher: The master game sheet, rules and game suggestions are on pages 179 and 180.

Statements for Alabama Bingo

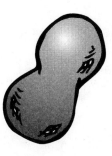

- One of Alabama's nicknames is **the Heart of Dixie**.
- The capital of Alabama is **Montgomery**.
- **George Washington Carver** became famous for making more than 300 new products from peanuts.
- The **Gulf of Mexico** is south of Alabama.
- **Dolphins** swim in the waters of the Gulf of Mexico.
- **Georgia** is east of Alabama.
- The **yellowhammer** is Alabama's state bird.
- **Mississippi** is west of Alabama.
- **Alligators** can be found in Alabama's swamps and bayous.
- **Tennessee** is north of Alabama.
- Steel and iron are made in **Birmingham**.

- **Opossums** live in the forests of Alabama.
- Alabama's state fish is the **largemouth bass**.
- Alabama was named for the **Alibamus**.
- The **Cherokee** lived in Alabama when white settlers first arrived.
- The first Europeans in Alabama were **Spanish explorers**.
- **Hank Aaron** was a famous baseball player from Alabama.
- **Rosa Parks** was arrested in 1955 for sitting in the "whites only" section of a bus in Montgomery.
- **Dr. Martin Luther King, Jr.** led African Americans to fight for Civil Rights in Alabama.
- In 1956 the Supreme Court declared that **segregation** was not legal.
- Alabama was one of the states to secede from the Union during the **Civil War**.
  - **Peanuts** are an important crop in Alabama.
  - **Jesse Owens** won four gold medals in track at the 1936 Olympics.
  - The **boll weevil** is an insect that destroyed much of Alabama's cotton crop.

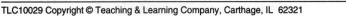

Alabama Puzzler

Research to fill in the puzzle using the clues.

Across

3. Helicopter collection at Fort _____
7. _____ of Dixie
9. Marsupial found in Alabama woods
10. Alabama state flower

Down

1. Alabama state rock
2. Confederate submarine
4. Alabama was named for this Native American tribe
5. Alabama state saltwater fish
6. Cave where people lived over 9,000 years ago
8. This city claims first Mardi Gras

Silly Sayings

Use the letters in the word *Alabama* as the first letters of words in a silly saying. Here's an example:

Alvin **l**iked **A**nn, **b**ut **A**nn **m**arried **A**ndy.

Write your silly saying below:

A_____ l_____ a_____ b_____ a_____ m_____ a_____

An Alabama Report Card

Wouldn't it be nice to get a report card with as many *A*s as there are in *Alabama*? Not many words have four *A*s. Here are a few:

Appalachian

Casablanca

Extravaganza

Madagascar

Maharajah

Panamanian

Can you think of any other words that have several *A*s?

Alaska

Nickname: The Last Frontier • State Bird: Willow Ptarmigan • Capital: Juneau

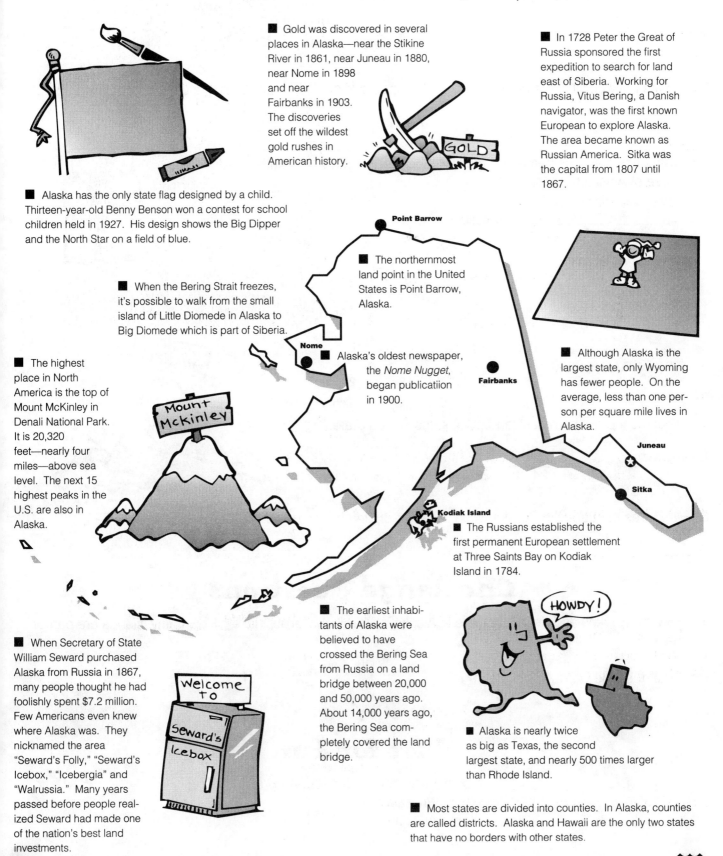

■ Gold was discovered in several places in Alaska—near the Stikine River in 1861, near Juneau in 1880, near Nome in 1898 and near Fairbanks in 1903. The discoveries set off the wildest gold rushes in American history.

■ In 1728 Peter the Great of Russia sponsored the first expedition to search for land east of Siberia. Working for Russia, Vitus Bering, a Danish navigator, was the first known European to explore Alaska. The area became known as Russian America. Sitka was the capital from 1807 until 1867.

■ Alaska has the only state flag designed by a child. Thirteen-year-old Benny Benson won a contest for school children held in 1927. His design shows the Big Dipper and the North Star on a field of blue.

■ When the Bering Strait freezes, it's possible to walk from the small island of Little Diomede in Alaska to Big Diomede which is part of Siberia.

■ The northernmost land point in the United States is Point Barrow, Alaska.

Point Barrow

Nome

■ Alaska's oldest newspaper, the *Nome Nugget*, began publicatiion in 1900.

Fairbanks

■ Although Alaska is the largest state, only Wyoming has fewer people. On the average, less than one person per square mile lives in Alaska.

■ The highest place in North America is the top of Mount McKinley in Denali National Park. It is 20,320 feet—nearly four miles—above sea level. The next 15 highest peaks in the U.S. are also in Alaska.

Mount McKinley

Juneau

Sitka

Kodiak Island

■ The Russians established the first permanent European settlement at Three Saints Bay on Kodiak Island in 1784.

■ When Secretary of State William Seward purchased Alaska from Russia in 1867, many people thought he had foolishly spent $7.2 million. Few Americans even knew where Alaska was. They nicknamed the area "Seward's Folly," "Seward's Icebox," "Icebergia" and "Walrussia." Many years passed before people realized Seward had made one of the nation's best land investments.

Welcome to Seward's Icebox

■ The earliest inhabitants of Alaska were believed to have crossed the Bering Sea from Russia on a land bridge between 20,000 and 50,000 years ago. About 14,000 years ago, the Bering Sea completely covered the land bridge.

HOWDY!

■ Alaska is nearly twice as big as Texas, the second largest state, and nearly 500 times larger than Rhode Island.

■ Most states are divided into counties. In Alaska, counties are called districts. Alaska and Hawaii are the only two states that have no borders with other states.

5

Look Along the Coast

What can be seen along the coast of Alaska but never found along the coast of Nebraska?

$$\overline{\quad}\ \overline{\quad}\ \overline{\quad}\ \overline{\quad}\ \overline{\quad}\ \overline{\quad}$$
$$3\quad 14\quad 4\quad 19\quad 2\quad 27$$

To find the answer, fill in the blanks below. Write the letter that corresponds with the number below each blank.

1. What peninsula was named for the U.S. Secretary of State who authorized the purchase of Alaska from Russia?

$$\overline{1}\ \overline{2}\ \overline{3}\ \overline{4}\ \overline{5}\ \overline{6}$$ Peninsula

2. When this was discovered in Alaska, it started one of the wildest

$$\overline{7}\ \overline{8}\ \overline{9}\ \overline{10}\qquad \overline{11}\ \overline{12}\ \overline{13}\ \overline{14}\ \overline{15}\ \overline{16}$$ in American history.

3. Where is Mount McKinley? $$\overline{15}\ \overline{16}\ \overline{17}\ \overline{18}\ \overline{19}\ \overline{20}$$ National Park

4. Where is the northernmost land point in the United States?

Point $$\overline{21}\ \overline{22}\ \overline{23}\ \overline{24}\ \overline{25}\ \overline{26}$$

5. What was the capital of Alaska when it was controlled by the Russians? $$\overline{27}\ \overline{28}\ \overline{29}\ \overline{30}\ \overline{31}$$

Challenge Questions

1. How many lakes and rivers are there in Alaska? What is the largest lake? How many islands are part of Alaska?

2. What does the word *Alaska* mean?

Just for Fun

Kym: I was born in Juneau, Alaska.
Tim: What part?
Kym: All of me.

TLC10029 Copyright © Teaching & Learning Company, Carthage, IL 62321

Let It Snow!
Let It Snow!
Let It Snow!

Parts of Alaska average 20 feet of snow in the winter. During one 24-hour period in 1963, 74 inches of snow fell at Mile 47 Camp.

How many feet of snow would that be? _____

Measure 74 inches on a wall and mark it. Stand next to the mark. How far above your head is the mark?

Scientists say that no two snowflakes are exactly alike, but here is an exception. Two of the snowflakes below are exactly alike. Which two?

One of a Kind Snowflakes

Make your own snowflakes. Fold a piece of lightweight white paper in half, then in half again. Fold it a third time so it is triangular.

Cut various shapes from the folded paper, being careful not to cut the bottom point of the triangle.

Unfold the paper to see your "one of a kind" snowflake.

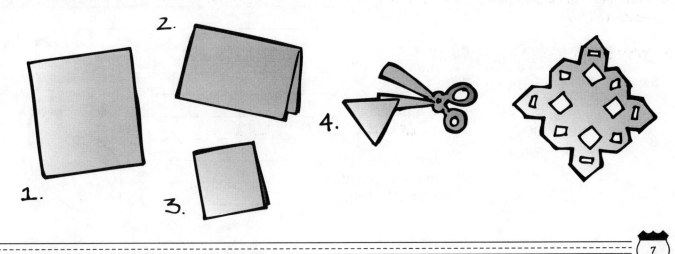

Mixed-Up Nature

Unscramble these groups of letters to discover some of the wildlife found in Alaska.

Mammals

1. DIOAKK EARBS _____
2. CLAKB RABSE _____
3. LAPRO ABSER _____
4. ZGIRZYL SABER _____
5. SOMOE _____
6. KLE _____
7. ROBCIUA _____
8. LOVESW _____
9. TAIMNOUN TOGAS _____
10. BRAVESE _____
11. CUPROPNSIE _____
12. EXOSF _____
13. LOVERWNISE _____
14. SEALSWE _____

Birds

15. PATMIRNGAS _____
16. NETRS _____
17. FUFNIPS _____
18. SLOON _____
19. EEEGS _____
20. LADB LEGEAS _____

Sea Animals

21. LAWSEH _____
22. PINSHLOD _____
23. LEASS _____
24. MOLNSA _____
25. BUTILAH _____
26. SLACM _____
27. DOC _____
28. BRCAS _____
29. PRIMSH _____
30. RINGHER _____

Arizona

Nickname: Grand Canyon State • State Bird: Cactus Wren • Capital: Phoenix

■ The Hopi village of Oraibi was settled over 800 years ago. People still live there making it the oldest settlement in the U.S. that has been lived in continuously.

■ The Apaches were nomadic hunters in the mountains of Arizona. They lived in cone-shaped homes, covered with reeds and grass called wickiups.

■ About 1,000 years ago the Anasazi built their homes in Arizona's cliffs on the northern plateau. Anasazi homes looked much like modern apartment buildings. Instead of stairs or elevators, they used ladders to climb from one level to another.

■ Other prehistoric Arizonans, the Salados and the Sinaguas, were also cliff dwellers. A Sinagua ruin now called Montezuma Castle was five stories high. Nearby is a 100-room Sinagua pueblo.

■ The Navajo hunted and farmed in open country on the Colorado plateau. They lived in log homes covered with earth called hogans.

■ Arizona is sometimes called the Valentine State because it became the 48th state on February 14, 1912.

■ London Bridge was brought to Lake Havasu City, Arizona, from England in 1968. It took three years to reassemble the 952-foot bridge piece by piece.

Lake Havasu City

■ The first known explorer in Arizona was a Spanish friar, Marco de Niza in 1539. The area was ruled as part of New Spain from 1598 to 1821.

■ Bola ties were invented in Arizona. They became so popular they were named the state's official neckwear. Many bola ties are decorated with silver, copper and turquoise, three of Arizona's natural resources.

■ The name *Arizona* may have come from the Papago Indian word *ari-zonac*, meaning "small spring" or from the Aztec word *arizuma*, meaning "silver-bearing."

Phoenix ✪

■ Temperatures frequently dip below 0° in Arizona's snow-capped mountains. A reading of -40°F was recorded at Hawley Lake on January 7, 1971.

■ Wyatt Earp and Doc Holliday had their famous shoot-out at the OK Corral with the Clanton gang in 1881 at Tombstone, Arizona.

● **Tombstone**

■ People settled in Arizona at least 12,000 years ago. The early inhabitants hunted mastodons, wooly mammoths and other prehistoric creatures across the Southwest.

■ The Hohokams were great builders. They dug a complex network of canals from rivers to carry water to their fields. Nearly 700 years ago they built Casa Grande (large house), a 40-foot high building. People have called it America's First Skyscraper.

Life in the Desert

■ Temperatures in the Arizona desert often climb over 100 degrees. On July 7, 1905, the temperature reached 127°F in Parker.

■ Elf owls and gilded flickers nest in saguaro cactus.

■ The cactus wren builds its nest in cholla cactus. Some types of cholla cactus have sprawling arms several yards long. Other types are tree-like and grow up to 15 feet tall.

■ Native Americans used yucca plants to make soap, rope and sandals. Sap from mesquite plants provided medicine for sore throats.

■ Yucca plants, organ-pipe cactus and mesquite grow in abundance in the desert.

■ A two-foot poisonous lizard, the Gila monster, hides in burrows during the day. This colorful lizard hunts for its prey at night when the temperature is cooler.

■ The Sonoran Desert covers most of south-western Arizona and receives little rain—only about two inches a year. It may look empty at first, but the desert is home to thousands of types of plants, mammals, insects, reptiles, birds and amphibians.

■ The two-foot long roadrunner would rather run than fly. For short distances, it can run up to 15 miles per hour.

■ Kangaroo rats live on the tiny amount of water found in the plants they eat. They never need to drink.

■ Seventy kinds of cactus grow in Arizona's deserts. The saguaro cactus, one of the slowest growing plants in the world, can grow 50 feet tall. It grows about one inch a year. Saguaros do not bloom until they are 50 to 75 years old. The largest saguaros may be 200 years old and weigh over 10 tons.

■ The large ears of black-tailed jackrabbits warn them of predators and help remove heat from their bodies.

■ The Grand Canyon is over 200 miles long, about 10 miles across and 1 mile deep. If you stacked four buildings the height of the Empire State Building on top of one another, they wouldn't reach from the bottom to the top of the Grand Canyon.

■ Hundreds of canyons mark the northwest corner of Arizona, but the granddaddy of all is the Grand Canyon. For millions of years, the Colorado River has slowly been forming the largest canyon in the world. Marine fossils found in the limestone walls show that a deep sea once covered the site of the Grand Canyon over 300 million years ago.

TLC10029 Copyright © Teaching & Learning Company, Carthage, IL 62321

Natural Wonders

Besides the spectacular Grand Canyon, Arizona is home to many other beautiful and unusual natural wonders. Two of them are listed below.

__ __ __ __ __ __ __   __ __ __ __ __ __
1 18 49 54 29 44 23   36 57 14 31 20 56

__ __ __ __ __ __ __ __ __   __ __ __ __ __ __
9 4 29 40 30 45 6 24 42   45 53 40 13 17 56

To find the answer, fill in the blanks below. Write the letter that corresponds with the number below each blank.

1. The capital of Arizona is __ __ __ __ __ __ __.
                     1 2 3 4 5 6 7

2. Who were the nomadic hunters who lived in the Arizona mountains? __ __ __ __ __ __ __
              8 9 10 11 12 13 14

3. The Hohokams built a 40-foot high dwelling called

   __ __ __ __   __ __ __ __ __ __.
   15 16 17 18   19 20 21 22 23 24

4. Arizona's state neckwear are __ __ __ __   __ __ __ __.
                       25 26 27 28   29 30 31 32

5. It used to cross the Thames River, now it is at Lake

   Havasu. What is it? __ __ __ __ __ __   __ __ __ __ __ __
                    33 34 35 36 37 38   39 40 41 42 43 44

6. Roadrunners would rather run than __ __ __.
                           45 46 47

7. This two-foot poisonous lizard hunts by night in the desert.

   What is it called? __ __ __ __   __ __ __ __ __ __ __
                  48 49 50 51   52 53 54 55 56 57 58

Challenge Questions

1. Which four states meet at the place known as Four Corners?

2. Turquoise, copper and silver are three of Arizona's natural resources. Select one. Where is it found? How is it mined?

Just for Fun

Why do mother kangaroos in the Phoenix Zoo hate rainy days?

Arizona Bingo

To the Teacher: The master game sheet, rules and game suggestions are on pages 179 and 180.

Statements for Arizona Bingo

- People lived in Arizona at least **12,000** years ago.
- The blossom of the **saguaro cactus** is Arizona's state flower.
- Saguaro cactus grow about **one inch** per year.
- The **cactus wren** is Arizona's state bird.
- The **Gila monster** is a two-foot long poisonous lizard.
- The **paloverde** is Arizona's state tree.
- **London Bridge** now stands at Lake Havasu City, Arizona.
- Arizona's state mammal is the **ring-tailed cat**.
- Kangaroo rats never need to **drink**.
- The **ridge-nosed rattlesnake** is Arizona's state reptile.
- The **Arizona tree frog** is the state's official amphibian.
- A **roadrunner** can run up to 15 MPH.
- **Petrified wood** is Arizona's state fossil.
- **Phoenix** is the capital of Arizona.
- One nickname for Arizona is the **Grand Canyon State**.
- The **Apaches** were nomadic hunters who lived in Arizona's mountains.
- Because it became a state on February 14, Arizona is sometimes called the **Valentine State**.
- Doc Holliday and Wyatt Earp had a shoot-out at **Tombstone**, Arizona.
- **Bola ties** are Arizona's official state neckwear.
- The **Grand Canyon** is the largest canyon in the world.
- The Grand Canyon was formed by the **Colorado River** over millions of years.
- The Anasazi used **ladders** to climb to different levels in their homes.
- A Sinagua ruin called **Montezuma Castle** is five stories high.
- The Navajo lived in homes called **hogans**.

Arkansas

Nickname: Land of Opportunity • State Bird: Mockingbird • Capital: Little Rock

■ The first people to live in Arkansas arrived about 12,000 years ago. Known as the Bluff Dwellers, they lived in caves or under rock shelves.

■ Millions of years ago, most of Arkansas was under water. Fossils of fish have been discovered far from any water. Mosasaurs (giant lizards), huge wolves and mastodons roamed the land.

■ Each October, Yellville, Arkansas, holds the National Wild Turkey Calling Contest.

Yellville

Mammoth Springs

■ Springs bubble up in the Ozark and Ouachita mountain regions. Mammoth Springs is one of the largest in the country. The city of Hot Springs is known for its 47 hot mineral springs.

■ In 1817, Fort Smith was the last outpost of American civilization. During the California gold rush, Fort Smith became a supply base for those traveling west to seek their fortunes.

Fort Smith

■ When it was built in 1986, the Sesquicentennial Sundial in North Little Rock was the largest in the world. Stones from all over the world were donated to create this master timepiece in honor of Arkansas's 150th birthday.

■ The word *Arkansas* came from the French translation of the word *Ugaxpa*, the name for the Quapaws. The word means "downstream people."

■ Toltec Mounds are the remains of a large ceremonial complex built between 700 and 950 A.D. by the people of the Plum Bayou Culture.

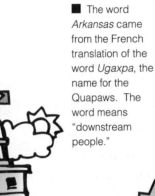

Little Rock

■ The capitol building at Little Rock is a one-quarter size replica of the U.S. Capitol in Washington, D.C.

■ Bauxite, an important mineral used in making aluminum, was discovered near Little Rock in 1887.

■ The Arkansas state bird, the mockingbird, mocks (imitates) the songs of other birds.

■ The vine-ripened pink tomato was named the official state fruit and vegetable of Arkansas in 1987. Although most people think it's a vegetable, tomatoes are really fruit.

■ Reverend Cephas Washburn started the first school in the Arkansas Territory in 1820 to teach Cherokee children.

■ Traditional Ozark folk music is played on autoharps, mandolins and dulcimers. Members of Arkansas "kitchen bands" play tunes on pots and pans, washboards, wash tubs and other kitchen items.

■ Hernando de Soto explored Arkansas for Spain in 1541, but France was the first country to claim the area. Both France and Spain claimed the land at different times over the next 262 years until the U.S. acquired Arkansas as part of the Louisiana Purchase in 1803 at a cost of 15 million dollars, about 3 cents an acre.

■ Milk is the official state drink of Arkansas.

TLC10029 Copyright © Teaching & Learning Company, Carthage, IL 62321

Finders, Keepers

The only active diamond mine in North America is located in a state park near Murfreesboro, Arkansas. Visitors to the park can hunt for and keep any diamonds they find. What is this state park called?

$\overline{38}$ $\overline{8}$ $\overline{16}$ $\overline{50}$ $\overline{33}$ $\overline{45}$ $\overline{11}$ $\overline{47}$ $\overline{46}$ $\overline{44}$ $\overline{4}$ $\overline{32}$ $\overline{37}$ $\overline{41}$ $\overline{27}$ $\overline{51}$

$\overline{5}$ $\overline{54}$ $\overline{24}$ $\overline{50}$ $\overline{26}$ $\overline{19}$ $\overline{6}$ $\overline{34}$ $\overline{39}$

To find the answer, fill in the blanks below. Write the letter that corresponds with the number below each blank.

1. $\overline{}_{1}$ $\overline{}_{2}$ $\overline{}_{3}$ $\overline{}_{4}$ $\overline{}_{5}$ $\overline{}_{6}$ $\overline{}_{7}$ $\overline{}_{8}$ $\overline{}_{9}$ were giant lizards that once lived in Arkansas.

2. Arkansas became part of the U.S. in 1803 as part of the

$\overline{10}$ $\overline{11}$ $\overline{12}$ $\overline{13}$ $\overline{14}$ $\overline{15}$ $\overline{16}$ $\overline{17}$ $\overline{18}$ $\overline{19}$ $\overline{20}$ $\overline{21}$ $\overline{22}$ $\overline{23}$ $\overline{24}$ $\overline{25}$ $\overline{26}$.

3. Traditional Ozark Mountain music is played on autoharps,

mandolins and $\overline{27}$ $\overline{28}$ $\overline{29}$ $\overline{30}$ $\overline{31}$ $\overline{32}$ $\overline{33}$ $\overline{34}$ $\overline{35}$.

4. The $\overline{36}$ $\overline{37}$ $\overline{38}$ $\overline{39}$ $\overline{40}$ $\overline{41}$ $\overline{42}$ $\overline{43}$ $\overline{44}$ $\overline{45}$ $\overline{46}$ is the state bird of Arkansas.

5. $\overline{47}$ $\overline{48}$ $\overline{49}$ $\overline{50}$ $\overline{51}$ $\overline{52}$ $\overline{53}$ $\overline{54}$ $\overline{55}$ was the last outpost of American civilization.

Challenge Questions

1. What was the capital of Arkansas when it first became a territory in 1819?

2. Arkansas was one of the states formed from the area known as the Louisiana Purchase. Name four other states.

Just for Fun

Why don't people in Arkansas like turnips?

TLC10029 Copyright © Teaching & Learning Company, Carthage, IL 62321

Name _____

Musical Words

Arkansas is famous for its folk music, blues, ballads, bluegrass, country music, old-time fiddling and banjo picking. Traditional Ozark folk music is played on autoharps, mandolins and dulcimers.

Music is based on notes with letter names: A, B, C, D, E, F and G. Each line and each space between the lines on the staff is named for a letter. The bottom line is E. The space between the two bottom lines is F. The next line is G. Then the alphabet starts over at A.

D E F G A B C D E

Find the words formed by the notes by writing the letter name of each note on the line below it.

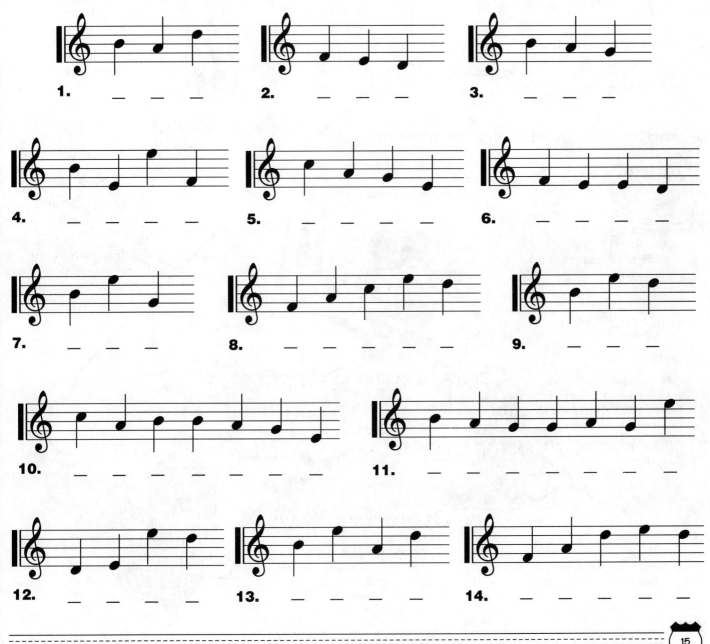

1. __ __ __

2. __ __ __

3. __ __ __

4. __ __ __ __

5. __ __ __ __

6. __ __ __ __

7. __ __ __

8. __ __ __ __

9. __ __ __

10. __ __ __ __ __ __

11. __ __ __ __ __ __

12. __ __ __ __

13. __ __ __ __

14. __ __ __ __

California

Nickname: The Golden State • State Bird: California Valley Quail • Capital: Sacramento

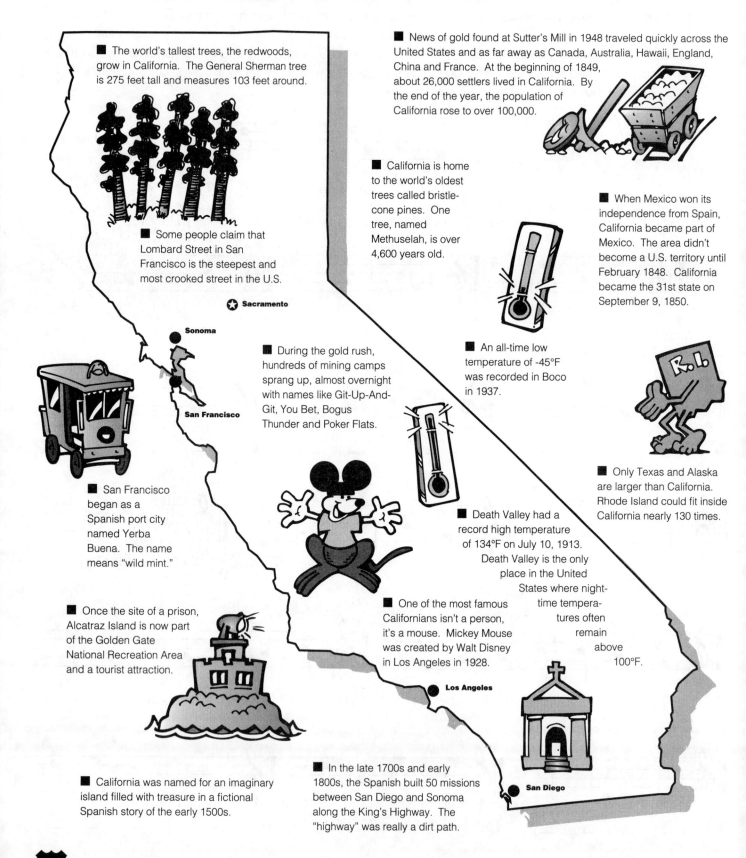

■ The world's tallest trees, the redwoods, grow in California. The General Sherman tree is 275 feet tall and measures 103 feet around.

■ News of gold found at Sutter's Mill in 1948 traveled quickly across the United States and as far away as Canada, Australia, Hawaii, England, China and France. At the beginning of 1849, about 26,000 settlers lived in California. By the end of the year, the population of California rose to over 100,000.

■ California is home to the world's oldest trees called bristle-cone pines. One tree, named Methuselah, is over 4,600 years old.

■ Some people claim that Lombard Street in San Francisco is the steepest and most crooked street in the U.S.

■ When Mexico won its independence from Spain, California became part of Mexico. The area didn't become a U.S. territory until February 1848. California became the 31st state on September 9, 1850.

Sacramento

Sonoma

San Francisco

■ During the gold rush, hundreds of mining camps sprang up, almost overnight with names like Git-Up-And-Git, You Bet, Bogus Thunder and Poker Flats.

■ An all-time low temperature of -45°F was recorded in Boco in 1937.

■ San Francisco began as a Spanish port city named Yerba Buena. The name means "wild mint."

■ Only Texas and Alaska are larger than California. Rhode Island could fit inside California nearly 130 times.

■ Death Valley had a record high temperature of 134°F on July 10, 1913. Death Valley is the only place in the United States where night-time temperatures often remain above 100°F.

■ Once the site of a prison, Alcatraz Island is now part of the Golden Gate National Recreation Area and a tourist attraction.

■ One of the most famous Californians isn't a person, it's a mouse. Mickey Mouse was created by Walt Disney in Los Angeles in 1928.

Los Angeles

■ California was named for an imaginary island filled with treasure in a fictional Spanish story of the early 1500s.

■ In the late 1700s and early 1800s, the Spanish built 50 missions between San Diego and Sonoma along the King's Highway. The "highway" was really a dirt path.

San Diego

Birds and Bees

Where in California would you find a large collection of birds, reptiles and mammals from all over the world in simulated natural habitats?

$\overline{13}$ $\overline{37}$ $\overline{20}$ $\overline{33}$ $\overline{2}$ $\overline{19}$ $\overline{23}$ $\overline{28}$ $\overline{41}$ $\overline{22}$ $\overline{24}$

To find the answer, fill in the blanks below. Write the letter that corresponds with the number below each blank.

1. What was the name of the old road between San Diego and Sonoma?

$\overline{1}$ $\overline{2}$ $\overline{3}$ $\overline{4}$ $\overline{5}$ $\overline{6}$ $\overline{7}$ $\overline{8}$ $\overline{9}$ $\overline{10}$ $\overline{11}$ $\overline{12}$

2. What is the capital of California?

$\overline{13}$ $\overline{14}$ $\overline{15}$ $\overline{16}$ $\overline{17}$ $\overline{18}$ $\overline{19}$ $\overline{20}$ $\overline{21}$ $\overline{22}$

3. What was discovered at Sutter's Mill in 1848? $\overline{23}$ $\overline{24}$ $\overline{25}$ $\overline{26}$

4. Name the crookedest, steepest street in San Francisco.

$\overline{27}$ $\overline{28}$ $\overline{29}$ $\overline{30}$ $\overline{31}$ $\overline{32}$ $\overline{33}$ Street

5. Name the California island that was once a prison.

$\overline{34}$ $\overline{35}$ $\overline{36}$ $\overline{37}$ $\overline{38}$ $\overline{39}$ $\overline{40}$ $\overline{41}$ Island.

Challenge Questions

1. What famous place in California features handprints, footprints and even paw prints of movie stars in its famous cement courtyard?

2. Describe what scientists discovered trapped in the La Brea tar pits.

Just for Fun

Why would a barber in California rather cut hair for 10 men from San Diego
than for one man from San Francisco?

All Mixed Up

Somehow, all the letters except the first ones got mixed up. Perhaps it was a minor earthquake. Can you sort them out to form the names of 25 cities in California?

Hint: The California state map could be very helpful in solving this puzzle.

1. AANEMHI _____

2. BEELYRV SHILL _____

3. BUNBARK _____

4. CAMELR _____

5. EOINCN _____

6. FORESN _____

7. GALELEND _____

8. HOODWOYLL _____

9. IWOLEGNOD _____

10. LSO SANGLEE _____

11. LGNO CHEAB _____

12. MAILUB _____

13. NEOWRPT CHEAB _____

14. OKADANL _____

15. PENAAASD _____

16. PLAM RINGSPS _____

17. SAMECRNTOA _____

18. SNAILSA _____

19. SNA DAREBNOIN _____

20. SAN IEDOG _____

21. SNA CRANFICOS _____

22. SNA SOJE _____

23. STAAN RABBARA _____

24. SALEYUNNV _____

25. VNA YUNS _____

Places to Visit,
Things to See
—In California

Look up, down, backwards, forwards and diagonally to find the 31 words listed below. Only words in CAPITAL letters are hidden in the puzzle.

Write the unused letters on the blanks below to find the name of a place to watch sea lions and seals.

```
S  S  E  Q  U  O  I  A  R  Y  L  O  N  G
A  S  U  T  C  A  C  U  E  A  N  F  M  F
U  B  I  L  A  M  S  R  G  K  I  O  D  D
R  A  P  N  K  G  E  U  N  S  J  O  O  I
N  L  A  C  I  T  N  O  H  A  O  O  A  S
A  W  L  B  N  A  T  E  V  W  W  I  T  N
P  O  O  O  G  T  R  E  D  Y  S  N  S  E
A  B  M  T  S  M  T  E  L  L  L  Y  A  Y
V  E  E  I  A  I  R  L  A  A  O  O  H  L
A  S  R  N  M  N  O  M  S  U  B  G  S  A
L  O  S  E  E  H  I  S  L  L  H  R  S  N
L  R  S  C  K  N  E  H  A  A  L  S  E  D
E  O  O  B  A  N  A  B  C  Y  P  A  O  A
Y  T  R  O  L  L  E  Y  C  A  R  S  F  J
```

Unused letters: __ __ __   __ __ __ __ __ __ __ __ __   __ __ __ __

ANIMALS	JOSHUA Tree National Monument	NAPA VALLEY
BALBOA Park	KINGS Canyon	PALM Canyon
BIG SUR	KNOTTS Berry Farm	PALOMER Observatory
Bridalveil FALLS	LA BREA Tar Pits	REDWOOD National Park
CACTUS	LAGUNA Beach	ROSE BOWL Parade
CHINATOWN	LAKE Manzanita	SEQUOIA National Park
DISNEYLAND	LASSEN Volcanic National Park	SHASTA Dam
FISHERMAN'S Wharf	LONG Beach	TROLLEY CARS
GOLDEN GATE Bridge	MALIBU	YOSEMITE National Park
HOLLYWOOD	MOJAVE Desert	
INYO National Forest	MONTEREY Peninsula	

Colorado

Nickname: Centennial State • State Bird: Lark Bunting • Capital: Denver

■ The first gold strike in Colorado occurred in 1858. As news of the discovery spread, people rushed to Colorado to get rich. Denver, Golden, Boulder and Colorado City began as gold mining towns. Prices were high in the booming gold rush towns of Colorado. Eggs cost a dollar each and a sack of potatoes sold for $15.

■ By the 1870s people were finding little gold, but in 1878 a "silver rush" began when several silver strikes were made. Leadville and Aspen became important silver mining towns. A silver nugget weighing about 1,840 pounds was discovered in Aspen in 1894.

■ Boulder was named for the rocks and boulders in the area.

■ More than 50 types of dinosaurs once lived in western Colorado including brachiosaurus, tyrannosaurus rex, apatosaurus and stegosaurus. Colorado even has a city named Dinosaur.

Dinosaur

■ The water in the bubbling spring at Steamboat Springs sounds like a steamboat whistle.

Steamboat Springs

■ Greeley was named for a New York newspaperman, Horace Greeley, who was credited with giving the advice, "Go West, young man."

Greeley

Boulder

Denver ☆

■ The U.S. Mint in Denver produces 5 billion coins a year. Coins stamped with a *D* were made at the mint in Denver.

Aurora

■ Denver is nicknamed the "Mile High City." The 13th step at the state capitol is 5,280 feet above sea level—exactly one mile high. About half of all the people in Colorado live in the Denver area.

■ Although he was born in New Mexico, Henry John Deutschendorf, Jr. loved the Mile High City so much he changed his name to John Denver.

Aspen

Guffey

■ The town of Guffey has about 26 people and a most unusual mayor. In 1987 the people elected Paisley, a cat. The town has had a cat for a mayor ever since.

Colorado Springs

■ Colorado Springs was named for the nearby springs. Many Olympic athletes train at the city's U.S. Olympic Training Complex. The Pro Rodeo Hall of Fame and World Figure Skating Hall of Fame are in Colorado Springs.

■ A second gold rush started in 1890 when Bob Womack found gold in a cow pasture. He sold his claim for $300. Half a billion dollars was mined from that pasture.

■ In the 1950s, only about 2,000 people lived in Aurora. After the discovery of "black gold" (oil) the population shot up to over 220,000.

Colorado Trivia

■ Cliff Palace contains open plazas, stone houses two to three stories high and more than 200 rooms. To get from one level to another, the people climbed ropes and ladders. To protect the treasures found at Mesa Verde, the area became a national park in 1906.

■ The oldest fossil of a flowering plant found in the U.S. was discovered in Colorado in 1953. It dates back about 65 million years.

■ The Royal Gorge Bridge, the world's highest suspension bridge above water, hangs 1,053 feet above the Arkansas River.

■ While searching for stray cattle in 1888 on Mesa Verde, two men discovered a magnificent city built under an overhanging cliff. They named it Cliff Palace. Once home to the Anasazi, Cliff Palace and other nearby cliff cities were deserted nearly 700 years ago.

■ Colorado is known as the "Centennial State" because it joined the Union in 1876, 100 years after the founding of our nation.

■ Seven hundred-year-old dried beans left by the Anasazi were preserved by the dry weather. When planted, they grew. In 1983 two men from Colorado started Adobe Milling, a company that sells Anasazi beans.

■ In 1893 Colorado became the second state to grant women the right to vote. Most states didn't allow women to vote until 1920.

■ The view from the 14,110-foot high Pike's Peak in 1893 inspired Katharine Lee Bates to write a poem we know as the song, "America, the Beautiful." Colorado has 56 peaks over 14,000 feet high.

■ More than 1,000 peaks in Colorado are over two miles high. The highest point in Colorado is Mount Elba, 14,433 feet above sea level.

■ The Garden of the Gods near Colorado Springs has huge rocks named the Sleeping Giant and the Kissing Camels. A Ute legend says the rocks were once giants who were turned to stone by the Great Spirit for invading Ute lands.

■ Archaeologists have found black on white pottery, woven blankets, stone and bone tools, clothing, bows and arrows at Cliff Palace. The Anasazi grew corn, beans and squash; hunted deer and rabbits; and kept dogs and turkeys.

■ Gold and silver were important during the history of the Centennial State, but red was the color that gave Colorado its name. The word *colorado* is Spanish, meaning the color red.

■ North America's tallest sand dunes are found at Sand Dunes National Monument. Some dunes are 700 feet tall.

TLC10029 Copyright © Teaching & Learning Company, Carthage, IL 62321

The Source

Cascade Falls empties into Colorado's largest natural lake, the starting point of the Colorado River. What is it called?

$$\overline{22}\ \overline{24}\ \overline{7}\ \overline{18}\ \overline{25}\qquad \overline{2}\ \overline{35}\ \overline{30}\ \overline{13}$$

To find the answer, fill in the blanks below. Write the letter that corresponds with the number below each blank.

1. Once home to the Anasazi, $\overline{}\ \overline{}\ \overline{}\ \overline{}\ \overline{}\quad \overline{}\ \overline{}\ \overline{}\ \overline{}\ \overline{}\ \overline{}$
   1 2 3 4 5   6 7 8 9 10 11

   contains open plazas and over 200 rooms on Mesa Verde.

2. Colorado is known as the $\overline{}\ \overline{}\ \overline{}\ \overline{}\ \overline{}\ \overline{}\ \overline{}\ \overline{}\ \overline{}\ \overline{}$
   12 13 14 15 16 17 18 19 20 21

   State because it joined the Union in 1876.

3. Rocks called the Sleeping Giant and the Kissing Camels can

   be seen at the $\overline{}\ \overline{}\ \overline{}\ \overline{}\ \overline{}\ \overline{}$ of the Gods.
   22 23 24 25 26 27

4. The view from $\overline{}\ \overline{}\ \overline{}\ \overline{}'\overline{}\quad \overline{}\ \overline{}\ \overline{}\ \overline{}$
   28 29 30 31 32   33 34 35 36

   inspired the song "America, the Beautiful."

Challenge Questions

1. Seven states border Colorado. What are they?

2. Colorado's state song is "Where the Columbines Grow." Where do columbines grow? What is a columbine? Draw a colored picture of this plant.

Just for Fun

What's the difference between an old ten dollar bill and a new one?

In Pursuit of Colorado Trivia

To play, divide into teams of two to four players. Your teacher will shake a die and read a question from that numbered section. As a team, decide on the answer and write it on a blank line. (Only one answer per team per question is allowed.) When all teams have written their answers, your teacher will give you the correct answer. If your team's answer is correct, color in the matching numbered section of the circle.

Write your answers here.

_____

_____

_____

_____

_____

_____

_____

_____

_____

_____

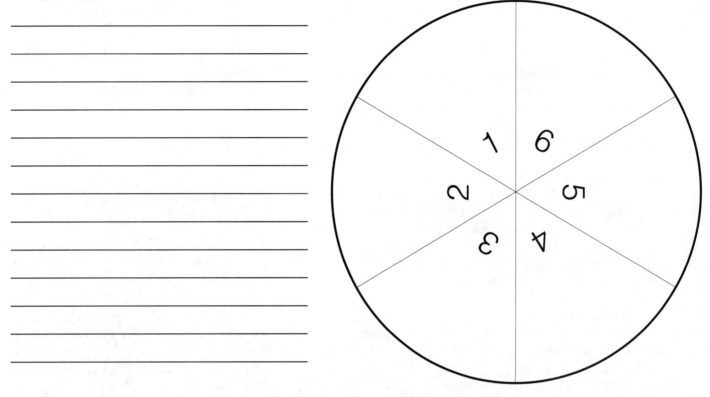

Bonus Section

If you correctly answer more than one question with the same number, draw a triangle here. Each triangle is worth one bonus point.

The first team to color all six sections of their circle wins. In the event of a tie, the team with the most bonus points wins.

To the Teacher

Question list for In Pursuit of Colorado Trivia game.

Section 1

Colorado is nicknamed the . . .
Denver is nicknamed the . . .
Colorado's state flower is . . .
Colorado's state tree is . . .
What vegetable was grown from 700-year-old seeds?

Answers

Centennial State
Mile High City
Rocky Mountain columbine
Colorado blue spruce
Beans

Section 2

Colorado's state bird is . . .
Colorado's state animal is . . .
Colorado's state gem is . . .
Colorado's state song is . . .
The world's highest suspension bridge over water is . . .

Lark bunting
Rocky Mountain bighorn sheep
Aquamarine
"Where the Columbines Grow"
Royal Gorge Bridge

Section 3

The water in Colorado Springs sounds like a . . .
What is unusual about the mayor of Guffey?
When did Colorado become a state?
The view of Pike's Peak inspired what song?
How did the Anasazi get from one level
    to another at Cliff Palace?

Steamboat whistle
The mayor is a cat.
1876
"America, the Beautiful"

By ropes and ladders

Section 4

What does the word *colorado* mean in Spanish?
The highest point in Colorado is . . .
What is black gold?
Greeley, Colorado, was named for . . .
More than half the people in Colorado live where?

The color red
Mount Elba
Oil
Horace Greeley
Denver area

Section 5

Bob Womack struck gold in a . . .
What name do we know Henry John Deutschendorf, Jr. by?
Colorado was the ___ state to allow women to vote.
What city's population went from 2,000 to
    220,00 after oil was discovered?
Once home to the Anasazi, this cliff
    dwelling has over 200 rooms . . .

Cow pasture
John Denver
2nd

Aurora

Cliff Palace

Section 6

Colorado's state fossil is . . .
The capital of Colorado is . . .
Apatosaurus is a type of . . .
Discovered near Aspen, it weighed 1,840
    pounds. What was it?
North America's highest sand dunes are at . . .

Stegosaurus
Denver
Dinosaur

A silver nugget
Sand Dunes National Monument

Connecticut

Nickname: Nutmeg State • State Bird: Robin • Capital: Hartford

■ In the 1800s, ships from Connecticut traveled all over the world, trading in spices and other goods, giving the state its nickname, "Nutmeg State."

■ King Charles II granted the Puritans a charter in 1662 that allowed them to elect their governor and gave the colony other rights. In 1697, the royal governor of New York tried to take over Connecticut colony. He demanded the colonists hand over the charter from the king. The colonists refused to return the document and hid it in a hollow oak tree. The tree became known as the Charter Oak.

■ Connecticut is the only state with an official state hero. Nathan Hale served as a spy for George Washington until he was captured by the British and executed. His famous last words were: "I only regret that I have but one life to lose for my country."

■ Beginning on March 1, 1784, all children born into slavery in Connecticut were freed when they turned 25. Slavery ended in Connecticut in 1848.

■ Footprints of dinosaurs that roamed Connecticut 185 million years ago are preserved under plexiglass at Dinosaur State Park.

Hartford ✪

■ In 1852, Harriet Beecher Stowe wrote *Uncle Tom's Cabin*, a widely read novel about the evils of slavery.

■ The word *Connecticut* came from a Native American word, *quinnehtukgut* meaning "beside the long tidal river."

■ The Nut Museum in Old Lyme features a bride and groom carved from a walnut and an eight-foot long nutcracker.

Old Lyme ●

■ Connecticut is the third smallest state. Fifty-three states the size of Connecticut could easily fit inside the state of Texas.

■ During the 1830s and '40s, a movement for the abolition of slavery arose in Connecticut. Through a secret network of "stations" along the Underground Railroad, Connecticut men and women sheltered escaped slaves and helped them escape to freedom.

■ Until 1765, Connecticut remained almost completely independent from England. When their freedom was threatened by the passage of several laws demanding the payment of taxes, two men from Connecticut formed a patriotic group called the Sons of Liberty.

■ Sixty percent of Connecticut is covered with forests of oak, beech, birch, hickory, maple, oak, pine and hemlock.

■ Connecticut was the fifth of the original 13 colonies to ratify the Constitution on January 9, 1788.

■ The Puritans established the Connecticut colony as a theocracy—a community ruled by the church. They believed that people should be allowed to elect their leaders. In 1639, they wrote a code of laws called the Fundamental Orders that became the first constitution in the New World. That is why Connecticut is also nicknamed the Constitution State.

Connecticut Connections

Connect the items in the first column by drawing a line to the correct answer in the second column.

1. Connecticut nickname
2. State flower
3. Capital of Connecticut
4. Hiding place of Connecticut charter
5. State tree
6. State bird
7. Wrote *Uncle Tom's Cabin*
8. State animal
9. Route used by escaped slaves
10. State insect
11. Patriotic group
12. State mineral
13. State ship
14. State hero
15. State song

A. Charter oak
B. Constitution State
C. Garnet
D. Harriet Beecher Stowe
E. Hartford
F. Nathan Hale
G. Mountain laurel
H. Praying mantis
I. Robin
J. Sons of Liberty
K. Sperm whale
L. Underground Railroad
M. *USS Nautilus*
N. White oak
O. "Yankee Doodle"

Challenge Questions

1. The First Presbyterian Church in Stamford has a very unusual shape for a church. What is it shaped like?

2. What are the Quinebaug, Housatonic and Naugatuck?

Just for Fun

Why don't penguins fly to Connecticut?

Connecticut Bingo

To the Teacher: The master game sheet, rules and game suggestions are on pages 179 and 180.

Statements for Connecticut Bingo

- **Yale University** in New Haven is world famous for its libraries and art museums.
- Connecticut's state song is **"Yankee Doodle."**
- Nearly 2,000 acres of land in **Bridgeport** have been set aside as city parks.
- Connecticut's state bird is the **robin**.
- **Norwalk's** seafaring days are remembered in the Maritime History Museum on the waterfront.
- The **mountain laurel** is Connecticut's state flower.
- At one time, **Waterbury** was known as Brass City. It was the center of America's brass industry.

- The **white oak** is Connecticut's state tree.
- The city of **Danbury** was once the hat-making capital of America.
- The **sperm whale** is Connecticut's state animal.
- The **Dutch** established a colony at the site of present-day Hartford in 1633.
- Connecticut's state insect is the **praying mantis**.
- The first atomic submarine, the *USS Nautilus* was built at **Groton** and launched in 1954.
- The **garnet** is the state mineral.
- Connecticut has an official state ship, the ***USS Nautilus***.
- **Nathan Hale** is Connecticut's state hero.
- Connecticut is nicknamed the **Constitution State**.
- **Hartford** has been the capital since 1875.
- 185 million-year-old footprints are preserved at **Dinosaur State Park**.

- A **theocracy** is a community ruled by the church.
- Harriet Beecher Stowe wrote ***Uncle Tom's Cabin*** in 1852.
- Slavery ended in Connecticut in **1848**.
- The **Underground Railroad** provided an escape route for runaway slaves.
- Connecticut was the **fifth** colony to ratify the Constitution.

Delaware

Nickname: First State • State Bird: Blue Hen Chicken • Capital: Dover

■ Fort Christina became the heart of New Sweden, a string of settlements along the Delaware River from Wilmington nearly to Philadelphia.

■ Cooch's Bridge, near Newark, was the site of Delaware's only Revolutionary War battle. According to tradition, Betsy Ross's flag was first raised in battle here.

■ Delaware was the first to form a convention to write a state constitution which called for election of a president, banned importation of slaves and guaranteed freedom of religion and freedom of the press.

■ Delaware is the second smallest state. From north to south, the greatest distance in Delaware is only 96 miles. From east to west, the state measures only 39 miles wide. Delaware shares the Delmarva Peninsula with part of Maryland and Virginia. Delmarva comes from the words **Del**aware, **Mar**yland and **V**irginia.

Wilmington

Newark

■ Delaware was the first of the 13 original colonies to ratify the Constitution on December 7, 1787, giving it the nickname, "First State."

WE'RE #1

Dover ✪

■ Barratt's Chapel was the birthplace of the Methodist Episcopal Church in 1784. The town of Frederica has been called the "Cradle of Methodism in America."

■ The governor of Delaware tried to persuade the state legislature to join the southern states that seceded from the Union. The state remained with the Union, but hundreds from Delaware joined the Confederate Army.

■ The English navigator, Henry Hudson working for the Netherlands, was the first European known to reach Delaware. He and his crew explored Delaware Bay in 1609.

■ Led by Peter Minuit, Dutch and Swedish colonists landed at a place known as The Rocks. Fort Christina, named for the Queen of Sweden, became the first permanent European settlement in Delaware. The town was later renamed Wilmington.

■ In 1610, Samuel Argall, a Virginia colonist, was swept off course during a storm and took shelter in a bay. He named it De La Warr Bay after Sir Thomas West, Lord De La Warr, the governor of Virginia.

■ Although it became illegal in 1776 to import slaves, slavery remained legal in Delaware. The Emancipation Proclamation freed all slaves in the Confederate states. Slavery in the Union states was still legal. Slaves in Delaware and Kansas were not freed until the Thirteenth Amendment to the Constitution passed in 1865.

■ Cornelius Mey and Cornelius Henderson explored the land around Delaware Bay for the Netherlands in 1614 and 1616. A small group of Dutch colonists began a settlement called Zwaanendael (Valley of the Swans) in 1631, but only one member of the group survived.

■ Swedish pioneers built log cabins which kept out the cold better than the lumber houses built by English colonists.

Let There Be Light

An historic lighthouse built in 1857 can be seen on an island in the Atlantic Ocean. What is the name of the island?

$\overline{31}$ $\overline{15}$ $\overline{12}$ $\overline{27}$ $\overline{11}$ $\overline{5}$ $\overline{30}$ $\overline{32}$ $\overline{34}$ $\overline{20}$ $\overline{13}$ $\overline{25}$ $\overline{23}$

To find the answer, fill in the blanks below. Write the letter that corresponds with the number below each blank.

1. $\overline{}$ $\overline{}$ $\overline{}$ $\overline{}$ $\overline{}$ $\overline{}$ $\overline{}$ $\overline{}$ $\overline{}$ $\overline{}$ $\overline{}$ $\overline{}$ $\overline{}$ was named for the Queen of Sweden.
   1 2 3 4   5 6 7 8 9 10 11 12 13

2. Although he was English, Henry Hudson was working for another country when he explored Delaware

   Bay. What country sent him to the New World? $\overline{14}$ $\overline{15}$ $\overline{16}$ $\overline{17}$ $\overline{18}$ $\overline{19}$ $\overline{20}$ $\overline{21}$ $\overline{22}$ $\overline{23}$ $\overline{24}$

3. Cooch's Bridge, near $\overline{25}$ $\overline{26}$ $\overline{27}$ $\overline{28}$ $\overline{29}$ $\overline{30}$ was the site of the

   only Revolutionary War battle in Delaware.

4. Delaware is nicknamed $\overline{31}$ $\overline{32}$ $\overline{33}$ $\overline{34}$ $\overline{35}$ State because it was

   the first one to ratify the Constitution.

Challenge Questions

1. The governor of New Sweden from 1643 to 1653 was reported to be a large man—seven feet tall and weighing over 400 pounds. He is remembered in this nursery rhyme:

   > No governor of Delaware, before or since,
   > Has weighed as much as _____.

   What was the governor's name?

2. What was the name of the island where Confederate soldiers were kept in a prison at Fort Delaware?

Just for Fun

What did the lady from Delaware get when she crossed a kangaroo with a calendar?

What Can You Find in *Delaware?*

How many words can you make using the letters in DELAWARE? Words must be three or more letters.
Write your words on a separate sheet of paper.

Delaware Bingo

To the Teacher: The master game sheet, rules and game suggestions are on pages 179 and 180.

Statements for Delaware Bingo

- Delaware was nicknamed **First State** because it was the first to ratify the Constitution.
- **Liberty and Independence** is Delaware's state motto.
- Delaware's state flower is the **peach blossom**.
- **Fort Christina** was named for the Queen of Sweden.
- The **American holly** is Delaware's state tree.
- Delaware's state bird is the **blue hen chicken**.
- Fort Christina was later renamed **Wilmington**.
- The **weakfish** is Delaware's state fish.
- According to tradition, Betsy Ross's flag first flew at the battle of **Cooch's Bridge** during the Revolutionary War.
- **Dover** is the capital of Delaware.
- Only one member of the first Dutch colony Zwaanendael survived. *Zwaanendael* means **"Valley of the Swans."**

- **Henry Hudson** was the first European known to reach Delaware.
- The **ladybug** is Delaware's state insect.
- Delaware is the **second** smallest state.
- Delaware's state mineral is **sillimanite**.
- **Wilmington** is the largest city in Delaware.
- Delaware Bay and the **Atlantic Ocean** form the state's eastern border.
- Barratt's Chapel near Frederica is the birthplace of the **Methodist Episcopal Church** in America.
- Delaware was named for Sir Thomas West, **Lord De La Warr**.
- **Colonial blue and buff** are Delaware's state colors.

  - **Milk** is Delaware's state beverage.
  - **"Our Delaware"** is the state song.
  - Slavery remained legal in Delaware until the **13th Amendment** was passed in 1865.
  - Swedish pioneers built **log cabins** which kept out the cold better than English style lumber houses.

Florida

Nickname: Peninsula State • State Bird: Mockingbird • Capital: Tallahassee

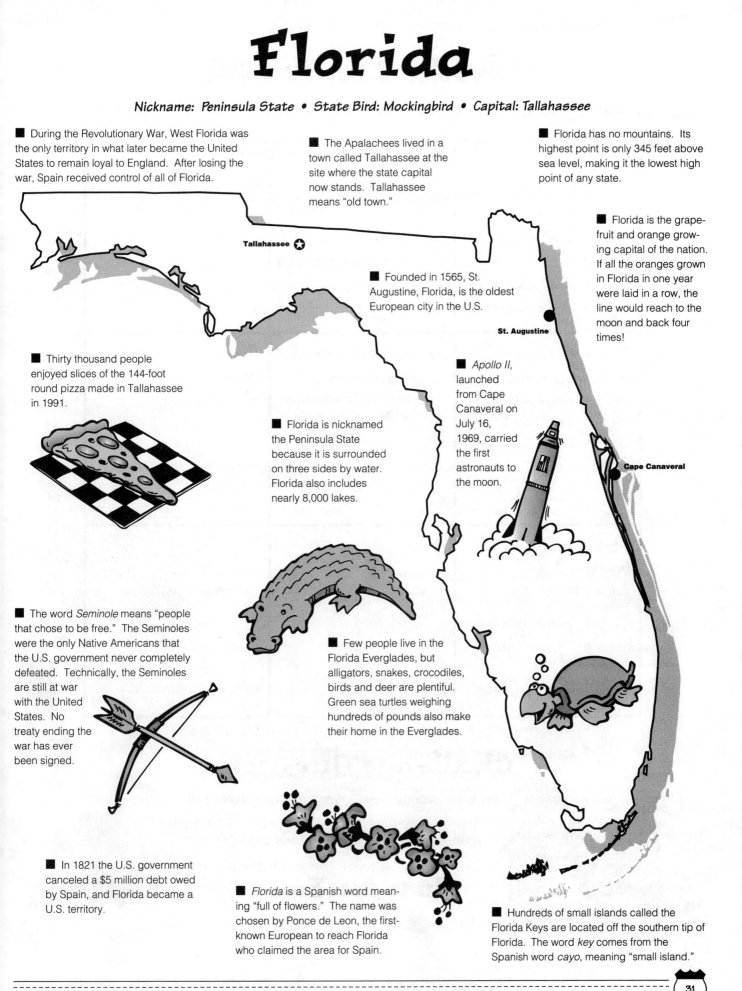

■ During the Revolutionary War, West Florida was the only territory in what later became the United States to remain loyal to England. After losing the war, Spain received control of all of Florida.

■ The Apalachees lived in a town called Tallahassee at the site where the state capital now stands. Tallahassee means "old town."

■ Florida has no mountains. Its highest point is only 345 feet above sea level, making it the lowest high point of any state.

■ Florida is the grape-fruit and orange grow-ing capital of the nation. If all the oranges grown in Florida in one year were laid in a row, the line would reach to the moon and back four times!

Tallahassee ⭐

■ Founded in 1565, St. Augustine, Florida, is the oldest European city in the U.S.

St. Augustine

■ Thirty thousand people enjoyed slices of the 144-foot round pizza made in Tallahassee in 1991.

■ *Apollo II*, launched from Cape Canaveral on July 16, 1969, carried the first astronauts to the moon.

Cape Canaveral

■ Florida is nicknamed the Peninsula State because it is surrounded on three sides by water. Florida also includes nearly 8,000 lakes.

■ The word *Seminole* means "people that chose to be free." The Seminoles were the only Native Americans that the U.S. government never completely defeated. Technically, the Seminoles are still at war with the United States. No treaty ending the war has ever been signed.

■ Few people live in the Florida Everglades, but alligators, snakes, crocodiles, birds and deer are plentiful. Green sea turtles weighing hundreds of pounds also make their home in the Everglades.

■ In 1821 the U.S. government canceled a $5 million debt owed by Spain, and Florida became a U.S. territory.

■ *Florida* is a Spanish word mean-ing "full of flowers." The name was chosen by Ponce de Leon, the first-known European to reach Florida who claimed the area for Spain.

■ Hundreds of small islands called the Florida Keys are located off the southern tip of Florida. The word *key* comes from the Spanish word *cayo*, meaning "small island."

31

Florida Tic-Tac-Toe

To play Florida Tic-Tac-Toe, answer three questions in a row: up and down, across or diagonally.

1. *Tallahassee* means _____	**2.** Florida has many famous mountain ranges. True or false? _____	**3.** What is the oldest European city in the United States? _____
4. In what year did Florida become a U.S. territory? _____	**5.** West Florida remained loyal to what country during the Revolutionary War? _____	**6.** What does the word *Florida* mean? _____
7. Who was the first European explorer in Florida? _____	**8.** What are the Florida Keys? _____	**9.** Why is Florida called the Peninsula State? _____

Challenge Questions

1. Describe the Overseas Highway to the Florida Keys. When and how was it built?

2. Describe several of the attractions at Walt Disney World or EPCOT Center.

Just for Fun

What's gray, has four legs and a trunk and is found in Florida?

TLC10029 Copyright © Teaching & Learning Company, Carthage, IL 62321

Enjoy the Wildlife in Florida

Florida is home to more than 350 types of trees, about 3,500 species of wild plants, 90 types of mammals and over 400 types of birds. About 200 types of freshwater fish and 1,200 kinds of marine fish also live in Florida's lakes and coastal waters.

Look up, down, backwards, forwards and diagonally to find 37 kinds of Florida wildlife hidden in the puzzle.

```
S  L  W  O  B  E  A  V  E  R  S  O  R  O
S  B  A  R  C  O  Y  S  T  E  R  A  N  D
S  K  R  O  T  S  E  S  L  O  D  I  E  S
S  F  U  O  N  L  N  I  O  E  L  E  O  P
S  I  O  N  T  A  D  S  C  R  R  A  I  O
R  S  O  R  K  O  P  B  A  W  O  G  O  N
O  H  U  E  C  R  O  M  H  N  E  L  O  G
T  T  S  O  E  B  A  A  O  O  E  E  O  E
A  C  R  Y  C  G  L  N  N  P  I  N  E  S
G  C  R  A  N  E  S  A  U  R  A  O  O  B
I  O  T  O  S  O  O  T  O  A  O  L  E  A
L  S  L  O  H  C  R  E  P  T  O  A  M  S
L  I  Q  U  A  I  L  E  E  G  R  E  T  S
A  C  Y  P  R  E  S  S  H  S  G  O  R  F
```

ALLIGATORS   OAKS
BASS   OSPREY
BEARS   OWLS
BEAVERS   OYSTER
BOBCATS   PALMS
CEDAR   PERCH
CRABS   PIGEON
CRANES   PINES
CROCODILES   POMPANO
CYPRESS   QUAIL
DEER   SKUNK
EAGLE   SNAKES
EGRETS   SPONGES
FISH   STORKS
FROGS   TARPON
HERON   TUPELO
MAGNOLIA   TURTLES
MANATEES   WHALES
MARLIN

Georgia

Nickname: Goober State • State Bird: Brown Thrasher • Capital: Atlanta

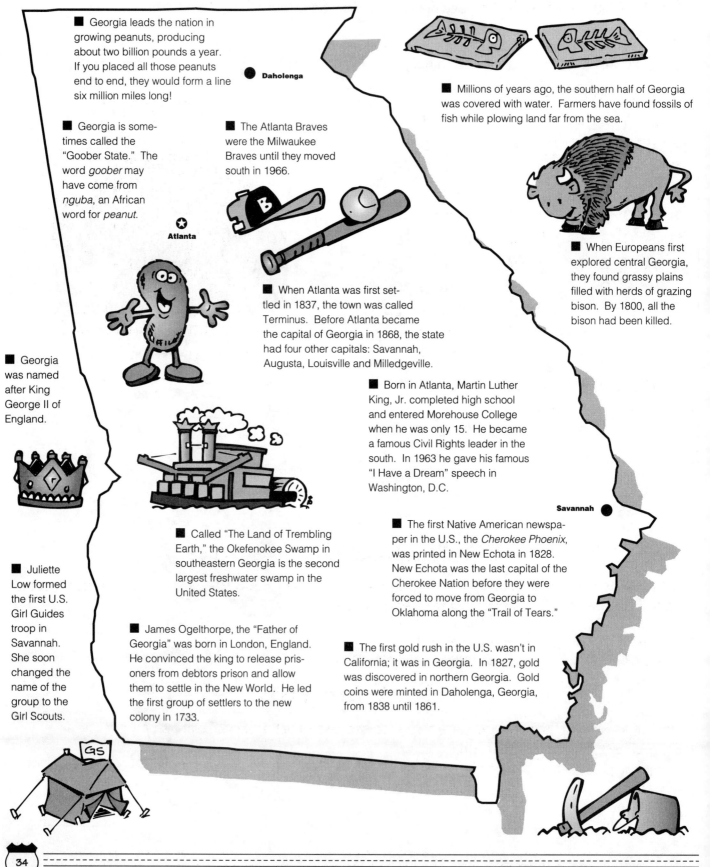

■ Georgia leads the nation in growing peanuts, producing about two billion pounds a year. If you placed all those peanuts end to end, they would form a line six million miles long!

■ Georgia is sometimes called the "Goober State." The word *goober* may have come from *nguba*, an African word for *peanut*.

■ Georgia was named after King George II of England.

■ Juliette Low formed the first U.S. Girl Guides troop in Savannah. She soon changed the name of the group to the Girl Scouts.

Daholenga

⭐ **Atlanta**

■ The Atlanta Braves were the Milwaukee Braves until they moved south in 1966.

■ When Atlanta was first settled in 1837, the town was called Terminus. Before Atlanta became the capital of Georgia in 1868, the state had four other capitals: Savannah, Augusta, Louisville and Milledgeville.

■ Called "The Land of Trembling Earth," the Okefenokee Swamp in southeastern Georgia is the second largest freshwater swamp in the United States.

■ James Ogelthorpe, the "Father of Georgia" was born in London, England. He convinced the king to release prisoners from debtors prison and allow them to settle in the New World. He led the first group of settlers to the new colony in 1733.

■ Millions of years ago, the southern half of Georgia was covered with water. Farmers have found fossils of fish while plowing land far from the sea.

■ When Europeans first explored central Georgia, they found grassy plains filled with herds of grazing bison. By 1800, all the bison had been killed.

■ Born in Atlanta, Martin Luther King, Jr. completed high school and entered Morehouse College when he was only 15. He became a famous Civil Rights leader in the south. In 1963 he gave his famous "I Have a Dream" speech in Washington, D.C.

Savannah ●

■ The first Native American newspaper in the U.S., the *Cherokee Phoenix*, was printed in New Echota in 1828. New Echota was the last capital of the Cherokee Nation before they were forced to move from Georgia to Oklahoma along the "Trail of Tears."

■ The first gold rush in the U.S. wasn't in California; it was in Georgia. In 1827, gold was discovered in northern Georgia. Gold coins were minted in Daholenga, Georgia, from 1838 until 1861.

Who Took the Vowels?

Someone took all the vowels except the *Ys* from the names of these cities in Georgia. It's a good thing this didn't happen in Hawaii. Without the vowels, most of the cities in Hawaii would disappear.

Find the names of these cities by adding *A, E, I, O* or *U.*

1. __ L B __ N Y
2. __ T L __ N T __
3. C __ L __ M B __ S
4. __ T H __ N S
5. __ __ G __ S T __
6. C __ __ R __
7. M __ C __ N
8. S __ N T __   C L __ __ S
9. S __ V __ N N __ H
10. N __ W __ C H __ T __
11. D __ H L __ N __ G __
12. L __ __ __ S V __ L L __
13. M __ L L __ D G __ V __ L L __
14. C __ M M __ R C __
15. C __ R D __ L __

Challenge Questions

1. Eli Whitney invented the cotton gin in 1793. What did the cotton gin do? How did his invention affect the production of cotton in Georgia and other southern states?

2. Jefferson Davis was the president of the Confederacy. Who was the Vice President?

Just for Fun

What do you get when you cross peanut butter with an elephant?

Georgia Bingo

To the Teacher: The master game sheet, rules and game suggestions are on pages 179 and 180.

Statements for Georgia Bingo

- **Atlanta** is the capital of Georgia.
- One of Georgia's nicknames is the **Peach State**.
- Georgia's state fossil is the **shark tooth**.
- The **live oak** is Georgia's state tree.
- **Quartz** is Georgia's state gem.
- Georgia has a state butterfly, the **tiger swallowtail**.
- The **honeybee** is Georgia's state insect.
- Georgia's state flower is the **Cherokee Rose**.
- **New Echota** was the last capital of the Cherokee Nation.
- Georgia was named for **King George II** of England.
- **James Ogelthorpe** is known as the "Father of Georgia."
- The city of Atlanta was once named **Terminus**.
- The **brown thrasher** is Georgia's state bird.
- Georgia is the **largest** state east of the Mississippi River.
- Georgia's state game bird is the **bobwhite quail**.
- The **largemouth bass** is Georgia's state fish.
- The **azalea** is the state's wildflower.
- The word *goober* came from an African word for *peanut*.
- The **Atlantic Ocean** forms Georgia's southeastern border.

- The **Appalachian Mountains** are in northern Georgia.
- The **Okefenokee Swamp** means "the land of trembling earth."
- Juliette Low started the first **Girl Scout troop**.
- The *Cherokee Phoenix* was the first Native American newspaper.
- Manatees, nicknamed **sea cows**, can be seen around Cumberland Island.

Hawaii

Nickname: Aloha State • State Bird: Hawaiian Goose (Nene) • Capital: Honolulu
The eight main islands in Hawaii each have their own official color and emblem.

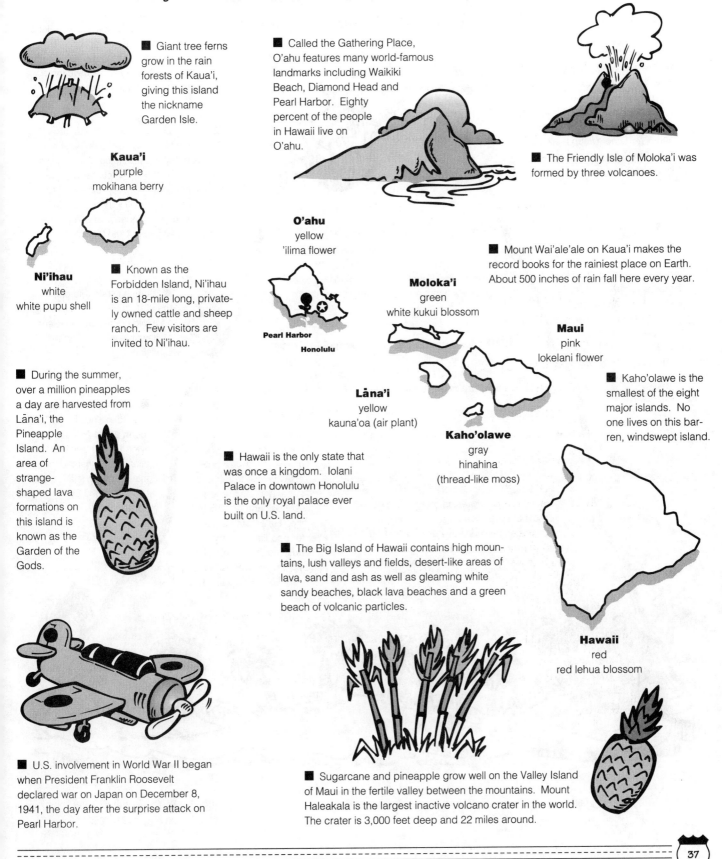

■ Giant tree ferns grow in the rain forests of Kaua'i, giving this island the nickname Garden Isle.

Kaua'i
purple
mokihana berry

Ni'ihau
white
white pupu shell

■ Known as the Forbidden Island, Ni'ihau is an 18-mile long, privately owned cattle and sheep ranch. Few visitors are invited to Ni'ihau.

■ Called the Gathering Place, O'ahu features many world-famous landmarks including Waikiki Beach, Diamond Head and Pearl Harbor. Eighty percent of the people in Hawaii live on O'ahu.

O'ahu
yellow
'ilima flower

Pearl Harbor

Honolulu

■ The Friendly Isle of Moloka'i was formed by three volcanoes.

■ Mount Wai'ale'ale on Kaua'i makes the record books for the rainiest place on Earth. About 500 inches of rain fall here every year.

Moloka'i
green
white kukui blossom

Maui
pink
lokelani flower

■ Kaho'olawe is the smallest of the eight major islands. No one lives on this barren, windswept island.

Lāna'i
yellow
kauna'oa (air plant)

Kaho'olawe
gray
hinahina
(thread-like moss)

■ During the summer, over a million pineapples a day are harvested from Lāna'i, the Pineapple Island. An area of strange-shaped lava formations on this island is known as the Garden of the Gods.

■ Hawaii is the only state that was once a kingdom. Iolani Palace in downtown Honolulu is the only royal palace ever built on U.S. land.

■ The Big Island of Hawaii contains high mountains, lush valleys and fields, desert-like areas of lava, sand and ash as well as gleaming white sandy beaches, black lava beaches and a green beach of volcanic particles.

Hawaii
red
red lehua blossom

■ U.S. involvement in World War II began when President Franklin Roosevelt declared war on Japan on December 8, 1941, the day after the surprise attack on Pearl Harbor.

■ Sugarcane and pineapple grow well on the Valley Island of Maui in the fertile valley between the mountains. Mount Haleakala is the largest inactive volcano crater in the world. The crater is 3,000 feet deep and 22 miles around.

Hawaii Trivia

■ Mauna Kea and Hualalai on the Big Island and Haleakala on Maui are called dormant volcanoes. *Dormant* means they haven't erupted for a long time, but they could erupt again in the future.

■ People from Europe, China, Japan, Korea, Samoa, New Zealand, Tonga and many other countries have settled in the Hawaiian Islands. As a result, the people have mixed ethnic and cultural backgrounds.

■ The first people to settle in the Hawaiian Islands came from the Polynesian islands more than 2,000 miles away. They traveled in large canoes, arriving about 300 A.D. Other groups, possibly from Tahiti, arrived 500 or 600 years later.

■ If the water were drained from the Pacific Ocean, you could see that the Hawaiian Islands are actually the tops of a chain of underwater mountains formed by volcanic activity. Two volcanoes on the Big Island are still very active. When Mauna Loa and Kilauea erupt, fountains of burning lava spout into the air.

■ According to legend, the Alakoko fish-pond was built by the **menehune**, an ancient race of little people who first inhabited Kaua'i. The menehune worked only at night and were rarely seen.

■ When missionaries arrived in Hawaii, they established phonetic spellings for Hawaiian words, using only 12 letters. Hawaiian words are spelled with five vowels: *A, E, I, O* and *U*; plus seven consonants: *H, K, L, M, N, P* and *W*.

■ Both the state and one of the islands are named Hawaii. To avoid confusion, the island of Hawaii is often called the Big Island.

■ The state of Hawaii is an archipelago—a chain of islands in the Pacific Ocean. The entire chain includes 132 islands and stretches 1,523 miles. Most of the islands are small and unpopulated.

■ When Captain Cook, first arrived in Kaua'i in 1778, he found about 250,000 people living in the Hawaiian Islands. He named them the Sandwich Islands after his patron, the Earl of Sandwich.

■ Many Hawaiian legends concern Maui, a man with god-like powers who invented the spear and the barbed fishhook and discovered fire. He created a place for people to live by pushing the sky high in the air. He was known as "Maui of a Thousand Tricks."

■ How did Hawaii get its name? One legend says the islands were named for Hawaii-loa, a Polynesian chief who discovered the islands long ago. The early Polynesian settlers may have named the islands for their South Pacific homeland which was called Hawaiki in ancient times.

■ The Big Island is the newest of the Hawaiian Islands. Southeast of the Big Island, a new volcanic island is forming. It should reach the surface in about 10,000 years.

■ Hawaii became the 50th state on August 21, 1959.

Tasty Treats

Hawaii is the nation's leading producer of sugarcane and pineapple. Although not native to the islands, Hawaii is also the principal producer of another delicious treat. What delicious, crunchy treat comes from Hawaii?

$\overline{16}$ $\overline{2}$ $\overline{11}$ $\overline{17}$ $\overline{28}$ $\overline{6}$ $\overline{16}$ $\overline{10}$ $\overline{26}$ $\overline{18}$ $\overline{4}$ $\overline{19}$ $\overline{24}$

To find the answer, fill in the blanks below. Write the letter that corresponds with the number below each blank.

1. Eighty percent of the people in Hawaii live on the island of $\underline{}'\underline{}\underline{}\underline{}$.
   $\;\;1\;\;2\;\;3\;\;4$

2. Captain James Cook named Hawaii the $\underline{}\underline{}\underline{}\underline{}\underline{}\underline{}\underline{}\underline{}$ Islands.
   $\;\;5\;\;6\;\;7\;\;8\;\;9\;\;10\;\;11\;\;12$

3. What word means that a volcano has not erupted in a long time? $\underline{}\underline{}\underline{}\underline{}\underline{}\underline{}\underline{}$
   $\;\;13\;\;14\;\;15\;\;16\;\;17\;\;18\;\;19$

4. The island of Hawaii is called the

   $\overline{20}\;\overline{21}\;\overline{22}$ $\quad\overline{23}\;\overline{24}\;\overline{25}\;\overline{26}\;\overline{27}\;\overline{28}$.

Challenge Questions

1. Draw a volcano. Label its parts, including the cinder cone, crater, lava, magma and vents. Explain how volcanoes erupt.

2. Kaummana Caves near Hilo on the Big Island are lava tubes that formed more than 100 years ago. What is a lava tube?

Just for Fun

What do cats in Hawaii have that no other animal has?

Hawaii Bingo

To the Teacher: The master game sheet, rules and game suggestions are on pages 179 and 180.

Statements for Hawaii Bingo

- The island of Hawaii is nicknamed the **Big Island**.
- **Captain James Cook** was the first European to visit Hawaii.
- Maui is known as the **Valley Island**.
- The first people to live on Hawaii came from the **Polynesian Islands**.
- Pineapples are plentiful on Lāna'i, the **Pineapple Island**.
- Captain Cook named Hawaii the **Sandwich Islands**.
- The **Friendly Island** of Moloka'i was formed by three volcanoes.
- The Hawaiian Islands are actually the tops of **underwater mountains** formed by volcanoes.
- O'ahu is known as the **Gathering Place**.
- A **dormant** volcano is one that has not erupted in a long time.
- Few people are invited to Ni'ihau, the **Forbidden Island**.
- Hawaii is an **archipelago**—a chain of islands.
- Giant ferns grow in the rain forests of Kaua'i, the **Garden Isle**.
- The state of Hawaii includes **132** islands.
- **Maui** is a legendary hero with great powers.
- Hawaii's nicknamed the **Aloha State**.
- The Hawaiian alphabet contains only **12** letters.
- Hawaii's state flower is the **hibiscus**.

- The state tree is the **candlenut**.
- The **Hawaiian goose** is the official state bird.
- Hawaii has two official state languages: **English** and **Hawaiian**.
- **Honolulu** is the capital of Hawaii.
- No one lives on **Kaho'olawe**, the smallest of the eight major islands.
- The Hawaiian Islands were formed by **volcanoes**.

Idaho

Nickname: Gem State • State Bird: Mountain Bluebird • Capital: Boise

■ The Nez Perce used digging sticks to gather kouse and camas bulbs. Kouse are bulb-like roots eaten raw that taste like turnips. Camas bulbs are a type of wild lily with blue and white flowers that grow about three feet high. The Nez Perce called them "quamash."

Lewiston

■ Cut by the Snake River over millions of years ago, Hells Canyon is the deepest canyon in North America.

■ Emerald Creek is one of the few places in the world where star garnets are found. Visitors are allowed to dig for these rare gems.

■ Fossil evidence indicates that people have lived in Idaho for more than 13,000 years. By the time white explorers arrived, several groups lived in the region including the Shoshone, Paiute and Nez Perce. (*Perce* is pronounced like *purse*.)

■ Millions of years ago, great earthquakes pushed up the mountains. Volcanoes erupted, spewing ash and lava across the land. Huge glaciers dug deep valleys between the mountains. These natural forces combined to make Idaho a land of contrasts and spectacular scenery.

■ The explorers, Lewis and Clark, crossed the Bitterroot Mountains to reach Idaho in 1805. They camped at the site of present-day Lewiston.

■ Potatoes are Idaho's best-known crop. Idaho farmers grow more spuds than any other state, producing 25% of the nation's potatoes.

★ **Boise**

■ The state capital in Boise is the only capitol building heated with geothermal hot water.

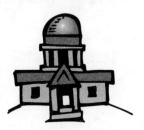

■ More than 2,000 natural lakes and 16,000 miles of rivers and streams cover the state. Forests cover 40% of Idaho. Some stands of red cedar date back hundreds of years. Millions of bison once roamed the grasslands of Idaho.

■ Trickling water freezes into unusual ice formations in Crystal Ice Cave, 155 feet deep inside the heart of a dormant volcano. Other spectacular ice formations can be seen in the lava tube of Shoshone Ice Cave. Minnetonka Cave contains dazzling ice crystal walls and fossils of prehistoric plants and animals.

■ *Nez Perce* is a French word meaning "pierced nose." They dug their homes, called lodges or dugouts, in the ground two to three feet deep. They used the scooped-out dirt to build walls. Posts along the sides and middle supported the roof. They covered the roofs with large mats of cattails sewn together.

■ The prospect of gold brought many miners to Idaho. By 1866 more than $24 million in gold had been discovered in the Boise Basin.

■ Irrigation ditches dug by the Mormons in 1855 have changed millions of acres of desert into productive cropland.

■ The word *Idaho* was invented by George Willig. He claimed it was a Native American word that meant "gem of the mountains." As far as anyone knows, no such word existed.

Out of This World

One of Idaho's most famous landmarks is an area where the land looks like the surface of the moon, complete with craters, lava flows, caves and tunnels. What is this place near Arco called?

$\overline{22}$ $\overline{2}$ $\overline{19}$ $\overline{9}$ $\overline{31}$ $\overline{18}$ $\overline{30}$ $\overline{12}$ $\overline{1}$ $\overline{11}$ $\overline{6}$ $\overline{24}$ $\overline{16}$ $\overline{8}$ $\overline{28}$ $\overline{4}$

To find the answer, fill in the blanks below. Write the letter that corresponds with the number below each blank.

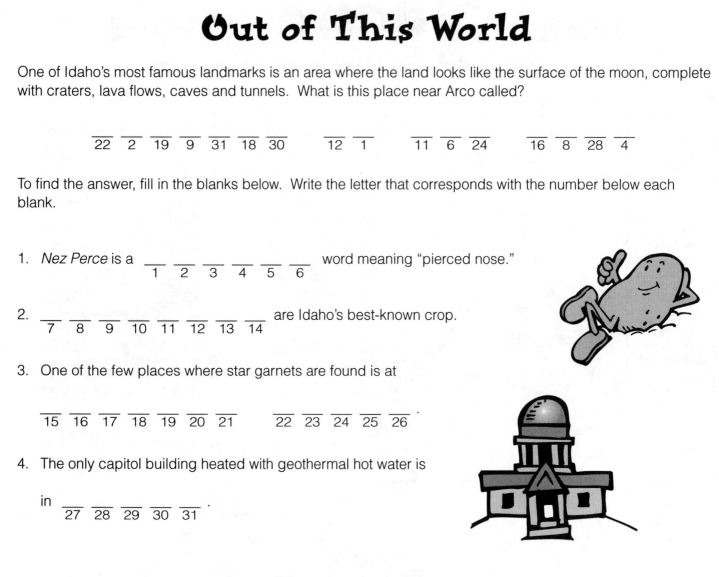

1. *Nez Perce* is a $\underset{1}{\rule{0.5cm}{0.4pt}}$ $\underset{2}{\rule{0.5cm}{0.4pt}}$ $\underset{3}{\rule{0.5cm}{0.4pt}}$ $\underset{4}{\rule{0.5cm}{0.4pt}}$ $\underset{5}{\rule{0.5cm}{0.4pt}}$ $\underset{6}{\rule{0.5cm}{0.4pt}}$ word meaning "pierced nose."

2. $\underset{7}{\rule{0.5cm}{0.4pt}}$ $\underset{8}{\rule{0.5cm}{0.4pt}}$ $\underset{9}{\rule{0.5cm}{0.4pt}}$ $\underset{10}{\rule{0.5cm}{0.4pt}}$ $\underset{11}{\rule{0.5cm}{0.4pt}}$ $\underset{12}{\rule{0.5cm}{0.4pt}}$ $\underset{13}{\rule{0.5cm}{0.4pt}}$ $\underset{14}{\rule{0.5cm}{0.4pt}}$ are Idaho's best-known crop.

3. One of the few places where star garnets are found is at

$\overline{15}$ $\overline{16}$ $\overline{17}$ $\overline{18}$ $\overline{19}$ $\overline{20}$ $\overline{21}$ $\overline{22}$ $\overline{23}$ $\overline{24}$ $\overline{25}$ $\overline{26}$.

4. The only capitol building heated with geothermal hot water is

in $\overline{27}$ $\overline{28}$ $\overline{29}$ $\overline{30}$ $\overline{31}$.

Challenge Questions

1. Chief Joseph led the Nez Perce on an 1,800-mile march towards Canada. Why were they going to Canada? What happened before they reached Canada?

2. Called the "Niagara of the West," its dazzling falls plunge more than 200 feet. What is the name of these falls in Idaho?

Just for Fun

What has eyes but cannot see?

Idaho Is a Five-Letter Word

Look up and down, backwards, forwards and diagonally to find these 44 places in Idaho.

B	O	I	S	E	A	R	I	M	O	P	E	B	R
O	U	H	T	R	I	F	Y	P	A	H	A	I	S
V	I	N	B	N	P	L	G	Y	A	K	G	S	U
I	I	O	K	A	D	I	R	M	E	B	L	M	T
L	N	O	R	O	O	E	E	R	Y	E	E	A	O
P	M	M	L	I	V	R	E	E	E	L	P	L	N
N	A	Y	R	A	E	D	R	S	G	M	C	L	S
E	A	R	S	E	R	A	S	A	A	E	I	A	K
W	N	N	I	T	C	D	S	N	D	D	N	D	N
B	N	O	E	S	A	N	O	T	E	T	I	P	A
L	I	E	T	M	H	O	E	C	A	R	G	M	B
I	W	A	G	S	T	C	I	D	A	H	O	U	L
S	R	I	R	I	E	K	R	U	B	U	Y	O	E
S	I	H	M	E	L	O	H	T	A	T	L	A	M

ARBON	EAGLE	MOORE
ARIMO	EMIDA	NAMPA
ATHOL	FIRTH	NOTUS
AVERY	FLIER	PARIS
BAKER	GRACE	PARMA
BANKS	GREER	RIGBY
BLISS	HAMER	RIRIE
BOISE	INKOM	SAGLE
BOVIL	IRWIN	SANTA
BURKE	LEMHI	SMALL
CAREY	LETHA	STONE
CONDA	MALTA	SWEET
DEARY	MELBA	TETON
DECLO	MENAN	VIOLA
DOVER	MIDAS	

All the places listed have two things in common:

1. They are all in Idaho.

2. What's the second thing they have in common?

_____

Illinois

Nickname: Land of Lincoln • State Bird: Cardinal • Capital: Springfield

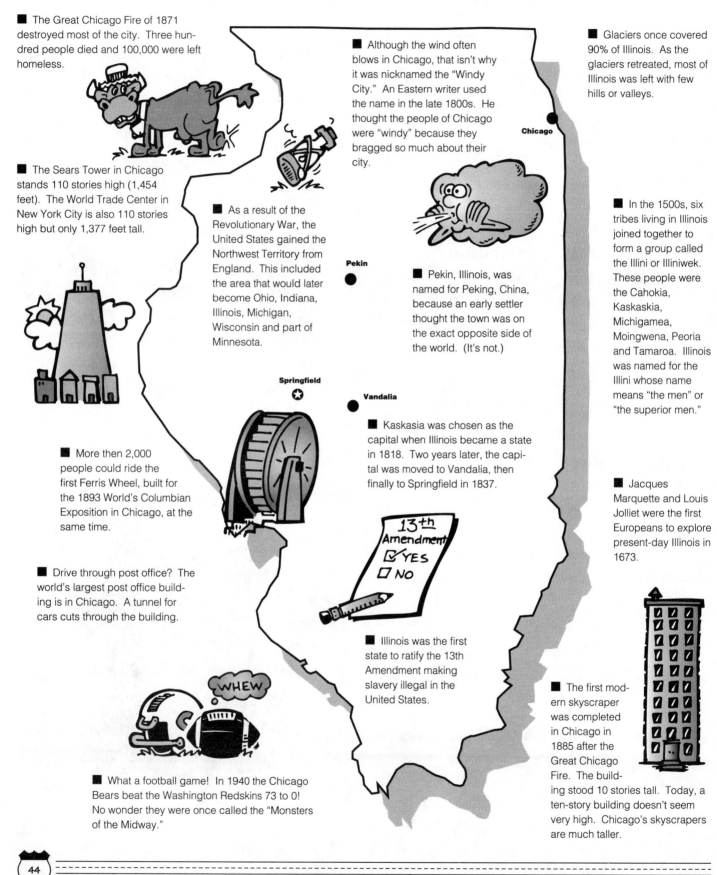

■ The Great Chicago Fire of 1871 destroyed most of the city. Three hundred people died and 100,000 were left homeless.

■ The Sears Tower in Chicago stands 110 stories high (1,454 feet). The World Trade Center in New York City is also 110 stories high but only 1,377 feet tall.

■ As a result of the Revolutionary War, the United States gained the Northwest Territory from England. This included the area that would later become Ohio, Indiana, Illinois, Michigan, Wisconsin and part of Minnesota.

■ Although the wind often blows in Chicago, that isn't why it was nicknamed the "Windy City." An Eastern writer used the name in the late 1800s. He thought the people of Chicago were "windy" because they bragged so much about their city.

■ Glaciers once covered 90% of Illinois. As the glaciers retreated, most of Illinois was left with few hills or valleys.

Chicago

Pekin

■ Pekin, Illinois, was named for Peking, China, because an early settler thought the town was on the exact opposite side of the world. (It's not.)

■ In the 1500s, six tribes living in Illinois joined together to form a group called the Illini or Illiniwek. These people were the Cahokia, Kaskaskia, Michigamea, Moingwena, Peoria and Tamaroa. Illinois was named for the Illini whose name means "the men" or "the superior men."

Springfield

Vandalia

■ Kaskasia was chosen as the capital when Illinois became a state in 1818. Two years later, the capital was moved to Vandalia, then finally to Springfield in 1837.

■ More then 2,000 people could ride the first Ferris Wheel, built for the 1893 World's Columbian Exposition in Chicago, at the same time.

■ Jacques Marquette and Louis Jolliet were the first Europeans to explore present-day Illinois in 1673.

13th Amendment
☑ YES
☐ NO

■ Drive through post office? The world's largest post office building is in Chicago. A tunnel for cars cuts through the building.

■ Illinois was the first state to ratify the 13th Amendment making slavery illegal in the United States.

WHEW

■ What a football game! In 1940 the Chicago Bears beat the Washington Redskins 73 to 0! No wonder they were once called the "Monsters of the Midway."

■ The first modern skyscraper was completed in Chicago in 1885 after the Great Chicago Fire. The building stood 10 stories tall. Today, a ten-story building doesn't seem very high. Chicago's skyscrapers are much taller.

44

Matchmaker

Match the items in the box by writing the correct letter in each blank. Watch out; some may have more than one answer and not all the answers may be used.

1. _____ Illinois nickname
2. _____ Capital of Illinois
3. _____ State motto
4. _____ State flower
5. _____ State tree
6. _____ State bird
7. _____ State animal
8. _____ State fish
9. _____ State insect
10. _____ State mineral
11. _____ State song
12. _____ Tallest building
13. _____ Windy City

A. Bluegill	L. Raccoon
B. Cardinal	M. Robin
C. Chicago	N. Sears Tower
D. Fluorite	O. Springfield
E. Honeybee	P. State Sovereignty, National Union
F. "Illinois"	
G. Land of Lincoln	Q. Tall State
H. Maple tree	R. Trout
I. Monarch butterfly	S. Violet
J. Morning glory	T. White oak
K. Prairie State	U. White-tailed deer

Challenge Questions

1. With a 1990 population of 2,783,726, Chicago isn't the largest city in the U.S., but it ranks near the top. How many U.S. cities are larger than Chicago? What are they?

2. Only one U.S. President was born in Illinois. Who was he?

Just for Fun

Which candles burn longer: white ones in Chicago or red ones in Springfield?

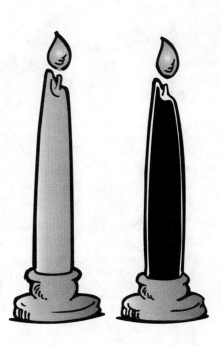

What Can You See in Illinois?

Study the pictures of these Illinois items for one minute. Then turn this page over. List all the items you can remember.

Illinois or Someplace Else?

Are you sure these cities are in Illinois? They sound like they should be someplace else. The names of 29 Illinois cities are hidden in the puzzle. Look up, down, backwards, forwards and diagonally to find them. Some letters in the puzzle will be part of more than one word. Words in parentheses are not in the puzzle.

Circle the words when you find them. When you finish the puzzle, write the unused letters on the blanks below. The unused letters will spell the name of a team from Illinois.

```
P  E  K  I  N  G  E  N  E  V  A  H
O  A  B  U  C  R  E  T  E  S  A  A
N  W  L  P  C  M  H  N  P  N  I  R
T  A  B  E  O  C  I  A  O  M  A  V
I  T  U  R  S  C  R  V  S  A  E  A
A  T  N  U  E  T  E  H  M  D  L  R
C  O  K  G  A  R  I  U  O  I  P  D
A  R  E  M  O  L  I  N  E  S  A  A
N  E  R  Z  O  G  B  E  E  O  S  L
T  G  I  H  L  E  N  O  D  N  O  L
O  O  A  E  P  A  R  I  S  R  S  A
N  N  B  N  A  L  I  M  E  L  A  S
```

BELGIUM	HANOVER	PEKING
BUNKER (Hill)	HARVARD	PERU
CANTON	LONDON (Mills)	PONTIAC
CRETE	MADISON	ROME
CUBA	MILAN	SALEM
DALLAS (City)	MOLINE	SHILOH
EL PASO	OREGON	SPARTA
ERIE	OTTAWA	VENICE
GENEVA	PALESTINE	ZION
GENOA	PARIS	

Unused letters: __ __ __ __ __ __ __ __ __ __ __

Indiana

Nickname: Hoosier State • State Bird: Cardinal • Capital: Indianapolis

■ Although the origin of the word is uncertain, almost everyone knows Indiana is the Hoosier State.

■ Before the early settlers arrived, forests covered over 80% of Indiana. Today, only 17% of the land remains forested.

■ Between 1900 and 1920, the automobile industry boomed in Indiana. More than 200 different makes of cars were produced including Duesenbergs, Auburns, Stutzes and Maxwells.

■ Part of Indiana's growth in the 1800s was due to a system of roads connecting it with other states. The National Road stretched from Cumberland, Maryland, to Vandalia, Illinois. Twelve different stagecoach lines ran through Indianapolis. The Michigan Road from Madison, Wisconsin, south to South Bend and back north to Michigan City also passed through Indianapolis. Today, more major highways intersect in Indiana than in any other state. No wonder Indiana's state motto is Crossroads of America.

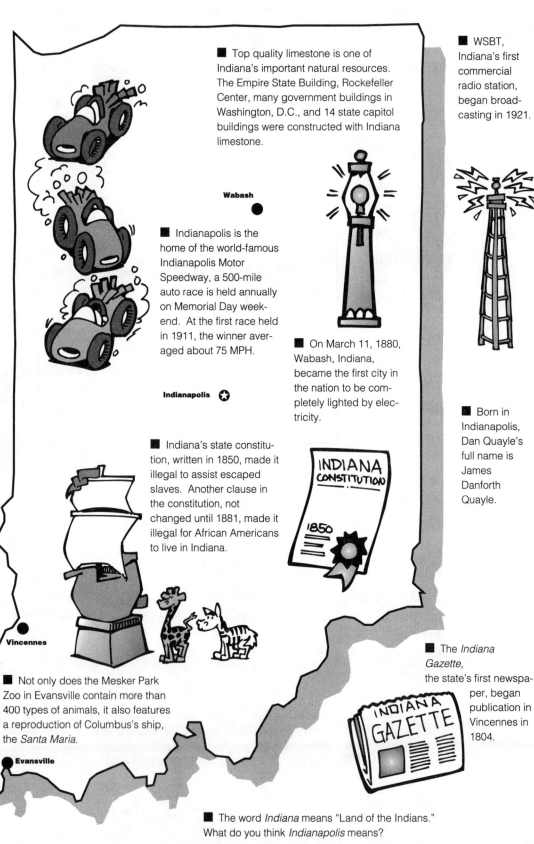

■ Top quality limestone is one of Indiana's important natural resources. The Empire State Building, Rockefeller Center, many government buildings in Washington, D.C., and 14 state capitol buildings were constructed with Indiana limestone.

Wabash ●

■ Indianapolis is the home of the world-famous Indianapolis Motor Speedway, a 500-mile auto race is held annually on Memorial Day weekend. At the first race held in 1911, the winner averaged about 75 MPH.

Indianapolis ☆

■ Indiana's state constitution, written in 1850, made it illegal to assist escaped slaves. Another clause in the constitution, not changed until 1881, made it illegal for African Americans to live in Indiana.

Vincennes ●

■ Not only does the Mesker Park Zoo in Evansville contain more than 400 types of animals, it also features a reproduction of Columbus's ship, the *Santa Maria*.

● **Evansville**

■ On March 11, 1880, Wabash, Indiana, became the first city in the nation to be completely lighted by electricity.

INDIANA CONSTITUTION

1850

INDIANA GAZETTE

■ WSBT, Indiana's first commercial radio station, began broadcasting in 1921.

■ Born in Indianapolis, Dan Quayle's full name is James Danforth Quayle.

■ The *Indiana Gazette,* the state's first newspaper, began publication in Vincennes in 1804.

■ The word *Indiana* means "Land of the Indians." What do you think *Indianapolis* means?

Underground

More than 700 of these have been discovered underground in southern Indiana. What are they?

$\overline{36}$ $\overline{32}$ $\overline{10}$ $\overline{5}$ $\overline{12}$ $\overline{31}$ $\overline{21}$ $\overline{34}$ $\overline{14}$ $\overline{4}$ $\overline{24}$ $\overline{1}$ $\overline{8}$ $\overline{27}$

To find the answer, fill in the blanks below. Write the letter that corresponds with the number below each blank.

1. The state's first newspaper, the *Indiana Gazette*, began

   publication in $\overline{1}$ $\overline{2}$ $\overline{3}$ $\overline{4}$ $\overline{5}$ $\overline{6}$ $\overline{7}$ $\overline{8}$ $\overline{9}$.

2. Where would you go in Indiana to see a reproduction of Columbus's ship, the *Santa Maria*?

   $\overline{10}$ $\overline{11}$ $\overline{12}$ $\overline{13}$ $\overline{14}$ $\overline{15}$ $\overline{16}$ $\overline{17}$ $\overline{18}$ $\overline{19}$ $\overline{20}$ $\overline{21}$ $\overline{22}$

3. What was the first city in the nation to be completely

   lighted by electricity? $\overline{23}$ $\overline{24}$ $\overline{25}$ $\overline{26}$ $\overline{27}$ $\overline{28}$

4. In 1834, people could travel from Cumberland, Maryland, to

   Vandalia, Illinois, on the $\overline{29}$ $\overline{30}$ $\overline{31}$ $\overline{32}$ $\overline{33}$ $\overline{34}$ $\overline{35}$ $\overline{36}$ Road.

Challenge Questions

1. Two brothers from Indiana made wheelbarrows and wagons in their factory before modernizing their company to build cars and trucks. Who were they?

2. The small community of Fountain City was known as the "Grand Central Station of the Underground Railroad." Why?

Just for Fun

What kind of beans don't grow from seeds in Indiana?

Indy 500

How many words can you make using the letters around the racetrack? Before you begin, check the rules.

Scoring

Add one lap for every word made.

Add five laps for every five-letter word.

Add 10 laps for every six-letter word.

Add 15 laps for every seven-letter word.

Add 20 laps for every eight-letter word.

Add 25 laps for every word of nine or more letters.

Deduct two laps for every letter not used.

Total laps: _____

Rules

1. Words must be three or more letters long. The longer the word, the more it's worth.
2. Cross out each letter as you use it.
3. Each letter may be used only once.

Write your words below. When you finish, tally your score. How close did you come to making 500 laps?

Indiana or Someplace Else?

Are you sure this is Indiana? These cities sound like they should be someplace else. The names of 27 cities in Indiana are hidden in the puzzle. Look up, down, backwards, forwards and diagonally to find them. Some letters in the puzzle will be part of more than one word. Words in parentheses are not in the puzzle.

Circle the words when you find them. When you finish the puzzle, write the unused letters on the blanks below. The unused letters will spell the name of a composer from Peru, Indiana, who wrote the words and music to many Broadway hit musicals.

```
W  M  E  L  A  S  R  E  I  G  L  A
A  H  C  N  O  N  R  E  V  T  M  T
T  U  O  O  N  O  L  M  E  S  O  L
E  D  S  L  A  R  U  O  P  I  R  A
R  S  O  T  L  K  A  R  R  R  O  N
L  O  T  Y  I  A  E  M  E  A  C  T
O  N  O  E  M  N  N  P  L  P  C  A
O  R  E  C  I  C  R  D  O  E  O  L
T  M  I  C  H  I  G  A  N  T  S  B
M  E  X  I  C  O  G  E  N  E  V  A
P  O  L  A  N  D  U  B  L  I  N  N
L  I  Z  A  R  B  U  N  K  E  R  Y
```

AKRON	DUBLIN	(New) PARIS
ALBANY	GENEVA	PERU
ALGIERS	HOLLAND	POLAND
ATLANTA	HUDSON	ROME (City)
AUSTIN	MEXICO	SALEM
BRAZIL	MICHIGAN (City)	SELMA
BUNKER (Hill)	MILAN	TOPEKA
CHILI	MOROCCO	TROY
CICERO	MT VERNON	WATERLOO

Unused letters: __ __ __ __   __ __ __ __ __

Iowa

Nickname: Hawkeye State • State Bird: Eastern Goldfinch • Capital: Des Moines

■ Nicknames for Iowa include: Hawkeye State, Corn State, Corn-Hog State and Land Where the Tall Corn Grows. The nickname "Hawkeye State" honors Chief Black Hawk, a Sauk leader who led an unsuccessful resistance against settlers in 1832.

■ Before the early settlers in Iowa could plant crops, the land had to be cleared and plowed. Prairie grass with long tangled roots covered most of the land. Many farmers hired professionals with enormous plows pulled by oxen to break up of the sod (dirt). Some farmers paid more per acre to have "sodbusters" plow the land than they did to purchase it.

■ Many early settlers in Iowa built homes by cutting up chunks of earth and using dirt "bricks" to build their homes. With walls three to four feet thick, sod houses stayed warm in winter and cool in summer.

■ Elk Horn and Kimballton were settled by people from Denmark. A statue of the Little Mermaid from the story by the Danish writer, Hans Christian Andersen, stands in the town square.

■ Sioux City

Kimballton

Elk Horn

Des Moines ✪

Dubuque

■ The world's largest popcorn processing plant is in Sioux City. Although most varieties of corn look similar, only one type actually pops. What makes it pop? Believe it or not—water. The kernel explodes when the moisture inside is heated. The pressure of steam inside the corn causes it to burst open.

Davenport

SNAKE ALLEY

■ Snake Alley in Burlington is said to be the crookedest street in the world, an honor also claimed by Lombard Street in San Francisco.

Burlington

■ Iowa was named for the Ioway Indians. One translation is "beautiful land."

■ Des Moines comes from the Native American word *moingona* meaning "river of the mounds." Davenport, founded in 1836, was named for George Davenport, a fur trader. Founded in 1833, Dubuque was named for Julian Dubuque, Iowa's first white settler. Sioux City, founded in 1854, was named for the Sioux.

■ Iowa is the nation's number one corn-growing state and one of the leading states for raising hogs. There are almost five times as many hogs in Iowa as there are people.

■ During a boundary dispute between Missouri and Iowa, a group of Missourians chopped down three hollow trees filled with wild honey in an area claimed by Iowa. The governors of both states called out the militia. By the time the Iowa militia, armed with pitchforks and squirrel guns, reached the border, the Missouri militia had gone home. The "Honey War" ended without a shot.

■ Shallow seas covered Iowa about 500 million years ago. Fossils of starfish and prehistoric amphibians similar to crocodiles have been found in Iowa.

TLC10029 Copyright © Teaching & Learning Company, Carthage, IL 62321

Iowa Tic-Tac-Toe

To play Iowa Tic-Tac-Toe, correctly answer three questions in a row: up and down, across or diagonally.

1. Who wrote the story of the Little Mermaid? _____	**2.** Iowa is the number one _____ growing state.	**3.** Before early settlers could plant crops, they had to _____ and _____ the land.
4. There are more than five times as many _____ in Iowa as people.	**5.** What makes popcorn pop? _____	**6.** The name Des Moines means _____
7. The nickname "Hawkeye State" honors _____	**8.** Iowa was named for the _____ Indians.	**9.** The world's largest popcorn processing plant is in _____

Challenge Questions

1. The Amana Colonies are a cluster of seven villages founded in the 1850s. Who founded the Amana Colonies? What was unique about the life-style of the people who lived there?

2. Who was the first President born west of the Mississippi River? Hint: He was born in West Branch, Iowa, in 1874.

Just for Fun

What's the best medicine for a pig with a sprained ankle?

Build by Number

In 1976, the people of Elk Horn, Iowa, brought a windmill from Denmark piece by piece and reassembled the mill's 30,000 numbered pieces.

Cut out the pieces of the windmill below and reassemble them by arranging them in numerical order, starting at the lower left corner.

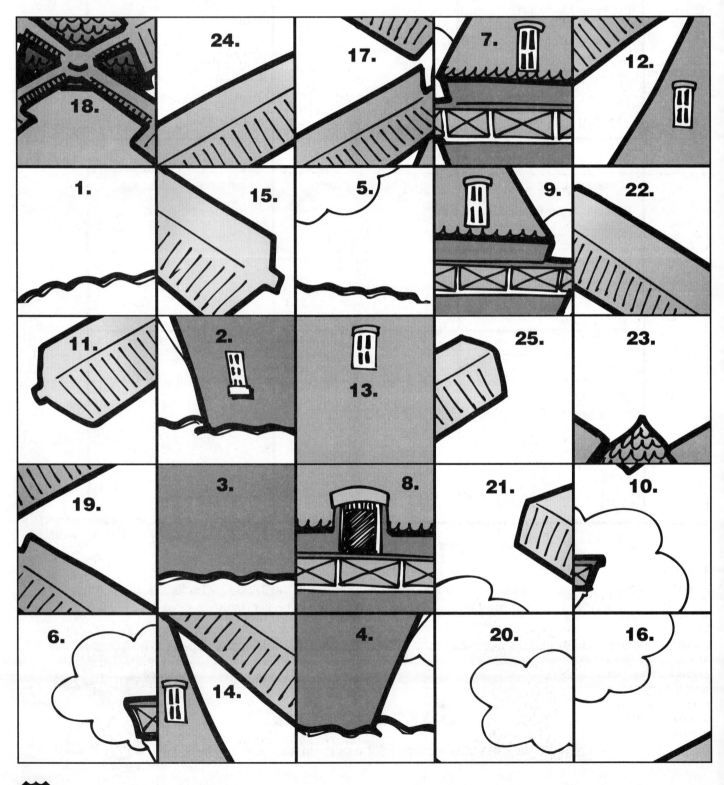

Kansas

Nickname: Sunflower State • State Bird: Western Meadowlark • Capital: Topeka

■ Millions of years ago, much of Kansas was covered by a great sea. Fossils of prehistoric fish, reptiles and swimming birds have been found along the Smoky Hill River.

■ In 1988, archaeologists digging near Bonner Springs along the Kansas River uncovered human bones 15,000 years old, evidence that people have lived in the area for at least that long.

■ Many settlers moved west to Kansas, lured by the promise of free land. The Homestead Act of 1862 gave 160 acres of federal land to any citizen who paid a $10 filing fee if he agreed to live on the land for five years and improve the property.

■ Kansas was named for the Native Americans known as the Kansa. *Kansa* means "people of the south wind." They lived in the northeast part of Kansas.

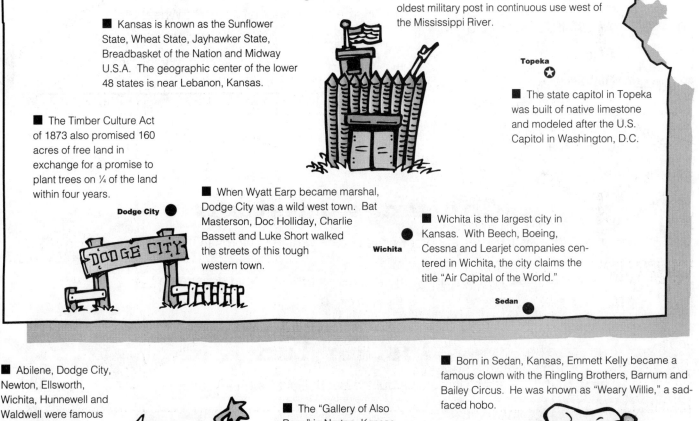

Norton ●   Lebanon ●

■ Kansas is known as the Sunflower State, Wheat State, Jayhawker State, Breadbasket of the Nation and Midway U.S.A. The geographic center of the lower 48 states is near Lebanon, Kansas.

■ Fort Leavenworth, built in 1827, is the oldest military post in continuous use west of the Mississippi River.

Topeka ✪

■ The state capitol in Topeka was built of native limestone and modeled after the U.S. Capitol in Washington, D.C.

■ The Timber Culture Act of 1873 also promised 160 acres of free land in exchange for a promise to plant trees on ¼ of the land within four years.

Dodge City ●

■ When Wyatt Earp became marshal, Dodge City was a wild west town. Bat Masterson, Doc Holliday, Charlie Bassett and Luke Short walked the streets of this tough western town.

Wichita ●

■ Wichita is the largest city in Kansas. With Beech, Boeing, Cessna and Learjet companies centered in Wichita, the city claims the title "Air Capital of the World."

Sedan ●

■ Abilene, Dodge City, Newton, Ellsworth, Wichita, Hunnewell and Waldwell were famous Kansas "cowtowns" in the 1870s and '80s. After long cattle drives, cowboys brought their cattle to towns along the railroad in Kansas for shipping to eastern markets.

■ The "Gallery of Also Rans" in Norton, Kansas, honors those who ran for President but were not elected.

■ Trees from all 50 states and from 33 countries grow in the International Forest of Friendship near Atchison, Kansas.

■ Born in Sedan, Kansas, Emmett Kelly became a famous clown with the Ringling Brothers, Barnum and Bailey Circus. He was known as "Weary Willie," a sad-faced hobo.

TLC10029 Copyright © Teaching & Learning Company, Carthage, IL 62321

Matchmaker

Match the items in the box by writing the correct letter in each blank. Watch out; some may have more than one answer, and not all the answers may be used.

1. ____   *Kansa* means . . .

2. ____   Marshall of Dodge City

3. ____   Kansas nickname

4. ____   State flower

5. ____   Known as "Weary Willie"

6. ____   State song

7. ____   Capital of Kansas

8. ____   Kansas Cowtown

9. ____   State bird

10. ____   Air Capital of the World

11. ____   State animal

12. ____   State tree

A. Abilene	K. People of the South Wind
B. Beautiful Kansas	L. Kansas quail
C. Breadbasket of the Nation	M. Roy Rogers
D. Buffalo	N. Sunflower
E. Cottonwood	O. Sunflower State
F. Daisy	P. Topeka
G. Emmett Kelly	Q. Western meadowlark
H. "Home on the Range"	R. Wheat State
I. Kansas City	S. Wichita
J. Midway U.S.A.	T. Wyatt Earp

Challenge Questions

1. "Home on the Range" is the state song of Kansas. Who wrote the words to this well-known song?

2. Born in Atchison, Kansas, Amelia Earhart made aviation history. What did she do?

Just for Fun

What's as large as a buffalo but doesn't weigh an ounce?

The Wind Blew

In 1931, a drought that lasted for several years began in Kansas and parts of neighboring states. Heat and dry weather ruined the crops and turned the land to dust. Kansas became a "dust bowl" as winds blew up great dust storms bad enough to cover roads, stop traffic and close schools. People could get lost in their own backyards when the howling winds brought the "black blizzards."

The letters of these Kansas cities have been blown out of order. Perhaps a big blast of wind was the cause, or maybe it was another cyclone like the one that sent Dorothy and Toto to Oz.

Rearrange the letters to correctly spell the names of 12 Kansas cities.

N L D O R E A V   R P K A   **T P A E K O**

1. _ _ _ _ _ _ _   _ _ _ _   7. _ _ _ _ _ _

T H U I O S C N N H   **H C T A I I W**

2. _ _ _ _ _ _ _ _ _   8. _ _ _ _ _ _ _

S S N A K A   I Y C T   **H L O T E A**

3. _ _ _ _ _ _   _ _ _ _   9. _ _ _ _ _ _

W E O L H E T R V N A   **L A A S N I**

4. _ _ _ _ _ _ _ _ _ _ _   10. _ _ _ _ _ _

N T N A T A A H M   **B I N A E E L**

5. _ _ _ _ _ _ _ _ _   11. _ _ _ _ _ _ _

D D E O G   T Y C I   **A R W C E E N L**

6. _ _ _ _ _ _ _ _ _   12. _ _ _ _ _ _ _ _

Kentucky

Nickname: Bluegrass State • State Bird: Kentucky Cardinal • Capital: Frankfort

■ About 300 million years ago, much of Kentucky was swampland. When the swamp plants died, they formed a thick layer of organic material which eventually turned into coal, an important natural resource.

■ The Church of Monte Cassino built in 1850 near Covington, Kentucky, is so small, only three people at a time can fit inside. The church contains three benches, large enough to hold only one person each. The church tower is so small that it cannot hold a bell.

■ Dozens of caverns lie underground in south-central and eastern Kentucky. Mammoth Cave is one of the largest in the world open to the public. *Mammoth* means "large." Three rivers, two lakes and a sea are part of Mammoth Cave. The temperature at Mammoth Cave stays at 54°F all year round.

■ Kentucky bluegrass isn't really blue. The grass itself is a lush, dark green. In spring, bluish-purple blossoms make lawns and fields of grass look blue.

■ Coffee doesn't grow on Kentucky coffee trees, but the early pioneers did make a drink from the tree's seeds.

■ Near Louisville, Kentucky's largest city, baseball bats called Louisville sluggers are made.

Frankfort ✪

Lexington

Louisville

Fort Knox

■ Horse farms surround the city of Lexington. Thoroughbreds and American Saddle Horses are raised in the "Horse Capital of the World."

■ About $6 billion in gold is stored at the U.S. Gold Depository at Fort Knox.

FORT KNOX
$

■ Best known as the Colonel of Kentucky Fried Chicken, Harlan Sanders was not actually born in Kentucky, but in Henryville, Indiana, in 1890.

■ Several Native American groups living in the area had words that sounded similar to Kentucky. Translated, the words meant "lands where we live," "meadowlands," "dark and bloody ground," "great meadows" or "land of tomorrow." The official name of Kentucky is the Commonwealth of Kentucky.

■ In 1776 Kentucky became a county in the state of Virginia. It didn't become a separate state until 16 years later.

■ It might say "Land of Lincoln" on Illinois license plates, but the famous 16th President of the United States, Abe Lincoln, was born in Hodgenville, Kentucky. He moved to Indiana with his family when he was seven years old, then to Illinois at age 21.

■ In 1966 Kentucky became the first southern state to adopt a Civil Rights law guaranteeing equal rights for African Americans.

Name _____

My Old Kentucky Home

After visiting relatives in Bardstown, this man wrote "My Old Kentucky Home," Kentucky's official state song. What was his name?

‾10‾ ‾21‾ ‾36‾ ‾15‾ ‾32‾ ‾17‾ ‾5‾   ‾18‾ ‾24‾ ‾10‾ ‾31‾ ‾3‾ ‾2‾

To find the answer, fill in the blanks below. Write the letter that corresponds with the number below each blank.

1. What color is Kentucky bluegrass?

‾1‾ ‾2‾ ‾3‾ ‾4‾ ‾5‾

2. What color are the blossoms of Kentucky bluegrass?

‾6‾ ‾7‾ ‾8‾ ‾9‾ ‾10‾ ‾11‾ - ‾12‾ ‾13‾ ‾14‾ ‾15‾ ‾16‾ ‾17‾

3. Where in Kentucky does the U.S. store much of its gold?

‾18‾ ‾19‾ ‾20‾ ‾21‾   ‾22‾ ‾23‾ ‾24‾ ‾25‾

4. Name the large cave in Kentucky that contains three rivers, two lakes and a sea.

‾26‾ ‾27‾ ‾28‾ ‾29‾ ‾30‾ ‾31‾ ‾32‾   ‾33‾ ‾34‾ ‾35‾ ‾36‾

Challenge Questions

1. What is a moonbow? Where would you go to see one?

2. What did the U.S. Supreme Court decide about the Civil Rights issue in the 1896 Plessy Decision?

Just for Fun

In Kentucky, which part of a horse is most important?

Would You Like to Visit Monkeys Eyebrow?

Kentucky has some places with rather unusual names, like Blue Heron Coal Camp, Barbourville, Bardstown and Berea.

Look up and down, backwards, forwards and diagonally to find the names of 33 places in Kentucky.

```
D B U T C H E R H O L L E R M
H R S O I Y D N A L S I T O A
A S Y T R N U E Y A R S N Y P
N L A R A N Y X L H K K R A D
G I E H I Y E T T O E C R W Q
R B B O T D L U O Y Y I V F U
A E N K N I G R S W S L I L I
P R N I C M B E E L N E C A C
E T G K O I Y B O L Y N C H K
V Y L U R E L U A Y U O O Y S
I T S E B R I T A R O B R E A
N I V R Z S A L N I N G A L N
E O O C A A C E H I Z I N P D
D W A R F O H R E R A B R I D
E I G H T Y E I G H T P O D W
```

BERRY

BIG BONE LICK

BROOKS

BUG

BUTCHER HOLLER

BUTLER

CLAY

DOVER

DRY RIDGE

DWARF

EIGHTY-EIGHT

GRAPEVINE

GUTHRIE

HALFWAY

HAZEL

INDEX

ISLAND

LIBERTY

LOUISA

LYNCH

MONKEYS EYEBROW

MOUSIE

NEON

PAINT LICK

PARIS

QUICKSAND

RABBIT HASH

SALT LICK

STAY

TINY TOWN

UNION

VICCO

WINGO

Louisiana

Nickname: Pelican State • State Bird: Eastern Brown Pelican • Capital: Baton Rouge

■ The highest point in Louisiana, Driskill Mountain, is only 535 feet above sea level. The lowest point is in New Orleans, 5 feet below sea level.

■ Louisiana covers approximately 47,752 square miles. The actual size changes because of flooding and erosion along the coast. If all of Louisiana's inlets, bays and islands are included, the state has over 7,700 miles of coastline.

■ Marshes, swamps and wetlands make up much of the state's coast. Half the ducks and geese in North America spend the winter along the Louisiana coast.

■ The Teche, Lafourche, Boeuf, Dorcheat, Dugdemona and D'Arbonne are Louisiana bayous. The word *bayou* comes from the Choctaw word *bayuk*, meaning "creek." A bayou is a slow-moving inlet or outlet of a lake, river or sea.

■ **Laissez les bons temps rouler!** as they say in Louisiana. Translated into English, it means "Let the good times roll!"

■ About 4,000 French colonists forced to leave Acadia (Nova Scotia) by the British in 1755 made their way to Louisiana. These people of Acadian descent are known as Cajuns.

■ Louisianans are a mix of many cultures and ethnic backgrounds. Many Native Americans, descendants of slaves and Hispanics intermarried with white settlers from France, Quebec and Spain. Their descendants are known as Creoles.

■ Because the land is so low, flooding is a continuous problem in Louisiana. Levees are thick walls of earth built along the banks of rivers to help control flooding.

■ News traveled slowly in the 1800s. The Battle of New Orleans, fought by troops led by Andrew Jackson in January 1815 against the British, ended in a major victory for the Americans. What none of the troops knew at the time was that the War of 1812 had ended 15 days before the battle was fought.

■ A 40-mile stretch north of New Orleans is called the German Coast because of the great number of German farmers who settled there in the 1720s. Many Irish and Italians migrated to Louisiana in the late 1800s.

■ The city of Baton Rouge means "red stick" in French. The city's name came from the tall red pole that once stood at the river's edge to mark the boundary of the Houmas hunting grounds.

■ The water in many Louisiana lakes is brackish — a combination of fresh water and salt water.

✪ **Baton Rouge**

● **New Orleans**

■ The most famous celebration in New Orleans is Mardi Gras. People wearing costumes sing and dance through the streets.

■ Louisiana has a humid, subtropical climate. Snow is so rare in the southern part that a park in New Orleans brings in truckloads of snow once a year as a special treat for the children.

■ New Orleans gave birth to a unique American form of music known as jazz, a combination of traditional African music, spirituals, slave work songs and brass marching bands. Louis Armstrong, one of the world's best-known jazz musicians, grew up in New Orleans.

Louisiana Question Game

To play Louisiana Question Game, read the answers, then finish the questions.

1. I am the Louisiana state bird.

   What is the _____?

2. Some of us are named the Teche, Lafourche, Boeuf, Dorcheat, Dugdemona and D'Arbonne.

   What are _____?

3. I am the Louisiana state gem.

   What is the _____?

4. Founded in 1719, the name of this city means "red stick."

   What is _____?

5. "Give Me Louisiana" and "You Are My Sunshine" are well known in Louisiana.

   What are Louisiana's two _____?

6. This battle was fought 15 days too late.

   What was the _____?

7. I am Louisiana's state insect.

   What is a _____?

8. Built along the banks of rivers, they reduce flooding.

   What are _____?

9. I am Louisiana's state tree.

   What is a _____?

10. Laissez les bons temps rouller! as they say in Louisiana.

    What is _____?

11. I am Louisiana's state flower.

    What is the _____?

12. These Louisianans are descendants of French colonists forced to leave Acadia (Nova Scotia) in 1755.

    Who are _____?

Challenge Questions

1. Why is New Orleans known as the "Crescent City"?

2. What are counties in Louisiana called?

Just for Fun

How can you tell the price of a pelican in Louisiana?

Louisiana Wildlife

All the wildlife in Louisiana isn't in New Orleans during Mardis Gras. The state's many swamps, forests, wet-lands, lakes, rivers and offshore waters provide year-round homes for a large variety of wildlife.

You'll find the letters you need in the letter bank below each group. Cross out the letters as you use them. Each letter will only be used once. All the letters will be used.

Plants and Trees

__ A S __ I N __
O __ C H I __ S
C __ P __ E S S
P A L __ E T T __
M A __ N __ L I A
H I __ I S C __ S
S P __ N I S __   M O __ S
P I T __ H E R   __ L A __ T S

Letter Bank:

A B D C E G H J M
M N O O P R R S U Y

Off the Coast

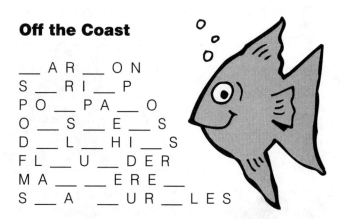

__ A R __ O N
S __ R I __ P
P O __ P A __ O
O __ S __ E __ S
D __ L __ H I __ S
F L __ U __ D E R
M A __ __ E R E __
S __ A __ U R __ L E S

Letter Bank:

C E H K L M M N N N
O O P P R T T T T Y

Four-Legged Creatures

M I N __
F O __ E __
N U __ R I __
__ T T __ R S
B __ B __ A T S
__ E A S E __ S
B E A __ E R __
__ A C __ O O N S
__ P O __ S __ M S
M __ S __ R A __ S
S __ U I __ R E __ S
B U __ L __ R O __ S
__ L __ I __ A __ O R S
W __ I T E - T __ I __ E D   D __ __ R

Letter Bank:

A A A C C E E E F G G H
K K L L L L L O O O Q R
R S S S T T T U U V W X

In the Air

O __ L S
G __ E __ E
__ U C __ S
Q U A __ L
D O __ E S
C __ O __ S
H A __ K S
S W __ N S
__ E R __ N S
E __ R E __ S
S T __ R __ S
__ R A __ E S
P __ L I __ A N S
B A __ D   __ A G __ E S

Letter Bank:

A C C D E E E G H I K K
L L O O N R S T V W W W

Maine

Nickname: Pine Tree State • State Bird: Chickadee • Capital: Augusta

■ Long before Christopher Columbus crossed the Atlantic Ocean, the Algonquian people lived in the forests along the coast from Canada south to present-day Virginia. They called themselves **Wabanaki**—people of the dawn.

■ An ancient legend claims that the Great Father sent a crow to the Algonquian people with a kernel of corn in one ear and a bean in the other. Beans and corn became their two most important crops.

■ *Wigwam* is the Algonquian word for *house*. The frame of a wigwam was built of tall young trees.

■ The Wedding Cake House at Kennebunk looks like a huge wedding cake. A sea captain built it for his bride in 1826.

■ The first sea battle of the Revolutionary War occurred in Maine on June 12, 1775, when patriots from Machias rowed out to the English ship *Margaretta*, attacked and captured it.

■ More potatoes are grown in Aroostook County than in any other county in the nation. Children are excused from school in the fall to help with the potato harvest.

■ Chester Greenwood of Farmington invented earmuffs in 1873. Farmington became the Earmuff Capital of the World.

■ The nation's first doughnuts were made in Camden in 1847. The first chewing gum made in the U.S. came from Bangor in 1848.

Bangor •

Farmington

■ Boston wasn't the only city to hold a tea party. The York Tea Party took place in 1774 when colonists from Maine destroyed British tea stored at York, Maine.

Machias •

■ New Hampshire is the only state that borders Maine. The other borders are formed by Quebec, New Brunswick and the Atlantic Ocean.

Augusta ✪

■ Portland was named the capital when Maine became a state in 1820. The majestic granite state capitol building in Augusta was built in 1829, but Augusta didn't become the capital until 1832.

Camden •

Portland •

Kennebunk •

York •

■ Besides having a state bird, animal, insect and fish, Maine also has an official state cat. The Maine coon cat looks like a raccoon and weighs up to 30 pounds when fully grown.

■ Sea mammals like seals, porpoises and even whales live along the Maine coast. The ocean also provides a home for cod, flounder, tuna, halibut, shellfish, clams, oysters and, of course, Maine lobsters. Bass, trout and salmon are abundant in freshwater lakes.

■ Hundreds of different types of animals make their homes in the Maine woods including deer, moose, black bears, bobcats, lynxes, beavers, otters, mink, martens and porcupine.

■ Forests of balsam, fir, basswood, beech, hemlock, oak, maple, spruce, birch, willow and pine cover nearly 90% of Maine. The Pine Tree State produces 50 billion wooden toothpicks a year.

Let There Be Light

During the Revolutionary War, the British often captured Maine ships at sea forcing the crew to join the British Navy. In protest, colonists of Maine shut off the lanterns in lighthouses along the rocky, treacherous coast. Then they hung lanterns around horses and let them wander up and down the shore at night. Local sailors could navigate by moonlight, but the British sailors who followed the lights crashed into the rocks and sank.

In Maine, a lighthouse is called a "light" for short. Maine's oldest lighthouse is a favorite subject for artists and photographers. What is it called?

___ ___ ___ ___ ___ ___ ___ ___   ___ ___ ___ ___   ___ ___ ___ ___ ___
12 18 26 21 16 11 6   1   5   22 33 1   16 30 31 5   8

To find the answer, fill in the blanks below. Write the letter that corresponds with the number below each blank.

1. The nation's first ___ ___ ___ ___ ___ ___ ___ ___ ___ were made in
                      1 2 3 4 5 6 7 8 9

   Camden, Maine, in 1847.

2. Augusta became the ___ ___ ___ ___ ___ ___ ___ of Maine in 1832.
                     10 11 12 13 14 15 16

3. In protest against the British tax on tea, Maine colonists

   held the ___ ___ ___ ___   ___ ___ ___   ___ ___ ___ ___ ___ in 1774.
            17 18 19 20   21 22 23   24 25 26 27 28

4. The Algonquian word for *house* is ___ ___ ___ ___ ___ ___ .
                          29 30 31 32 33 34

Challenge Questions

1. Born in Portland, he wrote "Paul Revere's Ride" and "Evangeline." What was the name of this famous poet from Maine?

2. Massachusetts purchased Maine from the Gorges family in 1677 for about $6,000. How long did Maine remain part of Massachusetts? Who were the Gorges family? How did they come to own Maine in the first place?

Just for Fun

What did the scientist from Maine get when she crossed a moose with a mouse?

What Rhymes with Maine?

Lots of words rhyme with *Maine*—like *airplane, obtain, reign* and *regain*.

Work with a partner to find as many words as you can that rhyme with *Maine*. You can use proper nouns like *Spain* and *Elaine*. Write your list of rhyming words here.

The rain in Maine
Falls mainly on Duane.

Couplets are two lines of poetry. The last word in the first line rhymes with the last word in the second line. Write the second line of these couplets, ending with words that rhyme with *Maine*.

Sasha wrapped the blueberry pie in cellophane

_____

Jayne looked through the rainy windowpane

_____

If the plane won't fly, we'll take a train

_____

I was surprised when I looked at the weather vane

_____

The hole in Maine was dug by a huge yellow crane

_____

Jane and Lorraine took a plane to Brisbane

_____

The dentist from Maine gave me novocaine

_____

A treasure chest! What does it contain?

_____

If you don't understand, I'll try to explain

_____

 TLC10029 Copyright © Teaching & Learning Company, Carthage, IL 62321

Maryland

Nickname: Free State • State Bird: Baltimore Oriole • Capital: Annapolis

■ Captain John Smith was one of the earliest Europeans to explore the Chesapeake Bay area.

■ Maryland was named for Henrietta Maria, wife of King Charles I of England.

■ King Charles I granted a land charter along the Chesapeake Bay to Cecil Calvert, the second Lord of Baltimore. Calvert hoped to establish a colony where Catholics and Protestants could live together in peace. Led by his younger brother, Leonard, colonists set sail for Maryland in 1633.

■ When Europeans first arrived, the Nanticoke, Choptan, Pocomoke, Wicomico, Yaoconaco, Anaco, Piscataway, Susquehannock and Patuxent lived in Maryland. Many were forced from their lands. Some died in battles. Native Americans had no natural immunities to European diseases, and terrible epidemics of smallpox, diphtheria and tuberculosis swept through their villages.

■ Some of the land claimed by the Maryland colony was also claimed by the Virginia and Pennsylvania colonies. These disputes were not settled until after 1767 when Charles Mason and Jeremiah Dixon determined a straight line, known as the Mason Dixon Line that became the border between Maryland and Pennsylvania.

■ Maryland was the seventh of the original 13 colonies to ratify the Constitution on April 28, 1788.

■ Originally called Anne Arundel Town, the city was renamed Annapolis in honor of Queen Anne. The octagon wooden dome of Maryland's capitol building at Annapolis was built entirely without nails.

■ Between 1776 and 1784, both Baltimore and Annapolis served briefly as the U.S. capital. The land for Washington, D.C., was originally part of Maryland.

■ Horse racing is a popular sport in Maryland. Every spring, race fans gather at Pimlico Race Course to watch the Preakness Stakes, the second of three races that make up the Triple Crown.

■ The sight of the American flag still waving the morning after the bombing of Baltimore's Fort McHenry in 1814, inspired Francis Scott Key to write "The Star-Spangled Banner" which became the national anthem in 1931.

■ Few states have an official state sport, and none have one as unusual as Maryland. Since 1842, Marylanders have held annual jousting tournaments. Galloping at full speed, riders try to spear dangling rings with a lance.

■ Maryland has only 31 miles of coastline along the Atlantic Ocean, but an additional 3,190 miles of coast lie along Chesapeake Bay.

■ A skipjack is the traditional wooden sailboat used to dredge for oysters in Chesapeake Bay. The skipjack is Maryland's official state boat.

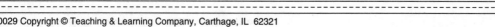

Name _____   *Maryland*

Matchmaker

Match the items in the box by writing the correct letter in each blank. Watch out; some may have more than one answer and not all the answers may be used.

1. ____ Maryland nickname
2. ____ State motto
3. ____ King Charles I
4. ____ State flower
5. ____ Briefly, U.S. capital
6. ____ State bird
7. ____ State dog
8. ____ The word *Maryland*
9. ____ State fish
10. ____ State boat
11. ____ Mason Dixon Line
12. ____ State insect
13. ____ Francis Scott Key
14. ____ State sport
15. ____ Capital of Maryland
16. ____ Anne Arundel Town

A. Annapolis
B. Baltimore
C. Baltimore oriole
D. Black-eyed Susan
E. Border between Maryland and Pennsylvania
F. Border between Maryland and Virginia
G. Canoe
H. Checkerspot butterfly
I. Chesapeake Bay retriever
J. Dalmatian
K. Free State
L. Granted land charter to Lord Baltimore
M. Jousting
N. Ladybug
O. Manly Deeds, Womanly Words
P. Named for Henrietta Maria
Q. Named for Queen Anne
R. Named for Lord Baltimore
S. Old Line State
T. Robin
U. Rockfish
V. Skipjack
W. Tuna
X. Wrote "Maryland, My Maryland"
Y. Wrote "The Star-Spangled Banner"
Z. Wrote "Yankee Doodle"

Challenge Questions

1. Why is one of Maryland's nicknames "Old Line State"?

2. Legend says this 90-year-old woman defied Stonewall Jackson's order to lower the Union flag as he marched through Frederick, Maryland, in 1862. She was immortalized in a poem by John Greeleaf Whittier with these words: Shoot if you must, this old gray head, But spare your country's flag . . ." What was her name?

Just for Fun

How can you tell the price of a Baltimore oriole?

TLC10029 Copyright © Teaching & Learning Company, Carthage, IL 62321

Weather Advice

Fishermen on Chesapeake Bay offer this weather advice:

When the wind is from the north,
Sailors don't go forth.
When the wind is from the east,
'Tis neither fair for man nor beast.
When the wind is from the south,
It blows the bait in the fish's mouth.
When the wind is from the west,
Then it's at its very best.

Finish the following weather poems with a word that rhymes.

When the leaves start to fall,

It's time to play _____.

When it starts to snow,

The roses won't _____.

When the north winds blow,

It will probably _____.

Make up some weather advice of your own and write it below. Your advice can rhyme, but it doesn't have to.

Some words you might want to use are *rain, wet, blizzard, snow, sleet, sun, sunny, sunshine, cold, hot, warm, chilly, ice, cloud, hail, north, south, east, west, blow, snow, June, May, fall, spring, summer, winter, thunder, boom.*

Massachusetts

Nickname: Bay State • State Bird: Chickadee • Capital: Boston

■ In 1845, owning a bathtub in Boston was against the law unless it was prescribed by a doctor.

■ The first shots of the Revolutionary War were fired at Lexington in 1775. At nearby Concord, the patriots won their first victory of the Revolutionary War.

■ The nation's first subway began in Boston in 1897.

■ A large statue known as the Gloucester Fishermen's Memorial in Gloucester honors fishermen who died at sea.

■ Harvard University, Radcliffe College and the Massachusetts Institute of Technology (MIT) are in Cambridge. Founded in 1636, Harvard was the first college in the New World.

■ The southeastern peninsula of Massachusetts is known as Cape Cod. Lief Erickson and his Vikings may have landed at Cape Cod as early as 1000 A.D. Martha's Vineyard and Nantucket Island are famous islands south of Cape Cod.

■ With the use of two peach baskets, James Naismith invented basketball in Springfield in 1891. This city is home to the Basketball Hall of Fame.

■ Boston is known as the "Cradle of Liberty" because the rebellion against England started there.

Gloucester

Cambridge   Boston

Springfield

■ Boston was once home to a professional baseball team called the Boston Beaneaters.

Plymouth

New Bedford

■ Salem was the first town founded by the Massachusetts Bay Colony in 1628.

■ The first town settled by the Pilgrims was Plymouth. The Pilgrims spelled it PLIMOTH. Although they sought religious freedom for themselves, the Puritans refused to allow others the same rights.

■ In 1852 a Massachusetts law required all children in the state between the ages of 8 and 14 to attend school at least 12 weeks a year. Six of the weeks had to be consecutive.

■ The state's official name is the Commonwealth of Massachusetts.

■ New Bedford was the world's leading whaling port in the 1800s.

■ The first American Thanksgiving, three days of prayer and feasting, was celebrated by the Plymouth colonists in 1621 to give thanks for their first harvest. They had survived a 65-day crossing of the Atlantic Ocean and many hardships in the New World.

■ In 1842, the governor of Massachusetts made it illegal for children under 12 to work more than 10 hours a day in factories.

■ Cranberry juice is the official state beverage of Massachusetts. The state colors are blue and gold.

TLC10029 Copyright © Teaching & Learning Company, Carthage, IL 62321

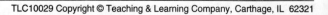

Name _____

Where in Massachusetts?

1. Name the city where basketball was invented. _____

2. The first shots in the Revolutionary War were fired at _____.

3. The American colonists won their first battle in the Revolutionary War at _____.

4. Name the city known as the "Cradle of Liberty." _____

5. The first college in the New World was in what city? _____

6. Where would you find a famous statue honoring fishermen who died at sea? _____

7. What was the first settlement founded by the Massachusetts Bay Colony? _____

8. The first town founded by the Pilgrims was _____.

9. What is the peninsula in southeastern Massachusetts called? _____

10. What Massachusetts town was the world's leading whaling port? _____

Challenge Questions

1. Susan B. Anthony was arrested and fined $100 for doing something unthinkable in 1872. What did she do?

2. A poem has been written about Paul Revere's famous ride from Boston. Where did he ride? Why did he make his famous ride?

Just for Fun

What did one pickle say to the other pickle?

What Can You Find in Massachusetts?

How many words can you make using the letters in MASSACHUSETTS? Words must be three or more letters. Words formed by adding *S* at the end cannot be used. Write your list of words below.

_____   _____   _____   _____

_____   _____   _____   _____

_____   _____   _____   _____

_____   _____   _____   _____

_____   _____   _____   _____

Look at the items below related to Massachusetts. Study the pictures for one minute. Turn the page over and list as many of the items as you can remember.

TLC10029 Copyright © Teaching & Learning Company, Carthage, IL 62321

Michigan

Nickname: Wolverine State • State Bird: Robin • Capital: Lansing

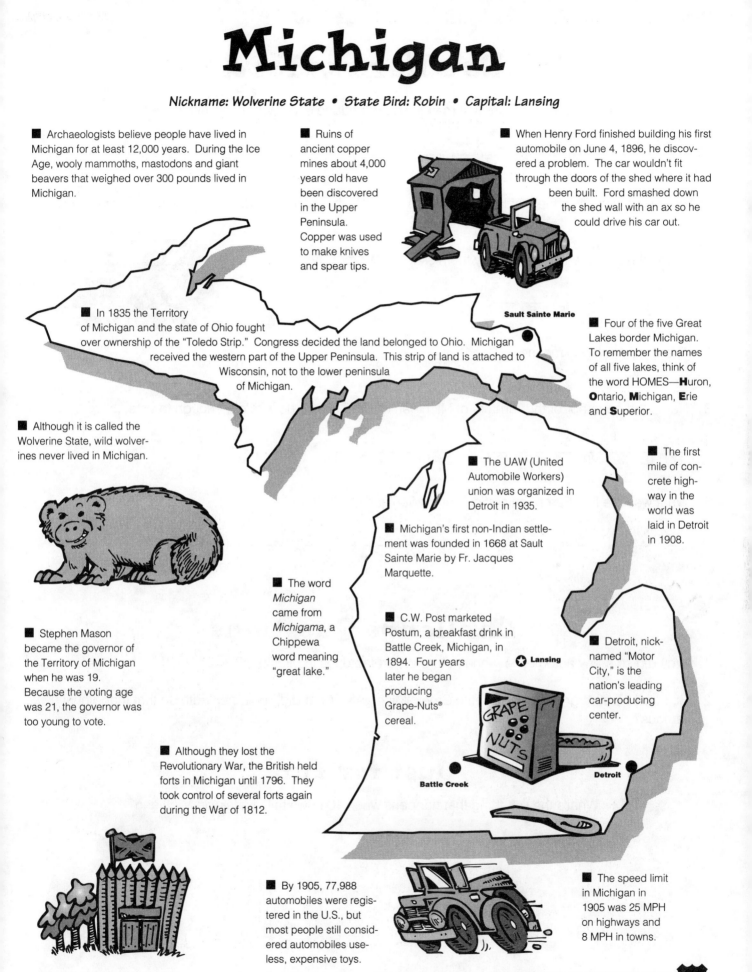

■ Archaeologists believe people have lived in Michigan for at least 12,000 years. During the Ice Age, wooly mammoths, mastodons and giant beavers that weighed over 300 pounds lived in Michigan.

■ Ruins of ancient copper mines about 4,000 years old have been discovered in the Upper Peninsula. Copper was used to make knives and spear tips.

■ When Henry Ford finished building his first automobile on June 4, 1896, he discovered a problem. The car wouldn't fit through the doors of the shed where it had been built. Ford smashed down the shed wall with an ax so he could drive his car out.

Sault Sainte Marie

■ In 1835 the Territory of Michigan and the state of Ohio fought over ownership of the "Toledo Strip." Congress decided the land belonged to Ohio. Michigan received the western part of the Upper Peninsula. This strip of land is attached to Wisconsin, not to the lower peninsula of Michigan.

■ Four of the five Great Lakes border Michigan. To remember the names of all five lakes, think of the word HOMES—Huron, Ontario, Michigan, Erie and Superior.

■ Although it is called the Wolverine State, wild wolverines never lived in Michigan.

■ The UAW (United Automobile Workers) union was organized in Detroit in 1935.

■ The first mile of concrete highway in the world was laid in Detroit in 1908.

■ Michigan's first non-Indian settlement was founded in 1668 at Sault Sainte Marie by Fr. Jacques Marquette.

■ Stephen Mason became the governor of the Territory of Michigan when he was 19. Because the voting age was 21, the governor was too young to vote.

■ The word *Michigan* came from *Michigama*, a Chippewa word meaning "great lake."

■ C.W. Post marketed Postum, a breakfast drink in Battle Creek, Michigan, in 1894. Four years later he began producing Grape-Nuts® cereal.

Lansing

■ Detroit, nicknamed "Motor City," is the nation's leading car-producing center.

Battle Creek

Detroit

■ Although they lost the Revolutionary War, the British held forts in Michigan until 1796. They took control of several forts again during the War of 1812.

■ By 1905, 77,988 automobiles were registered in the U.S., but most people still considered automobiles useless, expensive toys.

■ The speed limit in Michigan in 1905 was 25 MPH on highways and 8 MPH in towns.

73

Not Henry Ford

This machinist and inventor was the first man to mass produce cars. What was his name?

$\overline{42}$ $\overline{30}$ $\overline{28}$ $\overline{17}$ $\overline{5}$ $\overline{40}$ $\overline{19}$ $\overline{13}$ $\overline{36}$ $\overline{27}$ $\overline{32}$ $\overline{1}$ $\overline{26}$

To find the answer, fill in the blanks below. Write the letter that corresponds with the number below each blank.

1. Name the Michigan city known by the nickname "Motor City."

$\overline{1}$ $\overline{2}$ $\overline{3}$ $\overline{4}$ $\overline{5}$ $\overline{6}$ $\overline{7}$

2. The word *Michigan* means $\overline{8}$ $\overline{9}$ $\overline{10}$ $\overline{11}$ $\overline{12}$ $\overline{13}$ $\overline{14}$ $\overline{15}$ $\overline{16}$.

3. Name the governor of the Territory of Michigan elected before he was old enough to vote.

$\overline{17}$ $\overline{18}$ $\overline{19}$ $\overline{20}$ $\overline{21}$ $\overline{22}$ $\overline{23}$ $\overline{24}$ $\overline{25}$ $\overline{26}$ $\overline{27}$ $\overline{28}$

4. What was the first European settlement in Michigan?

$\overline{29}$ $\overline{30}$ $\overline{31}$ $\overline{32}$ $\overline{33}$ $\overline{34}$ $\overline{35}$ $\overline{36}$ $\overline{37}$ $\overline{38}$ $\overline{39}$ $\overline{40}$ $\overline{41}$ $\overline{42}$ $\overline{43}$ $\overline{44}$

Challenge Questions

1. Why did so many automobile manufacturers start factories in Michigan?

2. Sojourner Truth's grave is near Battle Creek, Michigan. What did Sojourner Truth do that made her famous?

Just for Fun

What's the first thing that happens when 10 cows fall in a lake in Michigan?

"C" These Sites in Michigan

If you go to Michigan, you can *C* these sites. The names of 26 places in Michigan beginning with *C* are hidden in the puzzle. Look up, down, backwards, forwards and diagonally to find them. Some letters in the puzzle will be part of more than one word. Words in parentheses are not in the puzzle.

When you finish the puzzle, write the unused letters on the blanks below. The unused letters will spell the name of an annual event in Holland, Michigan.

```
C C C A P A C O V E R T
A A C L I N T O N L C T
D L L E I N O T Y A L C
I U A E R M U L C T A E
L M W I D A A O A S R N
L E S P F O L X S Y K T
A T O E I D N C P R S E
C N N L W O O I I C T R
E E C A S L S T A O O P
D M T R O I V R N L N R
A E A M D R O C N O C A
R C A M B R I A A N L C
```

CADILLAC	CASS (River)	CLINTON
CALEDONIA	CEDAR (Springs)	CLIO
CALUMET	CEMENT (City)	COLDWATER
CAMBRIA	CENTER (Line)	COLOMA
CAPAC	CLARE	COLON
CARO	CLARKSTON	CONCORD
CARP (Lake)	CLAWSON	COVERT
CARSON (City)	CLAYTON	CRYSTAL
CASPIAN	CLIMAX	

Unused letters: __ __ __ __ __   __ __ __ __ __ __ __ __

Minnesota

Nickname: Gopher State • State Bird: Common Loon • Capital: St. Paul

■ Vikings may have explored Minnesota as early as 1362. Not all scientists believe the evidence, a stone carved in old Norse letters, is authentic.

■ Although gophers live in Minnesota, that isn't why the state is called the Gopher State. Promoters who worked to get state support for their railroads were pictured as gophers in top hats in an 1859 cartoon.

■ Minnesota is known as the North Star State. Its northern peninsula, called the Northwest Angle, extends farther north than any other place in the lower 48 states. This part of Minnesota can be reached only by taking a boat across Lake of the Woods or by driving through Canada.

■ Besides gophers, you'll find timber wolves, moose, deer, elk, bobcats, lynxes and black bears in the northern woods of the Gopher State.

■ Chippewa, Itasca, Jackson and Washington were some of the names suggested when Minnesota became a U.S. Territory. Finally, the name Minnesota was agreed upon.

■ Often called the "Nation's Icebox," January temperatures in International Falls range from an average high of 14°F to an average low of -8°F The city's 22-foot high thermometer provides the "cold facts" for everyone to see.

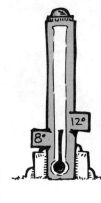

■ Lake Superior covers 31,700 square miles and is the largest lake in the world. Twenty-six states the size of Rhode Island would fit in the area covered by Lake Superior with room left over.

■ Minnesota's abundance of wheat, flour mills and dairy products earned it the nickname Bread and Butter State. Soybeans, beef cattle, sheep, poultry, oats, corn, sugar beets and potatoes are important agricultural products.

St. Paul
☆

■ Between 300 B.C. and 100 A.D. people in the southwestern corner of the state began to mine catlinite (pipestone). They carved **calumets** (peace pipes) from the red rock and traveled long distances to the sacred pipestone quarries.

■ The nickname "Land of Sky-Blue Waters" refers to the origin of the name Minnesota which came from a Dakota word meaning "sky-tinted water."

■ The Mississippi River begins in north-central Minnesota at Lake Itasca. As it starts its journey to the Gulf of Mexico, the Mississippi isn't very mighty. The Father of Waters begins as a narrow creek, so shallow that children can wade across it.

■ One nickname for Minnesota is "Land of 10,000 Lakes." There are actually 15,291 lakes in Minnesota. If you count small ponds, the number rises close to 22,000. More than 25,000 miles of lakes and streams crisscross the state. If all the lakes and streams were laid end to end, they would be long enough to go around the Earth at the equator.

Name _____

Go, Vikings, Go!

The Minnesota Vikings have a nickname that almost sounds like they might be aliens from another planet. What is the state's professional football team called?

$$\overline{11}\ \overline{4}\ \overline{27}\ \overline{22}\ \overline{3}\ \overline{13} \qquad \overline{11}\ \overline{6}\ \overline{10}\ \overline{22}\ \overline{16}\ \overline{31}$$

$$\overline{19}\ \overline{29}\ \overline{33}\ \overline{23}\ \overline{14}\ \overline{35}$$

To find the answer, fill in the blanks below. Write the letter that corresponds with the number below each blank.

1. Peace pipes carved from red rock were called

$$\overline{1}\ \overline{2}\ \overline{3}\ \overline{4}\ \overline{5}\ \overline{6}\ \overline{7}\ \overline{8}.$$

2. Railroad men were pictured as $\overline{9}\ \overline{10}\ \overline{11}\ \overline{12}\ \overline{13}\ \overline{14}\ \overline{15}$ wearing

    top hats in an 1859 cartoon.

3. The largest inland lake is

$$\overline{16}\ \overline{17}\ \overline{18}\ \overline{19} \qquad \overline{20}\ \overline{21}\ \overline{22}\ \overline{23}\ \overline{24}\ \overline{25}\ \overline{26}\ \overline{27}.$$

4. The mighty Mississippi River begins as a small stream at

$$\overline{28}\ \overline{29}\ \overline{30}\ \overline{31} \qquad \overline{32}\ \overline{33}\ \overline{34}\ \overline{35}\ \overline{36}\ \overline{37}$$ in north-central Minnesota.

Challenge Questions

1. What city in Minnesota is the busiest freshwater port in the United States?

2. All of Minnesota except the southeast corner was once covered by mile-thick glaciers that moved back and forth across the state. How did the glaciers affect the land in Minnesota?

Just for Fun

How do you get fur from a bear in Minnesota?

What Can You Find in Minnesota?

How many words can you make using the letters in *Minnesota*? Words must be three or more letters long. Words ending in *S* cannot be used. Write your list below.

_____   _____   _____   _____

_____   _____   _____   _____

_____   _____   _____   _____

_____   _____   _____   _____

_____   _____   _____   _____

_____   _____   _____   _____

What do you think of when you hear the word *Minnesota*? Draw at least 10 objects that remind you of the North Star State.

M Is for Minnesota

. . . and for 25 Minnesota place names hidden in the puzzle. Look up, down, backwards, forwards and diagonally to find them. Some letters in the puzzle will be part of more than one word. Words in parentheses are not in the puzzle.

Circle the words when you find them. When you finish the puzzle, write the unused letters on the blanks below. The unused letters spell the name of a man from Minnesota.

```
M  S  I  L  O  P  A  E  N  N  I  M
A  I  E  H  M  E  N  T  O  R  M  A
Z  R  S  D  R  A  N  Y  A  M  I  R
E  R  O  Q  U  B  B  E  R  T  L  S
P  O  O  M  U  S  K  E  G  E  A  H
P  M  M  H  M  A  D  E  L  I  N  A
A  I  O  U  M  R  H  B  Y  P  H  L
C  D  U  R  O  S  R  M  O  R  A  L
A  D  N  F  R  A  M  O  R  G  A  N
L  L  D  A  M  O  T  L  E  Y  E  M
I  E  M  M  A  R  I  E  T  T  A  Y
M  A  D  I  S  O  N  O  T  R  O  M
```

MABEL	MAYNARD	MISQUAH
MADELINA	MAZEPPA	MOOSE (Lake)
MADISON	MEDFORD	MORA
MARBLE	MENTOR	MORGAN
MARIETTA	MIDDLE (River)	MORRIS
MARSH (Lake)	MILACA	MORTON
MARSHALL	MILAN	MOTLEY
MARY (Lake)	MINNEAPOLIS	MOUND
		MUSKEG

Hint: The words MARSH and MARSHALL are two separate entries.

Unused letters: __ __ __ __ __ __   __ __ __ __ __ __

Mississippi

Nickname: Magnolia State • State Bird: Mockingbird • Capital: Jackson

■ In 1541, long before the Pilgrims landed at Plymouth Rock, Spanish explorers, led by Hernando de Soto, searched through Mississippi and other areas looking for gold. They hoped to claim new lands and riches for Spain.

■ The Pascagoula River makes a strange humming sound. Local legend claims the son of a Pascagoula chief fell in love with a princess from an enemy tribe, the Biloxi. The Biloxi attacked the Pascagoula. Knowing they could not win, the Pascagoula joined hands and walked to the river singing. They drowned in the river. People still hear their song today.

■ Both France and England fought to control a large part of the New World. The dispute over ownership of the land along the Mississippi was finally settled in 1763 when the Treaty of Paris was signed. The victor, England, received all French lands east of the Mississippi River.

■ Natchez began on the Mississippi River in 1716 as a center for trade in furs and bear grease.

■ Trade between the French and English with the Chickasaw, Choctaw and Natchez of Mississippi brought them many wonderful new tools and other items never seen by the Native Americans. The Europeans also brought diseases and war.

■ Pierre le Moyne started the first settlement in Mississippi at Ocean Springs in 1699.

■ Once Mississippi became a state in 1817, settlers moved in by the thousands, taking over the land by trickery, bribery and force. Finally, the Native Americans of Mississippi, like those of many other states, were forced to move from their home to the Indian Territory in Oklahoma. Few survived the forced march, blizzards, hunger and diseases along the Trail of Tears.

Tupelo

Columbus

Jackson

■ Jackson, the capital and largest city in Mississippi, was built on the bluffs of the Pearl River. The city boasts a bird sanctuary filled with blooming flowers and blossoming shrubs. Mynelle Gardens also contains tropical plants and a Japanese garden.

Natchez

■ The lighthouse at Biloxi was painted black after the Civil War by Mississippians who mourned the death of Abraham Lincoln.

Biloxi

■ The French explorer, LaSalle, traveled down the Mississippi River from Canada in 1682, claiming all the land along the river for France. He named the area Louisiana in honor of King Louis XIV.

■ The first Memorial Day celebration took place at Friendship Cemetery in Columbus. Women from the town decorated the graves of both Union and Confederate soldiers in 1866.

THANK YOU VERY MUCH!

■ Mississippi has had two famous "kings." Before the Civil War, cotton was "king"— the most important crop in the state. The other Mississippi "King" was Elvis Presley, born in Tupelo. A small museum in the house where the "King of Rock and Roll" was born is open to the public.

TLC10029 Copyright © Teaching & Learning Company, Carthage, IL 62321

Buried Treasure?

This Mississippi island in the Gulf of Mexico is the legendary hiding place of pirate treasure. Although many people believe treasure was hidden here, no one has ever found it. Where is the treasure supposed to be hidden?

—— —— —— ——   —— —— —— —— —— ——
36   6   18   14   11   40   28   21   1   36

To find the answer, fill in the blanks below. Write the letter that corresponds with the number below each blank.

1. __ __ __ __ __ __ __   started as a trading center for furs
     1   2   3   4   5   6   7

and bear grease.

2. Mississippi has had two "kings"—cotton and

__ __ __ __ __   __ __ __ __ __ __ __ .
 8   9   10   11   12   13   14   15   16   17   18   19

3. Which river in Mississippi makes a strange humming sound?

__ __ __ __ __ __ __ __ __ __   River
20   21   22   23   24   25   26   27   28   29

4. _____   ____   _____
    30 31 32 33 34 35 36 37   38 39   40 41 42 43

explored Mississippi in 1541, hoping to find new land and riches for Spain.

Challenge Questions

1. Early travelers followed a road called the Natchez Trace from Natchez, Mississippi, to what city in Tennessee?

2. Pecan, sweet gum, bald cypress, tupelo and magnolia trees flourish in Mississippi. Describe or draw one of these types of trees.

Just for Fun

What has a bed, but does not sleep?

Mississippi Counties

Look up and down, backwards, forwards and diagonally to find the names of 36 counties in Mississippi. Notice how many counties are named for people. There's even a Smith and a Jones!

```
A  S  A  M  I  T  E  N  E  E  R  G  E  S
S  R  E  T  S  B  E  W  N  G  N  O  P  D
C  H  O  C  T  A  W  O  G  O  R  I  K  N
A  L  O  N  N  E  T  J  T  N  K  O  M  I
T  T  A  T  I  S  A  W  O  E  L  O  E  H
T  N  O  R  L  C  E  M  A  N  A  T  C  G
A  L  N  I  K  N  A  R  O  Y  E  O  O  A
L  O  O  S  N  E  N  S  O  H  N  S  P  C
A  C  O  P  A  T  R  O  T  O  M  E  I  A
L  N  L  E  R  E  Z  I  I  A  R  D  A  L
C  I  E  A  F  A  M  N  D  R  T  L  H  H
O  L  O  F  Y  S  U  A  Y  A  A  E  I  O
R  T  E  D  L  L  A  H  S  R  A  M  M  U
N  J  A  S  P  E  R  M  A  D  I  S  O  N
```

ADAMS	GREENE	NEWTON
ALCORN	HINDS	PERRY
AMITE	JACKSON	PIKE
ATTALA	JASPER	RANKIN
CALHOUN	JEFFERSON	SCOTT
CHOCTAW	JONES	SMITH
CLARKE	LEE	STONE
CLAY	LINCOLN	TATE
COPIAH	MADISON	UNION
DE SOTO	MARION	WAYNE
FRANKLIN	MARSHALL	WEBSTER
GEORGE	MONROE	YAZOO

TLC10029 Copyright © Teaching & Learning Company, Carthage, IL 62321

Missouri

Nickname: *Show Me State* • State Bird: *Bluebird* • Capital: *Jefferson City*

■ If you enjoy spelunking, Missouri is a great place to explore caves. More than 5,000 caves have been discovered in Missouri, and 24 are open to the public.

■ "Buffalo Bill" Cody became a rider for the Pony Express at the age of 14. Another Pony Express rider was "Wild Bill" Hickok. The Pony Express charged $5.00 per half ounce to carry letters and $3.50 for a ten-word telegram.

■ Once the transcontinental telegraph was completed in October 1861, messages could be sent in a few seconds, and the Pony Express was no longer needed.

■ Fifty thousand miles of rivers and streams crisscross the Show Me State. The Missouri River is called "the Big Muddy." Farmers claim it is "too thick to drink and too thin to plow."

■ The area north of the Missouri River was once covered by glaciers.

Hannibal

■ Missouri was named for the Missouri Indians. The name means "people of the big canoe."

■ The fiddle is Missouri's state musical instrument.

■ Peanut butter was invented in 1890 by a doctor from St. Louis who mashed peanuts and spread them on bread.

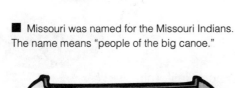

Jefferson City ✪

St. Louis

■ Young men, some only 14 and 15 years old, worked for the Pony Express, covering the distance between St. Joseph, Missouri, and San Francisco, California—2,000 miles in only 10 days. Relay stations were set up along the route. As one exhausted rider rushed in, the next rider grabbed the mail bags and galloped off on a fresh horse.

■ The Gateway Arch was built on the site of the first building in St. Louis, a trading post. The arch honors the role of St. Louis as the Gateway to the West for thousands of pioneers. Visitors can ride to an enclosed observation deck at the top of the 630-foot tall arch.

■ Missouri has a county named Texas, and Texas has a county named Missouri City.

■ Twenty million visitors to the 1904 St. Louis World's Fair explored 15 exposition halls and viewed exhibits from all over the world. Many sampled two newly invented treats—hot dogs and ice-cream cones. Visitors marveled at the exhibits in the Palace of Electricity; the Palace of Machinery and the Palace of Forestry, Fish and Game. After the World's Fair, the Palace of Fine Arts became the St. Louis Art Museum.

■ Mark Twain lived in Hannibal, Missouri, from 1839 until 1857. His two most famous characters, Tom Sawyer and Huckleberry Finn, were fictional residents of Hannibal. Each July, people in Hannibal celebrate National Tom Sawyer Days with frog jumping and fence painting contests.

Life on the Mississippi

Some cities and towns in Missouri have unusual names, like Fair Play, Tightwad, Devils Elbow and Humansville. Find the name of another Missouri town with an odd name.

$$\overline{15} \quad \overline{14} \quad \overline{35} \quad \overline{5} \quad \overline{13} \quad \overline{2} \quad \overline{31} \quad \overline{22}$$

To find the answer, fill in the blanks below. Write the letter that corresponds with the number below each blank.

1. What's a nickname for the Missouri River?

$$\overline{1} \quad \overline{2} \quad \overline{3} \qquad \overline{4} \quad \overline{5} \quad \overline{6} \quad \overline{7} \quad \overline{8}$$

2. What is Missouri's official state instrument?

$$\overline{9} \quad \overline{10} \quad \overline{11} \quad \overline{12} \quad \overline{13} \quad \overline{14}$$

3. Name the speedy mail service between Missouri and California.

$$\overline{15} \quad \overline{16} \quad \overline{17} \quad \overline{18} \qquad \overline{19} \quad \overline{20} \quad \overline{21} \quad \overline{22} \quad \overline{23} \quad \overline{24} \quad \overline{25}$$

4. What is built on the site of the first building in St. Louis?

$$\overline{26} \quad \overline{27} \quad \overline{28} \quad \overline{29} \quad \overline{30} \quad \overline{31} \quad \overline{32} \qquad \overline{33} \quad \overline{34} \quad \overline{35} \quad \overline{36}$$

Challenge Questions

1. What was the Dred Scott Decision? How did it affect slaves?

2. Something happened in southeastern Missouri in December 1811, January 1812 and February 1812 that destroyed cabins, created a large lake in Tennessee and caused the Mississippi River to flow backwards. What happened?

Just for Fun

What would you call a frog that's stuck in the mud in Missouri?

The Show Me State

Missouri is nicknamed the Show Me State. Below are drawings of items related to Missouri. Study the pictures for one minute. Then turn this page over. Make a list of all the items you can remember.

Montana

Nickname: Treasure State • State Bird: Western Meadowlark • Capital: Helena

■ The tyrannosaurus rex skeleton displayed at the New York American Museum of Natural History was found in Montana. Fossils of triceratops, pterosaurs and other dinosaurs have also been discovered in "Big Sky Country."

■ Paddlefish are an ancient type of fish that live in the Charles Russell Refuge. Their noses look like paddles.

■ *Montana* means "mountain" in Spanish. One of its nicknames is "Land of the Shining Mountains."

■ The 50 glaciers in Glacier National Park formed during the Ice Age. Iceberg Lake contains icebergs, even in the middle of summer. Moose, bighorn sheep, elk, mountain lions, grizzly bears and coyotes make their home in the park.

■ The temperature dipped to -70°F at Rogers Pass on January 20, 1954.

Eureka

■ Hundreds of thousands of Christmas trees are grown at Eureka, the Christmas Tree Capital of the World.

■ Montana has only about five people per square mile. The cattle population of the state is about three times larger than the people population. There are even more deer, elk, antelopes and bears in Montana than there are people.

Helena ★

■ A two-pound gold nugget was found near Butte, Montana, in 1989. Butte was named for Big Butte, a nearby volcanic mountain. Over 20 billion pounds of copper, 60 million pounds of silver and 240,000 pounds of gold have been discovered in the "Richest Hill on Earth."

Butte

■ At Pictograph Cave State Historical Site near Billings, a trail leads to drawings made on cave walls about 2,000 years ago. Eight thousand-year-old tools have been found in the cave.

Billings

■ Warm chinook winds blow across Montana in late winter and early spring, helping to melt the snow. The Blackfeet called these winds the "snow eater."

■ At first, the riches of fur trapping and trading brought people to Montana. Ranchers found the grassy plains ideal for raising cattle and sheep. When gold was discovered, thousands rushed to Montana to seek their fortune. Some found gold; others found silver, copper, rubies, garnets and sapphires. Major oil fields were discovered in the 1950s, and coal mining became important in the 1970s. These resources give Montana the nickname "Treasure State."

■ The Nez Perce, fleeing through Montana to Canada, met with U.S. troops only 30 miles from their destination, at Bears Paw Battlefield in 1877. They were defeated during a four-day battle with U.S. troops. Chief Joseph made a famous speech when he surrendered: "The little children are freezing to death. My heart is sick and sad. From where the sun now stands, I will fight no more forever."

■ In 1875 Native Americans of Montana were ordered to move to reservations. Under the leadership of Sitting Bull and Crazy Horse, they defeated General Custer and his troops at the Battle of Little Big Horn. Although they won that battle, they lost the war. By 1880 nearly all Native Americans in Montana lived on reservations.

Montana Question Game

To play Montana Question Game, read the answers, then finish the questions.

1. This skeleton from Montana can be seen at the New York American Museum of Natural History.

   What is _____?

2. This place features 2,000-year-old cave drawings.

   What is _____?

3. It's nickname is Christmas Tree Capital of the World.

   What is _____?

4. In Spanish, it means "mountain."

   What is _____?

5. Discoveries of gold, copper and silver helped give Montana this nickname.

   What is _____?

6. His famous words included these: "I will fight no more forever."

   Who was _____?

7. General Custer was defeated here by troops led by Sitting Bull and Crazy Horse.

   Where is _____?

8. Icebergs can be seen here, even in summer.

   What is _____?

9. Found in Glacier National Park, they were formed during the Ice Age.

   What are _____?

10. This ancient type of fish with a nose shaped like a paddle lives in Montana's Charles Russell Refuge.

    What are _____?

Challenge Questions

1. Helena was founded in 1864 by miners seeking gold and silver. What was the city's original name?

2. Two explorers were sent west by Thomas Jefferson to explore the land obtained from France through the Louisiana Purchase. Who were they? Who was the Shoshone woman who guided them through the wilderness?

Just for Fun

What makes more noise than a grizzly bear in Montana?

Treasures of Montana

Look up and down, backwards, forwards and diagonally to find 36 treasures of Montana.

Write the unused letters on the blanks below the puzzle to name two other resources found in Montana.

```
S A N D R E B M U L S T U S
E C N I Z A A C N C H G A T
I O G S R E R F O O O P G E
R S A I L T L E N P P A O E
R E T T F E E E R H P L L B
E E T E S L Y B I E O E D R
H A Y O N R O R D O V G R A
C N K I T R E U W A M L S G
L A N L G S A A R H E H I U
A R U B I E S G N E E L S S
Y O R E B M I T S E T A G A
P S E O T A T O P C L A T E
```

AGATES	GOLD	RUBIES
BARITE	GRAVEL	RYE
BARLEY	HAY	SAND
BEEF	HOGS	SAPPHIRES
CATTLE	HONEY	SHEEP
CHERRIES	LEAD	SILVER
CLAY	LUMBER	SUGAR BEETS
COAL	MILK	TALC
COPPER	OATS	TIMBER
EGGS	OIL	WHEAT
FLOUR	POTATOES	WOOL
GARNETS	POULTRY	ZINC

Unused letters: __ __ __ __ __ __ __ __

__ __ __ __ __ __ __ __

Nebraska

Nickname: Cornhusker State • State Bird: Meadowlark • Capital: Lincoln

■ Fossil evidence suggests that Nebraska once had a tropical climate. Scientists have discovered fossils of saber-toothed tigers, camels, rhinoceroses, turtles and crocodiles. Fossil remains show that horses once lived in Nebraska and other parts of the U.S. but died out millions of years ago.

■ Agate Fossil Beds National Monument near Harrison, one of the richest sources of fossils in the nation, includes the remains of 20 million-year-old mastodons and huge pigs.

■ Built in 1819, Fort Atkinson was the earliest military post west of the Missouri River. The outside walls measured 455 feet by 468 feet. (A football field is 300 feet long.) More than 1,000 soldiers were stationed there at a time. Fort Atkinson became the site of Nebraska's first school, farm, library, sawmill and hospital.

■ Few people settled in Nebraska in the early years. In 1854, the population of Nebraska Territory included only 2,732 whites. (Native Americans and Blacks were not counted.)

Harrison

■ Father Flanagan started Boys Town, a community for neglected and homeless boys, in 1917 as a home and school for boys. Based on his belief that "there is no such thing as a bad boy," he helped thousands of neglected and troubled boys. Today about 400 boys and girls live at Boys Town.

■ Between 1843 and 1858, about 500,000 pioneers crossed Nebraska in covered wagons. Known as the Great Platte River Road—the route along the Platte and North Platte Rivers became part of the Oregon Trail, the Mormon Trail and the California Trail.

Boys Town

■ Nebraska comes from the Oto word *Nebrathka* used to describe the Platte River. It means "flat water." Flowing westward across the state, the Platte is sometimes a mile wide and often quite shallow. Parts of the river may even dry up in the summer. Settlers called it the "mile-wide, inch deep river."

■ Nebraska has very little forested land—only about 2%. Much of the land is prairie where about 200 types of grasses grow.

■ Lincoln became the capital in 1867 when Nebraska joined the Union as the 37th state. A 400-foot domed tower tops the state capitol building.

Lincoln

■ The earliest people settled in Nebraska about 12,000 years ago. Over the centuries, various cultures grew, prospered and died out. Some people think all Native Americans of the past lived like the Plains Indians of the 1800s, riding horses and hunting bison. This image is only a small part of the history of people who lived in the area for 12,000 years.

■ In 1865 the Union Pacific Railroad began laying track at Omaha for the transcontinental railroad. They needed to build over 600 miles of track westward across a land with few trees. Crews traveled long distances, cutting every tree they could find to use for railroad ties. A state with few trees to begin with, had even less by the time the railroad was completed. Many early homes in Nebraska were made of sod (a layer of soil with a thick growth of grass and weeds). Cut into blocks to form walls, sod houses kept out the cold in winter and were fairly cool in summer.

Matchmaker

Match the items in the box by writing the correct letter in each blank. Watch out; some may have more than one answer and not all answers may be used.

1. ____ Nebraska nickname
2. ____ State fossil
3. ____ Capital of Nebraska
4. ____ State flower
5. ____ Early Nebraska pioneer homes
6. ____ State tree
7. ____ Fort Atkinson
8. ____ State bird
9. ____ Boys Town
10. ____ State insect
11. ____ State rock
12. ____ Wide, shallow river
13. ____ State song

A. "Beautiful Nebraska"	N. Mockingbird	
B. Cornhusker State	O. "My Nebraska"	
C. Cottonwood	Q. Nebraska River	
D. Gold	R. Pine	
E. Goldenrod	S. Prairie agate	
F. Goldenrod State	T. Platte River	
G. Home for troubled boys	U. Site of Nebraska's first school, hospital, library	
H Honeybee	V. Started by Father Flanagan	
I. Ladybug		
J. Lincoln	W. Sod houses	
K. Log cabins	X. Tyrannosaurus rex	
L. Mammoth		
M. Meadowlark		

Challenge Questions

1. Pioneers traveled through Nebraska on the Oregon Trail, the Mormon Trail and the California Trail. On a map, show the route of one of these three famous trails.

2. When did Nebraska officially become part of the territory of the United States?

Just for Fun

How do you stop your dog from barking in Nebraska?

Fort Tightfit

The year is 1825. The U.S. Army assigned you to design a new fort for the Western frontier. The outside of the fort has already been built. It is 300 feet on each side. Inside the walls you must provide living quarters for 500 soldiers, outhouses, kitchens and dining areas, a laundry area, bathing facilities, a store, a school, a church, a hospital, a barber shop, storage areas for supplies, a corral for 800 horses and mules, space for 100 cattle, vegetable gardens, a well, private quarters for five officers and their families, two VIP guest rooms and four offices. Don't forget to show where the large main gate will be located.

Using the grid below, design the fort. Label the locations of all items listed above. Each square is 10' x 10'.

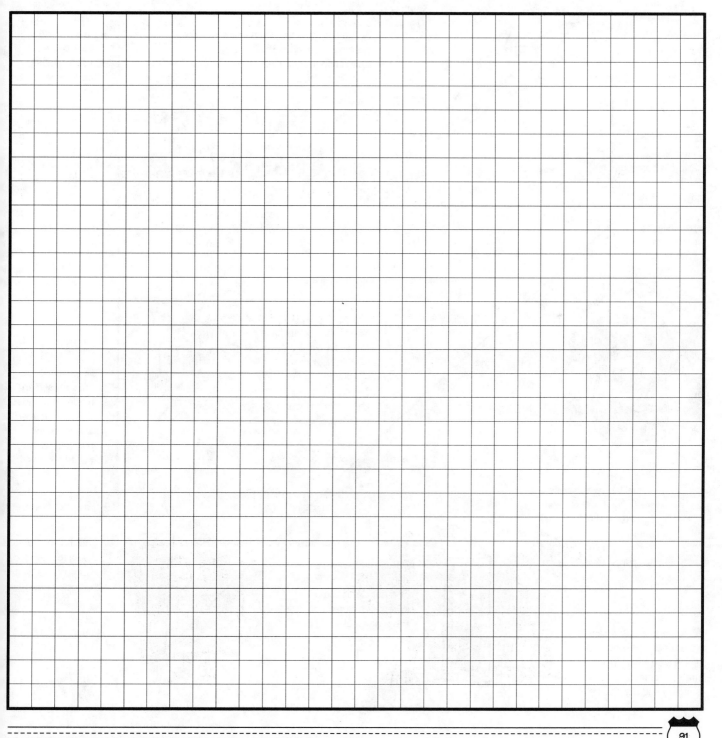

Nevada

Nickname: Silver State • State Bird: Mountain Bluebird • Capital: Carson City

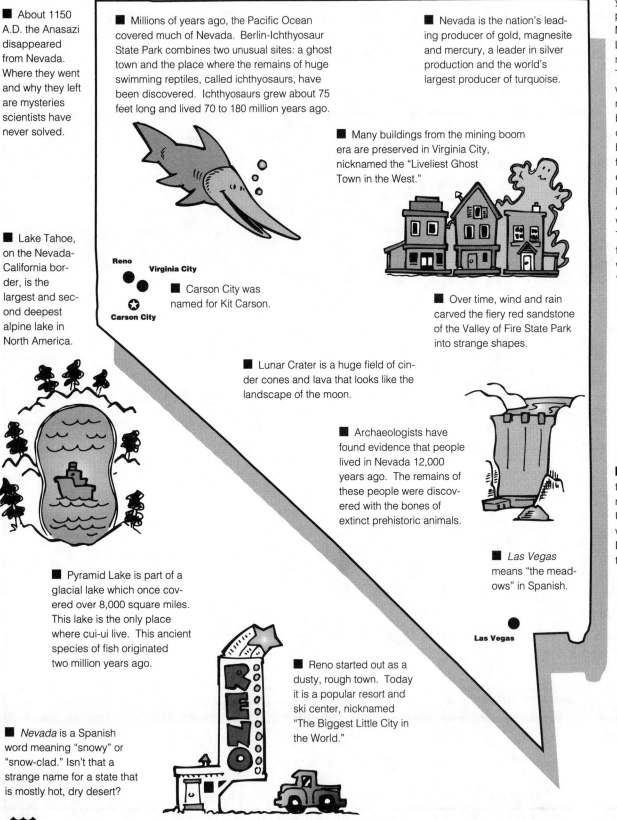

■ About 1150 A.D. the Anasazi disappeared from Nevada. Where they went and why they left are mysteries scientists have never solved.

■ Millions of years ago, the Pacific Ocean covered much of Nevada. Berlin-Ichthyosaur State Park combines two unusual sites: a ghost town and the place where the remains of huge swimming reptiles, called ichthyosaurs, have been discovered. Ichthyosaurs grew about 75 feet long and lived 70 to 180 million years ago.

■ Nevada is the nation's leading producer of gold, magnesite and mercury, a leader in silver production and the world's largest producer of turquoise.

■ About 3,000 years ago, people called Basket Makers lived near Lovelock Cave in northern Nevada. They were skillful weavers who made beautiful baskets and sandals from tree bark and plant fibers. These early people, known as the Anasazi, left no written records. Their name came from a Navajo word meaning "ancient ones."

■ Lake Tahoe, on the Nevada-California border, is the largest and second deepest alpine lake in North America.

■ Many buildings from the mining boom era are preserved in Virginia City, nicknamed the "Liveliest Ghost Town in the West."

Reno **Virginia City**

■ Carson City was named for Kit Carson.

Carson City

■ Over time, wind and rain carved the fiery red sandstone of the Valley of Fire State Park into strange shapes.

■ Lunar Crater is a huge field of cinder cones and lava that looks like the landscape of the moon.

■ Archaeologists have found evidence that people lived in Nevada 12,000 years ago. The remains of these people were discovered with the bones of extinct prehistoric animals.

■ *Las Vegas* means "the meadows" in Spanish.

Las Vegas

■ Lake Meade, the largest man-made lake in the U.S., was formed when Hoover Dam was built in the 1930s.

■ Pyramid Lake is part of a glacial lake which once covered over 8,000 square miles. This lake is the only place where cui-ui live. This ancient species of fish originated two million years ago.

■ Reno started out as a dusty, rough town. Today it is a popular resort and ski center, nicknamed "The Biggest Little City in the World."

■ If you're driving through the Silver State, you should know that in much of Nevada, cattle have the right of way.

■ *Nevada* is a Spanish word meaning "snowy" or "snow-clad." Isn't that a strange name for a state that is mostly hot, dry desert?

TLC10029 Copyright © Teaching & Learning Company, Carthage, IL 62321

Where in Nevada?

1. You are standing near the largest and second deepest alpine lake in North America.

   Where are you? _____

2. You stopped to look around the "Liveliest Ghost Town in the West.

   Where are you? _____

3. You are looking at the largest man-made lake in the nation.

   Where are you? _____

4. It's hard to believe this beautiful resort and ski center near Lake Tahoe began as a dusty, rough town. Today it's known as "The Biggest Little City in the World."

   Where are you? _____

5. You are in a city named for Kit Carson, the famous guide, frontiersman, hunter and soldier.

   Where are you? _____

6. In Spanish, the name of this city means "the meadows."

   Where are you? _____

7. Look around at the unusual shapes of the fiery red sandstone in the largest state park in Nevada.

   Where are you? _____

8. You may think you're on the moon as you look around at the cinder cones and lava, but you're not.

   Where are you? _____

9. At this state park you can visit a ghost town and see the site where "fish lizards," prehistoric ichthyosaurs, once swam.

   Where are you? _____

10. You are visiting a glacial lake that is the only known place where cui-ui live.

    Where are you? _____

Challenge Questions

1. An ancient type of fish called cui-ui live in Pyramid Lake. Fossils of ichthyosaurs have been found in Nevada. Draw an ichthyosaur or a cui-ui.

2. What was the Comstock Lode? Where and when was it discovered? How did it affect Nevada?

Just for Fun

What did the goat say when she ate a videotape in Nevada?

Ghost Dancers

By the 1850s most Native Americans had been affected by the advance of white settlers. Many had lost their lands and their traditional way of life. They were forced to flee to less desirable places or to live on reservations where they had little food and much sickness.

Wovoka, a Paiute living in Nevada, had visions in 1887 and 1889 while in a trance. He said he visited the land of the dead and returned with a message from the Great Spirit. He wanted all Native Americans to join in a ritual called the Spirit Dance. This dance would allow their ancestors to return to life in a world where game was plentiful and everyone would live together in the old way. Whites would be swept away by a great flood and the people would be free.

Sixty thousand members of over 30 different tribes joined in Wovoka's dance. Known as "ghost dancers" many of the dancers wore shirts decorated with eagles, buffalo and morning stars. They believed these symbols of powerful spirits would protect them from the soldiers' bullets.

What do you think these ghost dancers looked like? Draw a scene showing several dancers.

If you are interested in how another artist pictured the dancers, look at the painting *Ghost Dancers* by Oscar Howe, a famous Native American artist.

New Hampshire

Nickname: Granite State • State Bird: Purple Finch • Capital: Concord

■ New Hampshire was one of the 13 original colonies and the ninth state to ratify the Constitution on June 21, 1788.

■ The oldest family farm in the nation is in Dover, New Hampshire. Members of the Tuttle family have worked the farm since 1632.

■ New Hampshire has only 18 miles of coastline along the Atlantic Ocean.

■ Forests cover 80% of New Hampshire. Pine, spruce, fir, cedar, maple, birch, oak, ash and hickory trees grow here. In the fall, shades of red, yellow, orange and brown cover the forest. In spring, the bright blossoms of dogwoods, apple and cherry trees provide bright splashes of color.

■ The White Mountains of New Hampshire are part of the Appalachians. Many of the peaks are covered with snow much of the year. Sunlight reflecting off the rocks makes the mountains look white even in summer.

■ New Hampshire was named for the county of Hampshire in England.

■ Three of the Isles of Shoals are part of New Hampshire. The other six are part of Maine.

■ For a short time, part of northern New Hampshire was an independent country. In the 1800s, both the U.S. and Canada claimed the area. In 1832, the people formed their own country and called it Indian Stream Republic. Ten years later the Webster-Ashburton Treaty was signed, and the land became part of the U.S.

■ Five peaks in the White Mountains are named in honor of the first five Presidents: Washington, Adams, Jefferson, Madison and Monroe.

■ The movie, *On Golden Pond*, was filmed at New Hampshire's Squam Lake.

■ Relics of early settlers in New Hampshire over 9,000 years old have been found at Lake Winnipesaukee. *Winnipesaukee* is said to mean "the smile of the Great Spirit" or "beautiful water in a high place."

■ No one knows who built the place near North Salem called Mystery Hill. Sometimes called America's Stonehenge, it is filled with stone walls, passageways, chambers and carvings. Mystery Hill may have been an early European colony whose records have been lost.

■ Not only is it the highest peak in New England, Mount Washington also has the most remarkable weather. Scientists work year-round at a weather station where the temperature can drop to -30°F. Winter winds blow at 60 MPH or more. A world record for the strongest wind ever measured on Earth was recorded here on April 12, 1934. The winds reached 231 miles per hour.

■ A rock formation in the White Mountains of New Hampshire is called the Old Man of the Mountain because it looks like an old man's head. It has been New Hampshire's official emblem since 1945.

Concord ✪

● Dover

■ New Hampshire is also known as the Primary State because the first presidential primary has been held in New Hampshire since 1920. The primary elections determine the final candidates for President.

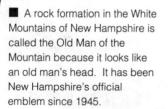

■ Although New Hampshire Reds are a breed of chickens developed in New Hampshire in the early 1900s and named for the state, the state bird is the purple finch.

Legendary Chief

The Pennacook people claimed he could change himself into fire and turn trees green in winter. When the English settlers arrived, he lost his powers. He said it was because their magic was stronger than his. He became a peacekeeper between his people and the white settlers.

The chief was about 100 years old when he died in 1665. According to legend, wolves pulled a sled carrying his body to the top of Mount Washington where everything disappeared in a cloud of fire. What was his name?

$\overline{44}$ $\overline{21}$ $\overline{1}$ $\overline{32}$ $\overline{41}$ $\overline{38}$ $\overline{5}$ $\overline{30}$ $\overline{20}$ $\overline{19}$ $\overline{44}$ $\overline{14}$ $\overline{27}$ $\overline{11}$ $\overline{18}$ $\overline{5}$ $\overline{34}$

To find the answer, fill in the blanks below. Write the letter that corresponds with the number below each blank.

1. For a short time, part of New Hampshire was an independent country called the

$\overline{1}$ $\overline{2}$ $\overline{3}$ $\overline{4}$ $\overline{5}$ $\overline{6}$ $\overline{7}$ $\overline{8}$ $\overline{9}$ $\overline{10}$ $\overline{11}$ $\overline{12}$ Republic

2. The highest, windiest place in New Hampshire is

$\overline{13}$ $\overline{14}$ $\overline{15}$ $\overline{16}$ $\overline{17}$ $\overline{18}$ $\overline{19}$ $\overline{20}$ $\overline{21}$ $\overline{22}$ $\overline{23}$ $\overline{24}$ $\overline{25}$ $\overline{26}$ $\overline{27}$.

3. No one knows who built the stone walls, passageways and

chambers at $\overline{28}$ $\overline{29}$ $\overline{30}$ $\overline{31}$ $\overline{32}$ $\overline{33}$ $\overline{34}$ Hill.

4. New Hampshire's state bird is the

$\overline{35}$ $\overline{36}$ $\overline{37}$ $\overline{38}$ $\overline{39}$ $\overline{40}$ $\overline{41}$ $\overline{42}$ $\overline{43}$ $\overline{44}$ $\overline{45}$.

Challenge Questions

1. The original names of two cities in New Hampshire were Derryfield and Pennycook. What are the names of those two cities today?

2. The first warship to fly the American flag was built in New Hampshire in 1777. What was the ship called? Who commanded it?

Just for Fun

Why were 1988 and 1992 good years for frogs in New Hampshire?

Where in New Hampshire?

Fill in the missing letters to correctly name 26 places in New Hampshire. Use each letter of the alphabet only once. Cross off the letters below as you use them.

A B C D E F G H I J K L M N O P Q R S T U V W X Y Z

1. ___ M H E R S T
2. B E ___ L I N
3. C H A R L E ___ T O N
4. C H E S T E R F ___ E L D
5. C L A R E ___ O N T
6. C O N ___ O R D
7. C ___ R N I S H
8. D O ___ E R
9. E ___ E T E R
10. F I T ___ W I L L I A M
11. ___ R A N C O N I A
12. F R A N ___ L I N
13. ___ E F F E R S O N

14. K E E ___ E
15. L O N ___ O N D E R R Y
16. M A N C H ___ S T E R
17. N A S ___ U A
18. N E W P O R ___
19. ___ E T E R S B O R O U G H
20. P I T T S B U R ___
21. P L ___ M O U T H
22. P O R T S M O ___ T H
23. S A ___ E M
24. S A L I S ___ U R Y
25. S A N D ___ I C H
26. S ___ U A M   L A K E

A Sign of the Times

As you travel through New Hampshire and other states, you'll see lots of different signs. Put the letter of each sign on the blank by its description.

1. ___ PICNIC SITE

2. ___ STOP

3. ___ YIELD

4. ___ MERGE

5. ___ PEDESTRIAN CROSSING

6. ___ CROSSROAD

7. ___ CURVE

8. ___ NO BICYCLES

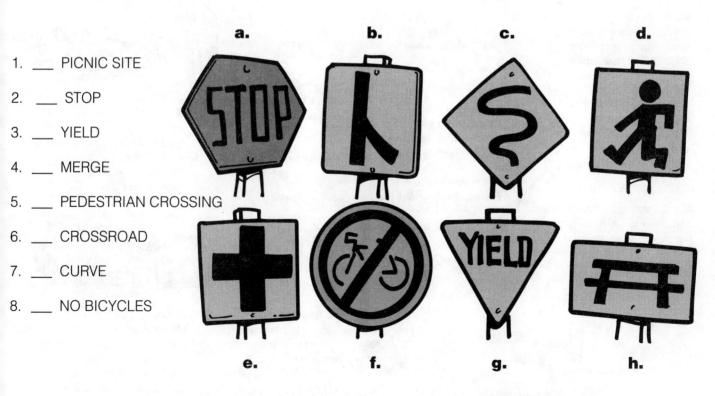

New Jersey

Nickname: Garden State • State Bird: Eastern Goldfinch • Capital: Trenton

■ The Lenni-Lenape, early settlers in New Jersey, lived in dome-shaped houses called wigwams. They were peaceful hunters and farmers. They gave food to strangers who stopped at their villages. Out of respect, other tribes called them "Our Grandparents."

■ In 1858 dinosaur bones were discovered at Haddonfield. Often called the "duck-billed" dinosaur, the hadrasaurus, adopted as New Jersey's official state dinosaur, grew about 30 feet long.

■ The first motion pictures showed events like people dancing, circus acts and a man sneezing. Fort Lee, New Jersey, became the nation's first movie capital.

■ The first motion picture that told a story was *The Great Train Robbery* filmed in New Jersey in 1903. The world's first drive-in movie theater opened near Camden in 1933.

■ Born in Elizabeth, Judy Blume wrote many popular books including *Tales of a Fourth Grade Nothing, Deenie* and *Blubber*.

■ New Jersey is one of two states that does not have a state song.

■ Although it is not an island, New Jersey was named for the English Isle of Jersey.

■ New Jersey averages about 995 people per square mile, the highest of the 50 states.

■ New Jersey was the third state to ratify the Constitution on December 18, 1787.

■ It takes about 400,000 people to keep the Garden State blooming. Orchids, roses, ornamental shrubs and other flowers are important money-making crops. Farms and forests cover two thirds of the state. New Jersey is one of the nation's leading producers of tomatoes, blueberries, cranberries, spinach and peaches.

■ Traffic in large cities would be a nightmare without the "cloverleaf." The first one was built in New Jersey in 1929.

■ New Jersey had two capitals for many years. Burlington became the capital of West New Jersey in 1677, and Perth Amboy became the capital of East New Jersey in 1686. Trenton became the single capital in 1790.

■ The Pinelands are a 1.3-million acre undeveloped wilderness covering about 20% of New Jersey. Nearly 13% of the state is covered with wetlands or marshes, including the Great Swamp, the Hackensack Meadowlands and the bogs and salt marshes of the Pinelands.

■ On November 6, 1869, Rutgers beat Princeton 6 to 4 in the first college football game ever played. The New York Nine beat the Knickerbocker Baseball Club at the first baseball game ever played. The New York team won 23 to 1 in Hoboken, New Jersey, on June 19, 1846.

■ Over 150 million Monopoly™ games have been sold in 23 different languages. Charles Darrow invented the game in 1930 and named the streets after those in Atlantic City, his favorite vacation spot.

■ In its state constitution in 1776, New Jersey became the first state to allow women to vote. In 1807, that right was taken away. Women in New Jersey were not allowed to vote until more than 100 years later.

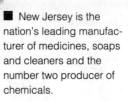

■ New Jersey is the nation's leading manufacturer of medicines, soaps and cleaners and the number two producer of chemicals.

■ Several teams play at the Meadowlands Sports Complex in East Rutherford, New Jersey, including the New York Giants, New York Jets (football), New York Nets (basketball) and New Jersey Devils (hockey).

Fort Lee
Hoboken
Elizabeth
Trenton ☆
Camden
Haddonfield
Atlantic City

New Jersey Tic-Tac-Toe

To play New Jersey Tic-Tac-Toe, correctly answer three questions in a row: up and down, across or diagonally.

1. What was the first motion picture that told a story? _____	**2.** What is New Jersey's state song? _____	**3.** What percent of New Jersey is covered with farms and forests? _____
4. Where do the Giants, Jets and Nets play ball? _____	**5.** What world-famous game is based on streets in Atlantic City? _____	**6.** What is the capital of New Jersey? _____
7. What is the official state dinosaur of New Jersey? _____	**8.** Who wrote *Tales of a Fourth Grade Nothing*? _____	**9.** On the average, how many people per square mile live in New Jersey? _____

Matchmaker

Match the items in the box by writing the correct letter in each blank. Some may have more than one answer and not all the answers may be used.

1. ____ State insect
2. ____ New Jersey nickname
3. ____ State flower
4. ____ State animal
5. ____ Pro hockey team
6. ____ State tree
7. ____ Former capital
8. ____ State bird
9. ____ New Jersey swamp
10. ____ State motto
11. ____ Duck-billed dinosaur
12. ____ Fort Lee, New Jersey
13. ____ New Jersey product

A. Blueberries	N. Nation's first movie capital
B. Burlington	O. New Jersey Devils
C. Chemicals	P. Orchids
D. Cockpit of the Revolution	Q. Perth Amboy
E. Eastern goldfinch	R. Purple violet
F. Faith, Hope and Charity	S. Raccoon
G. Garden State	T. Red oak
H. Hackensack Meadowlands	U. Roses
I. Hadrasaurus	V. Spinach
J. Honeybee	W. Stegosaurus
K. Horse	X. Trenton
L. Liberty and Prosperity	Y. Triceratops
M. Mockingbird	Z. Tulip

Challenge Questions

1. New Jersey has been the birthplace of many inventions and the manufacturing and developing site of products that have changed our lives. What are some items that have been invented or developed in New Jersey?

2. In 1881 James Lafferty, Jr. put up a six-story building in the shape of an animal. The building is now a national historic landmark. What animal is the building shaped like? What is the name of the building?

Just for Fun

What would you get if you crossed a porcupine with a skunk in New Jersey?

New Mexico

Nickname: Land of Enchantment • State Bird: Roadrunner • Capital: Santa Fe

■ People have lived in New Mexico for a long, long time. Ears of corn dating from 3000 to 2000 B.C. have been found in Bat Cave. Ten thousand-year-old spearheads were discovered in Folsom.

■ Unable to decide between the pinto bean and the chili pepper, the New Mexico state legislature declared both the official state vegetables in 1965.

Folsom

■ Apache medicine men wore turquoise. The Pueblos buried turquoise with their dead. Turquoise was used as ornaments and decorations in building and sometimes as money. In Pueblo Bonito, more than 50,000 pieces of handworked turquoise were found in one chamber.

Santa Fe ★

■ At over 2,000 feet above sea level, Santa Fe is the highest of the 50 state capitals. Founded in 1609, it is also the oldest capital in the country and has the nation's oldest office building. The Palace of the Governors, built in 1610 was used as administration headquarters for over 200 years.

■ Santa Fe also has the distinction of having the newest capitol building. Nicknamed the "Roundhouse" because it is shaped like a Pueblo kiva. The new capitol was completed in 1966. A kiva is a round room used for important ceremonies.

■ Found in rock deposits in New Mexico and other southwest states, turquoise has long been cherished by Native Americans. The Zunis said that turquoise came from the blue of the heavens, a gift of the sky and a protection from evil.

■ Carlsbad Caverns National Park features about 80 caves carved out by water and minerals 200 million years ago. Rock formations called Whale's Mouth, Frozen Waterfalls, Baby Hippo and Christmas Tree look much like their namesakes.

■ Twenty-seven giant satellite dishes make up the Very Large Array (VLA), the most powerful radio telescope in the world, located near Socorro.

Socorro

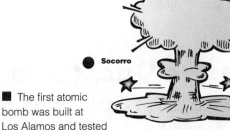

■ The first atomic bomb was built at Los Alamos and tested in the desert near Alamogordo, New Mexico, in 1945.

Alamogordo

Carlsbad

■ Archaeologists discovered cave dwellings at least 20,000 years old in the Sandia Mountains. In 1990, Dr. Richard MacNeish found tools in the Orogrande Caves dating back 55,000 years. This is the oldest evidence of humans found anywhere in the Americas.

■ The woman who wrote New Mexico's state song, "O, Fair New Mexico" couldn't see the "sky of azure," the "golden sunshine" the "deep canyons" or fields of "sweet alfalfa" described in the song. The daughter of Sheriff Pat Garrett who shot Billy the Kid, Elizabeth Garrett was blind.

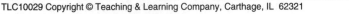

101

Matchmaker

Match the items in the box by writing the correct letter in each blank. Some may have more than one answer and not all the answers may be used.

1. ____ Capital of New Mexico
2. ____ New Mexico nickname
3. ____ State motto
4. ____ State flower
5. ____ State tree
6. ____ State bird
7. ____ State animal
8. ____ State insect
9. ____ State fish
10. ____ State vegetable
11. ____ State cookie
12. ____ State gem
13. ____ State fossil
14. ____ State song
15. ____ Original name

A. Albuquerque	L. Nuevo Mejico
B. Armadillo	M. "O, Fair New Mexico"
C. Barrel cactus	N. Oreos™
D. Biscochito	O. Piñon
E. Black bear	P. Pinto bean
F. Chili pepper	Q. Roadrunner
G. Coelophysis	R. Santa Fe
H. Cutthroat trout	S. Tacos
I. It Grows as It Goes	T. Tarantula hawk wasp
J. Land of Enchantment	U. Turquoise
K. Mosquito	V. Yucca flower

Challenge Questions

1. The Anasazi built pit houses by digging a large round hole a few feet deep. They built slanted walls and flat roofs of tree limbs, bark and dirt. A fireplace in the center allowed smoke from cooking fires to escape. To enter and leave their homes, they used ladders. Describe some advantages and disadvantages of this type of home.

2. A small bear cub found in 1950 in New Mexico's Lincoln National Forest after a fire destroyed his home became a national symbol. Who was that cub? What does he stand for? Where did he live after the fire?

Just for Fun

Why are prairie dogs in New Mexico such poor dancers?

Break the Code

Name _____

New Mexico

Break the Code

During World War II, the United States developed a secret code with the help of Navajos from New Mexico. The code was based on the Navajo language. Because few people in the world could speak their language, the code remained unbroken during the war.

To break the code and read the message below, fill in the letters given in the code chart. It may not be as easy as it seems. Symbols are given for all consonants but not for the vowels. Fill in the symbols for the vowels in the code chart as you discover them.

3 % ?   # % 7 ^ ! &   ^ 2   9 & # %   * &

$ 3 >>   () << $ ^ << ^ %   1 & @   * & ? 3 2.

* 9 %   * & ? 3 2   ! & 3 * $ ^ 3   # $ 3 >>

+ 3 1 % << @ << & + 3 1   ! & 3 3 % ! * ^ 3 @

~ + << << & ? 2. $ 6 * 9 & + @ 9   * 9 % >>

$ 33 % $ 2 & + 3 1   6 ^ 33 % $ 9 ^ @ 9-

() ^ * ! 9 % 1   ~ $ << 33'   () << $ ^ << ^ %

1 & @ 2 $ << %   3 & *   1 & @ 2   * 9 % >>

$ << %   # % # ~ % << 2   & 10   * 9 %

2 5 + ^ << << % 6   10 $ # ^ 6 >>.

Code Chart

A = $	E = %	I = ^	L = 6	O = &	R = <<	U = +	X = 7
B = ~	F = 10	J = 4	M = #	P = ()	S = 2	V = 8	Y = >>
C = !	G = @	K = 33	N = 3	Q = 5	T = *	W = ?	Z = []
D = 1	H = 9						

103

TLC10029 Copyright © Teaching & Learning Company, Carthage, IL 62321

Welcome to New Mexico

Welcome to New Mexico. Take a look around. There's lots to see. The names of 34 cities in New Mexico are hidden in the puzzle. Look up, down, backwards, forwards and diagonally to find them. Some letters in the puzzle will be part of more than one word.

Circle the words when you find them. When you finish the puzzle, write the unused letters on the blanks below. The unused letters will spell the names of three animals found in New Mexico.

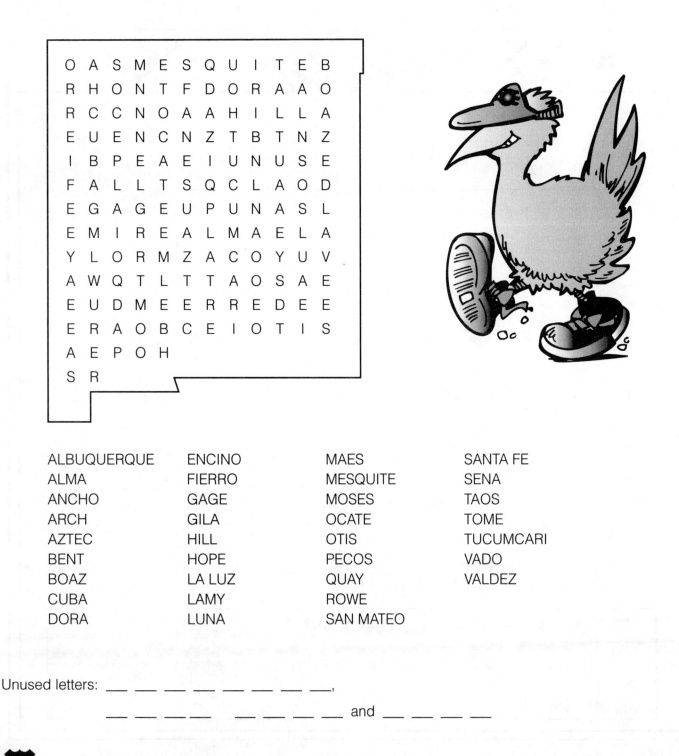

```
O A S M E S Q U I T E B
R H O N T F D O R A A O
R C C N O A A H I L L A
E U E N C N Z T B T N Z
I B P E A E I U N U S E
F A L L T S Q C L A O D
E G A G E U P U N A S L
E M I R E A L M A E L A
Y L O R M Z A C O Y U V
A W Q T L T T A O S A E
E U D M E E R R E D E E
E R A O B C E I O T I S
A E P O H
S R
```

ALBUQUERQUE	ENCINO	MAES	SANTA FE
ALMA	FIERRO	MESQUITE	SENA
ANCHO	GAGE	MOSES	TAOS
ARCH	GILA	OCATE	TOME
AZTEC	HILL	OTIS	TUCUMCARI
BENT	HOPE	PECOS	VADO
BOAZ	LA LUZ	QUAY	VALDEZ
CUBA	LAMY	ROWE	
DORA	LUNA	SAN MATEO	

Unused letters: __ __ __ __ __ __ __ __,

__ __ __ __ __ __ __ __ and __ __ __ __

New York

Nickname: Empire State • State Bird: Bluebird • Capital: Albany

■ During the Ice Age, glaciers covered most of New York. The moving mountains of ice were up to two miles thick. The glaciers carried rich soil across the state and created deep valleys which filled with water and became lakes. Prehistoric mastodons and mammoths roamed the state.

■ Henry Hudson searched for a shorter route to Asia. Instead of finding China, Hudson found New York. Although Hudson was English, he was working for the Dutch. Based on his explorations along the Hudson River, the Dutch claimed parts of New York, New Jersey, Connecticut and Delaware.

■ About 7.3 million people live in the Big Apple, the nation's largest city. Forty states have less total people than New York City. About 4 million people ride the subways of New York City every day.

■ New York City's Grand Central Terminal is the world's largest railroad station.

■ When the Empire State Building opened in 1931, it was the world's tallest building.

■ The first nomadic hunters reached New York about 11,000 years ago. Thousands of years later, many groups of Algonquian-speaking people and various groups of Iroquois settled in this area.

■ The English named the state New York for James, the Duke of York and Albany.

■ The Women's Rights National Historic Park was the site of the first Women's Rights Convention held in 1848. More than 300 people met in Seneca Falls to discuss the social condition of women.

■ The state capitol building in Albany looks like an old castle. Albany became the capital of New York in 1797.

■ Not everyone in the Empire State lives in a big city. More than 100,000 New Yorkers live and work on farms.

■ Slavery was outlawed in New York in 1827. About 10,000 slaves were set free 34 years before the Civil War began.

Cooperstown ●

■ New York was one of the 13 original colonies and the eleventh to ratify the Constitution on July 26, 1788.

■ The highest peak in New York is Mount Macy, 5,344 feet above sea level.

Albany ✪

■ The Smith Brothers, William and Andrew, started their cough drop business in Poughkeepsie in 1847.

Poughkeepsie ●

■ New York City is divided into five sections called boroughs. They are Manhattan, Queens, the Bronx, Brooklyn and Staten Island.

■ New York is home to nine professional teams: the Yankees, Mets (baseball); Bills, Giants, Jets (football); Sabres, Islanders, Rangers (hockey) and the Knicks (basketball). The National Baseball Hall of Fame is in Cooperstown.

■ New York City was the capital of the U.S. from 1785 to 1790.

New York City

■ The World Trade Center in New York City is the world's largest office center.

■ New York is the second most populous state. Only California has a larger population.

■ New York City has about 2,100 bridges, more than any other U.S. city. The Brooklyn Bridge was completed in 1883.

■ In the western part of the state, the Niagara River forms the New York-Canada border. Every year 15 million people visit the two huge falls and many smaller ones that make up Niagara Falls, one of the most spectacular natural sights in the world.

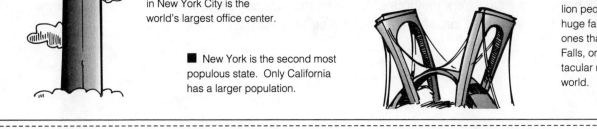

 105

The Peacemaker

According to legend, the five tribes of the Iroquois nation waged war against each other until the Peacemaker came in a canoe made of white stone. This mysterious stranger became friends with an Onondaga man. Together they convinced the five tribes to stop fighting and make a pact known as the Great Law of Peace. Many features of the U.S. Constitution are similar to the Iroquois system of government. Who was the Onondaga man befriended by the Peacemaker?

$$\overline{\text{22}} \ \overline{\text{36}} \ \overline{\text{12}} \ \overline{\text{7}} \ \overline{\text{26}} \ \overline{\text{37}} \ \overline{\text{17}} \ \overline{\text{8}}$$

To find the answer, fill in the blanks below. Write the letter that corresponds with the number below each blank.

1. New York's state motto is $\overline{\ \ }_1 \ \overline{\ \ }_2 \ \overline{\ \ }_3 \ \overline{\ \ }_4 \quad \overline{\ \ }_5 \ \overline{\ \ }_6 \ \overline{\ \ }_7 \ \overline{\ \ }_8 \ \overline{\ \ }_9 \ \overline{\ \ }_{10}$.

2. Long ago, prehistoric mastodons and $\overline{\ \ }_{11} \ \overline{\ \ }_{12} \ \overline{\ \ }_{13} \ \overline{\ \ }_{14} \ \overline{\ \ }_{15} \ \overline{\ \ }_{16} \ \overline{\ \ }_{17} \ \overline{\ \ }_{18}$

    lived in New York.

3. New York is divided into five boroughs: Queens, the Bronx,

    Brooklyn, Staten Island and $\overline{\ \ }_{19} \ \overline{\ \ }_{20} \ \overline{\ \ }_{21} \ \overline{\ \ }_{22} \ \overline{\ \ }_{23} \ \overline{\ \ }_{24} \ \overline{\ \ }_{25} \ \overline{\ \ }_{26} \ \overline{\ \ }_{27}$.

4. $\overline{\ \ }_{28} \ \overline{\ \ }_{29} \ \overline{\ \ }_{30} \quad \overline{\ \ }_{31} \ \overline{\ \ }_{32} \ \overline{\ \ }_{33} \ \overline{\ \ }_{34} \quad \overline{\ \ }_{35} \ \overline{\ \ }_{36} \ \overline{\ \ }_{37} \ \overline{\ \ }_{38}$ was the nation's

    capital between 1785 and 1790.

Challenge Questions

1. The Statue of Liberty was a gift to the United States from which country? What is the name of the island where the Statue of Liberty stands? Who was the sculptor who designed it?

2. Name the New York authors of these books: A. *The Legend of Sleepy Hollow*, B. *The Wizard of Oz*, C. *Moby Dick*, D. *Where the Wild Things Are*.

Just for Fun

At Carnegie Hall, home of the New York Philharmonic Orchestra, concerts are given by many well-known musicians. How do tuba players at Carnegie Hall clean their dirty tubas?

Snowsnakes

Snowsnake was a winter sport of skill and strength enjoyed by the Seneca and other Native Americans in New York and other parts of the northeast. In winter, the men and boys prepared for the game by dragging a smooth, heavy log through the snow until they formed a trough about 1,500 feet long and 10 to 12 inches deep.

The bottom and sides of the trough were packed to form a smooth icy surface. Then the boys and men made their snowsnakes—sticks 5 to 9 feet long made from hickory, maple or walnut. To give a stick additional weight, the head was tipped with lead. The sticks were about an inch wide at the front and tapered to less than half an inch at the back.

The name Snowsnake comes from the way the flexible sticks moved in a snake-like fashion as they sped along the trough.

The object was simply to see who could slide a snow stick for the longest distance. This sport wasn't as easy as it may seem at first, and the Seneca took the game very seriously. It required accurate sight, strong muscles and skill to place the snowsnake properly so it traveled straight and fast and far.

After reading the description of how the Seneca made their trough and their snowsnakes, can you picture what they looked like? Draw several snowsnakes speeding along a snow trough. You can add some people playing the game if you'd like.

If you live in an area where it doesn't snow, how could you play Snowsnake?

New York Lakes

New York has more than 8,000 lakes. Lakes Erie and Ontario form part of the international border between New York and Canada.

Look up and down, backwards, forwards and diagonally to find the names of 39 New York lakes.

```
C  H  A  M  P  L  A  I  N  L  O  N  G  D
M  R  B  O  Y  C  S  C  H  R  A  I  N  E
O  H  A  O  E  S  G  I  A  I  E  A  E  L
O  A  T  N  O  O  C  D  D  T  S  F  A  T
S  S  E  R  B  K  I  N  C  R  L  W  T  A
U  S  C  O  O  E  I  R  E  E  S  I  O  L
T  E  S  R  N  N  R  P  M  I  D  O  N  L
I  C  Y  O  A  T  M  R  L  U  C  A  O  I
T  C  L  C  P  A  A  V  Y  A  D  K  R  K
U  U  V  H  A  C  E  R  Y  L  C  E  W  S
P  S  A  A  R  R  R  U  I  A  D  I  A  K
P  E  N  Z  T  E  G  L  L  O  X  C  D  E
E  S  C  Y  E  A  A  B  G  E  O  R  G  E
R  G  A  K  U  E  K  X  O  D  A  R  A  P
```

AMPERSAND	EATON	ONEIDA
BLACK	ERIE	ONTARIO
BOG	FERN	PARADOX
BONAPARTE	GEORGE	PECK
CARMEL	HICKORY	PEEKSKILL
CATLIN	INDIAN	PLACID
CAYUGA	KEUKA	RED
CEDAR	LILA	SENECA
CHAMPLAIN	LONG	SILVER
CHAZY	LOWS	SUCCESS
CRANBERRY	MOON	SYLVAN
CROSS	MUD	TITUS
DELTA	NORTH	TUPPER

North Carolina

Nickname: Tarheel State • State Bird: Cardinal • Capital: Raleigh

■ Millions of years ago, most of eastern North Carolina was covered by the ocean. Mammoths and mastodons lived on the land. The first people arrived about 10,000 years ago. North and South Carolina were named in honor of King Charles I of England. *Carolina* comes from a Latin word, *Carolana*, meaning "land of Charles."

■ A group of 100 settlers landed at Roanoke Island in July 1587. On August 18, 1587, Virginia Dare was the first English child born in America. Shortly after, her grandfather Governor White returned to England for supplies. When he returned in 1590, he found the letters *CRO* carved on one tree and the word *CROATOAN* carved on another but no trace of the colonists. Historians have never learned the fate of the "Lost Colony."

■ In 1960, four African American college students sat at a "whites only" lunch counter in Greensboro. They refused to leave. "Sit-ins" became a way for African Americans to fight for civil rights.

■ The towns of Winston and Salem were separate cities until they joined in 1913 to become Winston-Salem.

■ New Bern was named for Bern, Switzerland. For a time, New Bern was the capital of North Carolina.

Greensboro

Raleigh

Winston-Salem

Charlotte

New Bern

■ Mount Mitchell in the Black Mountains, is the tallest peak in the U.S. east of the Mississippi River.

■ North Carolina's capital was named for Sir Walter Raleigh.

■ Charlotte was named for Queen Charlotte, wife of King George III.

■ The Venus flytrap grows in the wild in only two states: North and South Carolina. This unusual plant captures insects with its leaves, then produces a liquid that turns the insects into food it can eat.

■ The tallest lighthouse in the U.S. stands along the Atlantic coast at Cape Hatteras. The lighthouse is striped like a black and white barber's pole.

■ In 1934, the Great Smoky Mountains National Park was set up on a half million acres of wilderness in Tennessee and North Carolina. The park includes almost 900 miles of hiking trails and 270 miles of roads. Dozens of log houses, churches, barns, mills and school buildings are preserved in the park. Some of these historic buildings are "living museums" where the skills of our pioneer ancestors are demonstrated for visitors.

■ The Great Smoky Mountains are part of a larger range, the Appalachians. Their name comes from a Cherokee word, *shagonigei* which means "blue smoke place." Water vapor and natural plant oils released into the air by the forests form a blue smoky haze that usually blankets the mountains.

109

Name _____

Tea Party Time

Most people have heard of the Boston Tea Party. Another revolutionary tea party was held in North Carolina. In 1774 women in North Carolina protested the English tax on tea and pledged not to use British products. What did this boycott of English tea become known as?

$\overline{19}$ $\overline{33}$ $\overline{14}$ $\overline{9}$ $\overline{36}$ $\overline{8}$ $\overline{32}$　　$\overline{17}$ $\overline{28}$ $\overline{40}$　　$\overline{13}$ $\overline{21}$ $\overline{29}$ $\overline{4}$ $\overline{38}$

To find the answer, fill in the blanks below. Write the letter that corresponds with the number below each blank.

1. The North Carolina settlement on Roanoke Island is known as

the $\overline{1}$ $\overline{2}$ $\overline{3}$ $\overline{4}$　$\overline{5}$ $\overline{6}$ $\overline{7}$ $\overline{8}$ $\overline{9}$ $\overline{10}$.

2. The tallest lighthouse in the U.S. stands on the Atlantic

coast near $\overline{11}$ $\overline{12}$ $\overline{13}$ $\overline{14}$　$\overline{15}$ $\overline{16}$ $\overline{17}$ $\overline{18}$ $\overline{19}$ $\overline{20}$ $\overline{21}$ $\overline{22}$.

3. New Bern was named for a city in what country? $\overline{23}$ $\overline{24}$ $\overline{25}$ $\overline{26}$ $\overline{27}$ $\overline{28}$ $\overline{29}$ $\overline{30}$ $\overline{31}$ $\overline{32}$ $\overline{33}$

4. Where did the Wright brothers make their famous first

flight? $\overline{34}$ $\overline{35}$ $\overline{36}$ $\overline{37}$ $\overline{38}$　$\overline{39}$ $\overline{40}$ $\overline{41}$ $\overline{42}$

Challenge Questions

1. Pirates in North Carolina? That's right. Pirates were a problem in both North and South Carolina until 1718. They hid their ships in the Outer Banks, a region of sandbars and islands along the coast. When ships passed, the pirates raised their flag and attacked. Who were some well-known pirates who prowled along the North Carolina coast?

2. Wilbur and Orville Wright made history near Kitty Hawk, North Carolina, in 1903 when they flew the first powered, heavier-than-air plane. They didn't fly very high, very far, very fast or for very long, but they did fly! Part of the Wright brothers' original plane is now on the moon. A piece of it was taken there by astronauts Neil Armstrong and Buzz Aldrin when they made their first moon landing in 1969. What was the name of the Wright brothers' first plane?

Just for Fun

When do cardinals in North Carolina have four eyes?

Who's Who?

Look up and down, backwards, forwards and diagonally to find the last names of 27 well-known people born in North Carolina. Words in CAPITAL letters can be found in the puzzle.

Both North and South Carolina claim to be the birthplace of the seventh President of the U.S. Write the unused letters from the puzzle in the blanks below to find out this man's nickname and his last name.

```
O  M  A  D  I  S  O  N  L  N
L  A  P  D  H  S  I  C  Y  O
L  H  O  O  D  A  R  E  K  T
E  A  R  J  L  W  L  A  C  N
S  R  T  O  O  K  O  O  Y  E
O  G  E  R  N  H  L  L  R  B
C  G  R  I  U  T  N  H  F  L
Y  U  R  N  R  D  T  S  A  E
M  B  T  A  K  I  O  P  O  O
B  E  N  N  F  N  P  L  R  N
R  E  O  F  I  L  D  J  E  A
A  M  I  F  I  A  A  R  S  R
G  R  F  N  C  K  S  C  Y  D
G  O  G  T  L  A  R  U  K  B
C  S  C  R  U  G  G  S  O  N
```

Luke APPLING	Virginia DARE	Kay KYSER
Thomas Hart BENTON	Elizabeth DOLE	Ray (Sugar Ray) LEONARD
Braxton BRAGG	Donna FARGO	Dolley MADISON
David BRINKLEY	Roberta FLACK	Thelonious MONK
Betsy BYARS	Billy GRAHAM	Edward MURROW
Robert BYRD	Andy GRIFFITH	James POLK
Levi COFFIN	Jim "Catfish" HUNTER	William PORTER (O. Henry)
Levi COLTRANE	Andrew JOHNSON	Earl SCRUGGS
Howard COSELL	Charles KURALT	Thomas WOLFE

Unused letters: "__ __ __ __ __ __ __ __ __"

__ __ __ __ __ __ __

North Dakota

Nickname: Flickertail State • State Bird: Western Meadowlark • Capital: Bismarck

■ Millions of years ago, North Dakota was covered by a salt sea. When the sea dried up, it left deposits of limestone, sandstone and shale. Combined with the remains of plants and sea animals, oil and lignite coal were formed.

■ About a million years ago, the climate in North Dakota became colder. Year after year more snow fell. Winters became longer and longer until glaciers formed over the land. As they partially melted and froze, over and over, the powerful sheets of ice and snow moved across the state like a gigantic bulldozer.

■ North Dakota is the fourth smallest state in population. On the average, the state has only 9.2 people per square mile, according to the 1990 census. Only four cities in North Dakota have populations of over 20,000: Fargo, Bismarck, Grand Forks and Minot.

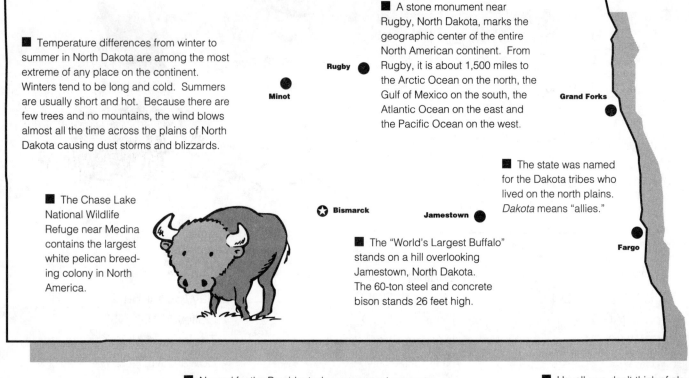

■ Temperature differences from winter to summer in North Dakota are among the most extreme of any place on the continent. Winters tend to be long and cold. Summers are usually short and hot. Because there are few trees and no mountains, the wind blows almost all the time across the plains of North Dakota causing dust storms and blizzards.

■ A stone monument near Rugby, North Dakota, marks the geographic center of the entire North American continent. From Rugby, it is about 1,500 miles to the Arctic Ocean on the north, the Gulf of Mexico on the south, the Atlantic Ocean on the east and the Pacific Ocean on the west.

Rugby ●

Minot ●

Grand Forks ●

■ The state was named for the Dakota tribes who lived on the north plains. *Dakota* means "allies."

■ The Chase Lake National Wildlife Refuge near Medina contains the largest white pelican breeding colony in North America.

★ Bismarck   Jamestown ●

■ The "World's Largest Buffalo" stands on a hill overlooking Jamestown, North Dakota. The 60-ton steel and concrete bison stands 26 feet high.

Fargo ●

■ North Dakota's nickname, the Flickertail State, came from another name for the Richardson ground squirrel that lives in the state. It is called the flickertail.

■ Named for the President who was a great conservationist, Theodore Roosevelt National Park covers 70,000 acres of North Dakota badlands and prairie.

■ The International Peace Garden is a 2,300-acre botanical garden on the border between North Dakota and Canada. Land for this project was donated by North Dakota and Manitoba. This huge garden, open to the public, commemorates the long friendship between the U.S. and Canada.

■ Usually we don't think of clay as a natural resource, but in North Dakota clay is mined and made into bricks and ceramic products. Salt is mined from deposits left by a salt sea that once covered the state.

Tales of the Wild West

This famous North Dakota writer of western fiction won several awards including the Rough Rider Award, the Congressional Gold Medal for literary achievement and the Presidential Medal of Freedom. His 86 western novels sold over 160 million copies. What was his name?

$\overline{~~~}$ $\overline{~~~}$ $\overline{~~~}$ $\overline{~~~}$ $\overline{~~~}$, $\overline{~~~}$ $\overline{~~~}$ $\overline{~~~}$ $\overline{~~~}$ $\overline{~~~}$ $\overline{~~~}$
  17   35   30   13   1   34   24   36   14   30   25

To find the answer, fill in the blanks below. Write the letter that corresponds with the number below each blank.

1. $\overline{~~~}$ $\overline{~~~}$ $\overline{~~~}$ $\overline{~~~}$ is mined from deposits left by a sea that once covered North Dakota.
     1   2   3   4

2. The $\overline{~~}$ $\overline{~~}$ $\overline{~~}$ $\overline{~~}$ $\overline{~~}$ $\overline{~~}$ $\overline{~~}$ $\overline{~~}$ $\overline{~~}$ $\overline{~~}$ $\overline{~~}$ $\overline{~~}$ $\overline{~~}$ $\overline{~~}$ $\overline{~~}$ $\overline{~~}$ $\overline{~~}$ $\overline{~~}$
          5   6   7   8   9   10 11 12 13 14 15 16 17   18 19 20 21 22

    $\overline{~~}$ $\overline{~~}$ $\overline{~~}$ $\overline{~~}$ $\overline{~~}$ $\overline{~~}$ commemorates the friendship between Canada and the U.S.
     23 24 25 26 27 28

3. This 60-ton statue standing on a hill overlooking Jamestown is

    known as the "World's Largest $\overline{~~}$ $\overline{~~}$ $\overline{~~}$ $\overline{~~}$ $\overline{~~}$ $\overline{~~}$ $\overline{~~}$."
                                    29 30 31 32 33 34 35

4. The only cities in North Dakota with a population over

    20,000 are Fargo, Bismarck, Grand Forks and $\overline{~~}$ $\overline{~~}$ $\overline{~~}$ $\overline{~~}$ $\overline{~~}$.
                                                  36 37 38 39 40

Challenge Questions

1. Important North Dakota crops include spring wheat, flaxseed, sunflowers, barley, pinto beans, rye and sugar beets. Learn more about one of these crops.

2. What are badlands?

Just for Fun

Why don't the buffalo in North Dakota ride tricycles?

North Dakota Wildlife

North Dakota may not have a large population of people, but many types of birds and other animals make their homes in the Flickertail State.

Look up and down, backwards, forwards and diagonally to find the names of 41 kinds of birds and animals that live in North Dakota.

```
R  L  P  E  E  H  S  N  R  O  H  G  I  B
E  N  A  C  I  L  E  P  R  C  N  L  I  O
E  A  R  R  L  Z  E  I  B  R  R  S  W  B
D  O  G  E  K  I  O  S  E  A  O  N  D  O
W  K  R  L  T  L  Z  A  A  N  H  I  U  L
O  W  E  R  E  N  N  A  R  E  T  B  C  I
R  A  B  B  I  T  C  A  R  P  W  O  K  N
R  H  E  N  E  R  W  O  L  D  Y  R  A  K
A  T  G  L  E  A  N  O  E  O  Y  J  N  D
P  I  O  I  L  U  V  V  T  L  E  U  K  E
S  P  R  A  T  E  O  E  Y  E  K  A  N  S
E  I  F  U  R  D  E  R  R  S  R  N  G  O
E  P  S  Q  U  I  R  R  E  L  U  U  I  O
B  P  A  R  T  R  I  D  G  E  T  O  A  M
```

ANTELOPE	FROG	QUAIL
BEAR	GREBE	RABBIT
BEAVER	HAWK	ROBIN
BIGHORN SHEEP	HERON	SKUNK
BISON	LARK	SNAKE
BOBOLINK	LIZARD	SPARROW
COYOTE	MINK	SQUIRREL
CRANE	MOOSE	TERN
CROW	ORIOLE	TOAD
DEER	OWL	TURKEY
DOVE	PARTRIDGE	TURTLE
DUCK	PELICAN	WEASEL
EAGLE	PIPIT	WREN
ELK	PLOVER	

Ohio

Nickname: Buckeye State • State Bird: Cardinal • Capital: Columbus

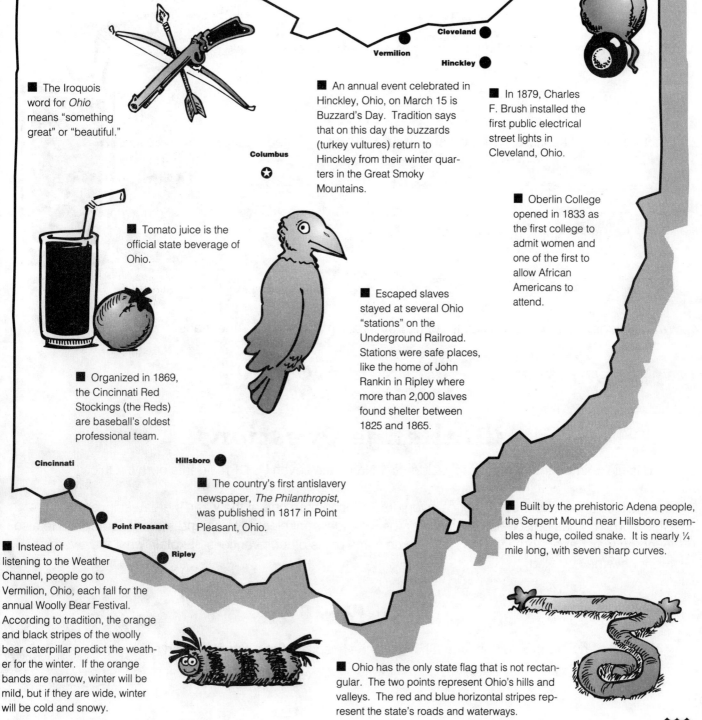

■ Millions of years ago, Ohio was covered with shallow seas and swamps. When the water receded, Ohio was left with deposits of sandstone, shale, salt, limestone, coal and oil.

■ Hunting was important to the early settlers of Ohio. Not only did they rely on hunting as a source of food, it also became a source of income. People in Amesville bought books for their library by selling raccoon pelts.

■ One of Ohio's nicknames is the "Buckeye State." What is a buckeye? It's a type of horse chestnut tree that grows in the Ohio River Valley. The large brown nut reminded early settlers of the eye of a male deer, thus the name buckeye.

Cleveland

Vermilion

Hinckley

■ The Iroquois word for *Ohio* means "something great" or "beautiful."

■ An annual event celebrated in Hinckley, Ohio, on March 15 is Buzzard's Day. Tradition says that on this day the buzzards (turkey vultures) return to Hinckley from their winter quarters in the Great Smoky Mountains.

■ In 1879, Charles F. Brush installed the first public electrical street lights in Cleveland, Ohio.

Columbus

■ Tomato juice is the official state beverage of Ohio.

■ Oberlin College opened in 1833 as the first college to admit women and one of the first to allow African Americans to attend.

■ Escaped slaves stayed at several Ohio "stations" on the Underground Railroad. Stations were safe places, like the home of John Rankin in Ripley where more than 2,000 slaves found shelter between 1825 and 1865.

■ Organized in 1869, the Cincinnati Red Stockings (the Reds) are baseball's oldest professional team.

Cincinnati

Hillsboro

■ The country's first antislavery newspaper, *The Philanthropist*, was published in 1817 in Point Pleasant, Ohio.

Point Pleasant

■ Instead of listening to the Weather Channel, people go to Vermilion, Ohio, each fall for the annual Woolly Bear Festival. According to tradition, the orange and black stripes of the woolly bear caterpillar predict the weather for the winter. If the orange bands are narrow, winter will be mild, but if they are wide, winter will be cold and snowy.

Ripley

■ Built by the prehistoric Adena people, the Serpent Mound near Hillsboro resembles a huge, coiled snake. It is nearly ¼ mile long, with seven sharp curves.

■ Ohio has the only state flag that is not rectangular. The two points represent Ohio's hills and valleys. The red and blue horizontal stripes represent the state's roads and waterways.

Ohio, the State with Many Nicknames

Most people will say they never heard of Phoebe Moses from Patterson, Ohio, because she was known by another, more famous name. What was her famous nickname?

$\overline{25}$ $\overline{13}$ $\overline{39}$ $\overline{30}$ $\overline{35}$ $\overline{27}$ $\overline{12}$ $\overline{4}$ $\overline{11}$ $\overline{32}$ $\overline{6}$

To find the answer, fill in the blanks below. Write the letter that corresponds with the number below each blank.

1. What Ohio nickname came from a type of horse chestnut tree?

   $\overline{}_{1}$ $\overline{}_{2}$ $\overline{}_{3}$ $\overline{}_{4}$ $\overline{}_{5}$ $\overline{}_{6}$ $\overline{}_{7}$ State

2. What was the first antislavery newspaper published in the United States?

   The $\overline{}_{8}$ $\overline{}_{9}$ $\overline{}_{10}$ $\overline{}_{11}$ $\overline{}_{12}$ $\overline{}_{13}$ $\overline{}_{14}$ $\overline{}_{15}$ $\overline{}_{16}$ $\overline{}_{17}$ $\overline{}_{18}$ $\overline{}_{19}$ $\overline{}_{20}$ $\overline{}_{21}$

3. Name the official state beverage of Ohio.

   $\overline{}_{22}$ $\overline{}_{23}$ $\overline{}_{24}$ $\overline{}_{25}$ $\overline{}_{26}$ $\overline{}_{27}$ $\overline{}_{28}$ $\overline{}_{29}$ $\overline{}_{30}$ $\overline{}_{31}$ $\overline{}_{32}$

4. What college in Ohio was the first to admit both women and African Americans?

   $\overline{}_{33}$ $\overline{}_{34}$ $\overline{}_{35}$ $\overline{}_{36}$ $\overline{}_{37}$ $\overline{}_{38}$ $\overline{}_{39}$ College

Challenge Questions

1. Ohio is nicknamed the "Mother of Presidents." Name the seven U.S. Presidents born in Ohio.

2. Ohio is also known as the "Mother of Inventors." Considered one of the world's greatest inventors, Ohio-born Thomas Edison held patents for the incandescent electric lamp and the phonograph. He also invented wax paper and a talking doll. Name some of his other inventions. Explain what they were used for or how they worked.

Just for Fun

Why did the woman from Ohio go to the hospital after a tomato fell on her head?

TLC10029 Copyright © Teaching & Learning Company, Carthage, IL 62321

Roughing It

You and your family are early pioneers in the Ohio wilderness. You have just arrived at the place where you plan to settle. There aren't any people within 50 miles, so you and your family will have to make everything you need. The date on the calendar is May 1, 1820.

You have only what you are carrying plus the following items in your wagon: one change of clothing for each person, a large keg of nails, two hammers, an ax, a hatchet, two rifles, shells, two bags of seed corn, some flower seeds, three books, two large feather pillows and two quilts, 100 feet of rope, fishhooks, a butter churn, a frying pan, a large cooking kettle and a large wooden tub.

You also have the two mules that pulled your wagon, a cow, two pigs, three chickens and a goat wandering around nearby.

Look around. What can you use to make your home? How will you keep warm in winter, cool in summer and dry when it rains? Where will you cook? Where will you bathe and wash clothes? What will you eat? How will you keep your animals safe? Where will you store your food?

List the three things you think you should do first.

1. _____

2. _____

3. _____

Draw your new home on the back of this page. Show both an inside and an outside view.

From A to Z

Ohio has cities and towns that begin with every letter of the alphabet—from A to Z.

Look up and down, backwards, forwards and diagonally to find the 26 Ohio cities and towns hidden in the puzzle.

```
Y  V  E  R  M  I  L  I  O  N  O  N
A  O  H  I  T  A  E  O  D  H  M  O
L  H  U  N  I  L  O  U  E  I  I  T
D  I  E  N  Y  E  R  N  L  R  L  L
N  K  E  R  G  B  O  H  O  Y  A  I
I  X  I  N  A  S  O  N  T  K  N  M
F  A  A  N  K  Y  T  I  R  S  H  A
T  R  A  C  E  O  C  O  O  U  N  H
O  N  A  L  N  R  N  O  W  D  A  K
O  J  P  I  E  H  R  C  P  N  R  O
O  I  I  K  S  E  L  A  Z  A  Y  H
R  H  A  O  V  Y  R  O  W  S  B  I
I  U  O  O  D  M  G  E  N  E  V  A
Q  O  D  E  A  Q  N  I  A  R  O  L
```

AKRON	JACKSON	SANDUSKY
BYRAN	KENT	TOLEDO
CLYDE	LORAIN	URBANA
DOVER	MILAN	VERMILION
ELYRIA	NEWARK	WARREN
FINDLAY	ORANGE	XENIA
GENEVA	PARMA	YOUNGSTOWN
HAMILTON	QUAKER CITY	ZALESKI
IRONTON	RIPLEY	

Oklahoma

Nickname: Sooner State • State Bird: Scissor-Tail Flycatcher • Capital: Oklahoma City

■ The earliest inhabitants of Oklahoma shared the land with mammoths, giant bisons, small horses and camels more than 15,000 years ago.

■ Over the centuries, Oklahoma's climate gradually changed and the people and animals living there also changed. Those who lived in Oklahoma after the Ice Age were known as the Paleo People. They hunted and gathered food which they stored in caves where they lived during the winter.

■ At the top of Poteau Mountain, in Heavener Runestone State Park, a stone stairway leads down to a small valley where a 12-foot high, 10-foot wide runestone is encased in glass. Some people believe the runes (letters) were carved by Norse explorers and may be translated as the date November 11, 1012 A.D. Two other inscriptions found nearby may mean November 11, 1017, and November 24, 1024.

■ Some cities in Oklahoma grew in one day. In March, 1889 President Benjamin Harrison announced that two million acres of land would be opened to white settlers at noon on April 22. When noon arrived, 50,000 settlers rushed across the border to claim land. Overnight, Oklahoma City became a tent city of 10,000. Gutherie acquired a population of 15,000 in a single day.

Guthrie

Oklahoma City

■ The "panhandle" is the long, thin strip of land in northwest Oklahoma that looks like the handle of a pan. The Panhandle was once known as No Man's Land.

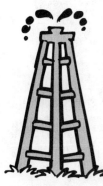

■ The first Oklahoma oil well was drilled near Chelsea in 1889. Oklahoma has the only state capitol with oil wells on the lawn and in the basement.

■ The National Cowboy Hall of Fame and Western Heritage Center in Oklahoma City houses John Wayne's collection of guns, knives, saddles, art and kachina dolls.

■ People who tried to sneak into the area sooner than the official starting time were nicknamed "Sooners." Some were caught and marched back across the border. Others pretended they had just arrived before others raced to the area. That's how Oklahoma came to be known as the Sooner State.

■ Promoters, called Boomers, were hired by businesses to convince people to settle in specific parts of Oklahoma, places where the companies wanted to open new businesses. That's how Oklahoma came to be known as the Boomer State.

■ The word *Oklahoma* came from two Native American words meaning "red people." Today, more people descended from Native Americans live in Oklahoma than in any other state except California.

■ Beginning in 1804, several laws were passed to force all Native Americans living anywhere east of the Mississippi River to move. More than 60 tribes were forced to move west to the Indian Territory of Oklahoma.

119

Matchmaker

Match the items in the box by writing the correct letter in each blank. Some may have more than one answer and not all answers may be used.

1. ____ Oklahoma nickname
2. ____ State flower
3. ____ State wildflower
4. ____ State bird
5. ____ "Overnight" cities
6. ____ State animal
7. ____ Early "inhabitants"
8. ____ State fish
9. ____ Rune site
10. ____ State rock
11. ____ Oklahoma panhandle
12. ____ State song
13. ____ Capital of Oklahoma
14. ____ Means "Oklahoma"
15. ____ State tree
16. ____ State motto

A. American bison
B. Bald eagle
C. Barite rose rock
D. Boomer State
E. Camels
F. Giraffes
G. Gutherie
H. Heavener Runestone State Park
I. Indian blanket
J. Labor Conquers All Things
K. Mammoths
L. Mistletoe
M. Oil Well State
N. "Oklahoma!"
O. Oklahoma City
P. Once known as "No Man's Land"
Q. Redbud
R. Red people
S. Scissor-tailed flycatcher
T. Sooner State
U. White bass
V. Zebras

Challenge Questions

1. Make up a story about the explorers who wrote the three dates on the Heavener runestones. Do you think they were written by one person who stayed in Oklahoma a long time or by explorers who visited on three separate occasions?

2. Born near Prague, Oklahoma, he became an international sports hero, winning medals in the pentathlon and decathlon in the 1912 Olympics. He was selected by sportswriters as the greatest athlete of the first half of the 20th century. What was his name? Where were the 1912 Olympics held?

Just for Fun

What animal should carry an oil can in Oklahoma?

Oklahoma Wildlife

Rocky Mountain elk and deer roam throughout the Wichita Mountains Wildlife Refuge near Lawton. The park has herds of bison, longhorn cattle and even a prairie dog town.

Millions of bison once roamed the Great Plains. Although many people call them buffalo, they are really bison. Every part of the bison was used by Native Americans. They dried and scraped the hide to make leather clothes and tepees. They ate fresh bison meat or dried and saved it for winter. They carved spoons from bison horns. Muscle sinews were used for thread and bow strings. Even buffalo droppings were dried and burned for fuel in areas where wood was scarce.

At one time over 30 million bison roamed the plains. Hunting reduced the once great herds to only 500 animals. Herds have slowly been increased by breeding on ranches and refuges. Bison now number between 35,000 to 50,000 and are no longer considered an endangered species.

You'll also find antelopes, rabbits, coyotes, horned lizards, opossums and armadillos in Oklahoma. The name *armadillo* comes from a Spanish word meaning "little armored one." Although they look something like scaly lizards, armadillos are mammals. Female armadillos always give birth to four identical quadruplets.

As many as 10 million crows arrive at the world's largest crow roost in Fort Cobb Recreation Area every October.

Once hunted for its long tail feathers, the scissor-tailed flycatcher, Oklahoma's state bird, is now protected by state law.

Almost every type of bird that lives between the Rocky Mountains and the Mississippi River makes its home in Oklahoma.

Write the number next to the animal beside its name below.

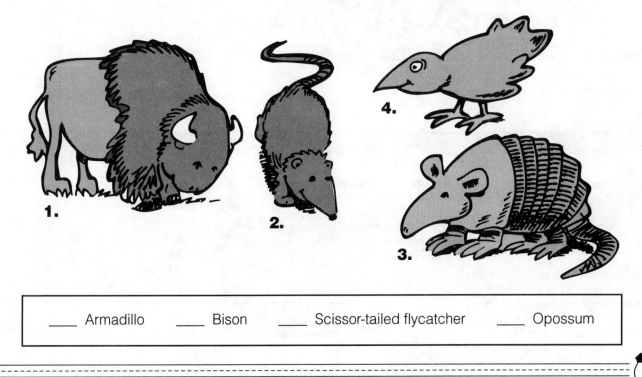

____ Armadillo   ____ Bison   ____ Scissor-tailed flycatcher   ____ Opossum

Oregon

Nickname: Beaver State • State Bird: Western Meadowlark • Capital: Salem

■ John Day Fossil Beds National Monument contains the fossilized bones of animals that lived in eastern Oregon 30 million years ago. Displays at the visitors center include remains of three-toed horses, giant pigs and saber-toothed cats.

■ Although salmon are the most valuable catch, tuna, flounder, oysters, rockfish and sturgeon are important to the commercial fishing industry.

■ Crater Lake, the deepest lake in the nation, lies in the crater of an extinct volcano. Formed about 6,000 years ago when an eruption blew the top off Mount Mazama, the water in this lake is extremely blue.

■ Oregon produces over 170 different crops including wheat, cranberries, hazelnuts, apples, pears, cherries, sugar beets and peppermint.

■ Astoria began as a trading post in 1811. It became the first permanent settlement in Oregon.

Astoria

Portland

■ When the capital was moved to Salem in 1852, it was a small village. For a time, Corvallis became the capital; then it was moved again, back to Salem.

Salem ★

■ The Chinooks lived and fished along the coast near the Columbia River. They traveled the coastal waters and swift rivers in cedar canoes. Food was plentiful. They became excellent fishermen, catching salmon with nets and traps, spearing them or shooting them with bows and arrows.

■ No written records, no large mounds and nor great temples or villages remain to tell us about the prehistoric people who lived in Oregon. A faded picture of a hunter on a cave wall at Fort Rock is one of the few pieces of evidence left by people who lived here as long ago as 15,000 years.

Eugene
●

■ Eugene was named for its first white settler, Eugene F. Skinner.

TRAIL

■ The Willamette River flows through the center of Portland, a city known for its beautiful parks and gardens. Washington Park includes a five-acre Japanese garden. Ten thousand rose bushes bloom in the Rose Test Garden. The 5,000-acre Forest Park contains 30 miles of hiking trails.

■ Oregon leads the nation in lumber production. To preserve the ecology, logging companies must plant trees to replace the ones they cut. Logging is not permitted in over 2,000,000 acres of forest.

■ The Beaver State is rich in natural resources: gold, silver, iron, copper, bauxite and timber.

■ To celebrate important events, the Chinooks and other groups along the northwest coast, held great feasts called potlatches. *Potlatch* is a Chinook word meaning "to give." At a potlatch, the host gave gifts to all his guests. By doing this, he showed how wealthy and important he was.

■ Lava Lands is a geological wonderland of volcanic formations including Lava Butte, a 500-foot cinder cone; Lava River Cave, a one-mile long lava tube and the world's largest forest of lava-cast trees.

The Deepest Gorge

Carved by the Snake River, this canyon in Oregon is the deepest gorge in North America. At some places it is 8,000 feet deep. What is it called?

$\overline{2}$ $\overline{31}$ $\overline{26}$ $\overline{20}$ $\overline{37}$, $\overline{1}$ $\overline{42}$ $\overline{4}$ $\overline{35}$ $\overline{9}$ $\overline{14}$

To find the answer, fill in the blanks below. Write the letter that corresponds with the number below each blank.

1. These Native Americans lived along the Oregon coast near the Columbia River.
    They celebrated important events with great feasts called potlatches. They were the

    $\overline{1}$ $\overline{2}$ $\overline{3}$ $\overline{4}$ $\overline{5}$ $\overline{6}$ $\overline{7}$ people.

2. The Willamette River flows through the center of this city known for its beautiful parks and gardens:

    $\overline{8}$ $\overline{9}$ $\overline{10}$ $\overline{11}$ $\overline{12}$ $\overline{13}$ $\overline{14}$ $\overline{15}$.

3. The official state insect is the Oregon

    $\overline{16}$ $\overline{17}$ $\overline{18}$ $\overline{19}$ $\overline{20}$ $\overline{21}$ $\overline{22}$ $\overline{23}$ $\overline{24}$ $\overline{25}$ $\overline{26}$ $\overline{27}$ $\overline{28}$ $\overline{29}$ $\overline{30}$ $\overline{31}$ $\overline{32}$ $\overline{33}$ $\overline{34}$ $\overline{35}$.

4. The first permanent settlement in Oregon, this city began as

    a trading post in 1811: $\overline{36}$ $\overline{37}$ $\overline{38}$ $\overline{39}$ $\overline{40}$ $\overline{41}$ $\overline{42}$.

Challenge Questions

1. This physician, explorer, fur trader and pioneer was called the Father of Oregon even though he was born in Canada and did not become a U.S. citizen until later in life. He assisted new arrivals to the territory with money, food and advice. What was his name?

2. How is Oregon's climate affected by the Pacific Ocean and the Cascade Mountains?

Believe It or Not

Portland, Oregon, received its name completely by chance. Two early settlers couldn't agree on the name for their new home. One wanted to call it Portland; the other wished to name it Boston. To settle the disagreement, they tossed a coin. Portland won.

Matchmaker

Match the items in the box by writing the correct letter in each blank. Some may have more than one answer and not all the answers may be used.

1. ____ State bird
2. ____ Oregon nickname
3. ____ State fish
4. ____ State dance
5. ____ State flower
6. ____ Natural resource
7. ____ State gem
8. ____ Oregon crop
9. ____ State insect
10. ____ Capital of Oregon
11. ____ State animal
12. ____ Means "to give"
13. ____ State tree
14. ____ Deepest lake
15. ____ State rock

A.	American bison	N.	"Oregon Waltz"
B.	Apples	O.	Polka
C.	Beaver	P.	Ponderosa pine
D.	Beaver State	Q.	Portland
E.	Chinook salmon	R.	Potlatch
F.	Coconuts	S.	Pronghorn antelope
G.	Crater Lake	T.	Salem
H.	Douglas fir	U.	Silver
I.	Fiesta	V.	Square dance
J.	Gold	W.	Sunstone
K.	Maple	X.	Thunder egg (geode)
L.	Oregon grape	Y.	Western meadowlark
M.	Oregon swallowtail butterfly	Z.	Wheat

What Can You Find
in the Columbia River?

Many types of fish, including Oregon's state fish, the Chinook salmon, live in the Columbia River. Look closer and see how many words you can find using the letters in *Columbia River*. Words must be three or more letters long. Write your list below. Try to think of at least 32 words.

_____   _____   _____   _____

_____   _____   _____   _____

_____   _____   _____   _____

_____   _____   _____   _____

_____   _____   _____   _____

_____   _____   _____   _____

_____   _____   _____   _____

Pennsylvania

Nickname: Keystone State • State Bird: Ruffed Grouse • Capital: Harrisburg

■ The name *Pennsylvania* means "Penn's Woods." The name was given by King Charles II of England in honor of Admiral William Penn. The king owed Penn a large sum of money. To repay his debt, he made Penn's son governor of more than 45,000 square miles of land in the New World.

■ Most of the more than six million dollars worth of coins issued at the Philadelphia Mint each year are pennies.

■ The Liberty Bell Shrine at Allentown commemorates the time the famous bell was hidden beneath the floorboards of Zion United Church of Christ during the Revolutionary War.

■ The first root beer made in the U.S. was made in Philadelphia in 1866. The ice-cream soda was invented in Philadelphia in 1874.

■ When Ben Franklin was 17, he was apprenticed to a printer in Boston. He ran away and became a prominent writer, inventor and diplomat in Philadelphia. Franklin established the first circulating library in the colonies and formed America's first volunteer fire department.

■ The official name of the state is the Commonwealth of Pennsylvania.

■ Pittsburgh began as a fur trading post in the 1600s. The city became the leading maker of American glassware by 1850 and later, the iron and steel center of the nation.

■ Philadelphia carpenters staged the nation's first strike in 1791. They demanded that their workday be shortened to 12 hours.

■ *Highlights for Children* is published in Honesdale.

Honesdale

Williamsport

Punxsutawney

■ New York was the U.S. capital from 1777 to 1778. Philadelphia served as the nation's capital from 1790 until 1800 when the center of government moved to Washington, D.C.

Allentown

Pittsburgh

Harrisburg ✪

Hershey

■ Hershey, home of the Hershey Chocolate factory, has a street named Chocolate Ave. with street lamps shaped like giant Hershey Kisses®.

■ Although the Liberty Bell hasn't rung since it cracked in 1835, this symbol of the U.S. is found in Philadelphia, the City of Brotherly Love.

Philadelphia

■ Much of the nation looks to Punxsutawney every Groundhog Day to see if Punxsutawney Phil, a well-known groundhog, will see his shadow.

■ In 1769, a 69-mile stone-surfaced road was completed between Philadelphia and Lancaster. To pay for the project, which cost nearly half a million dollars, travelers paid tolls at gates, called pikes, along the road. The toll collector turned the pike to let travelers continue on their way. The word *turnpike* came to mean "a toll road."

■ Boone County and Booneville, Kentucky, were named for Daniel Boone, a Quaker born in Pennsylvania.

■ The Little League Museum in Williamsport honors well-known people who once played Little League. The Little League World Series is played here each August.

TLC10029 Copyright © Teaching & Learning Company, Carthage, IL 62321

Where in Pennsylvania?

1. I am the City of Brotherly Love.

   What city am I? _____

2. I am the capital of Pennsylvania.

   What city am I? _____

3. I am the home of Phil, a famous groundhog.

   What city am I? _____

4. My streets have lights shaped like chocolate kisses.

   What city am I? _____

5. I was the nation's capital from 1790 until 1800.

   What city am I? _____

6. I was the nation's capital from 1777 until 1778.

   What city am I? _____

7. I host the Little League World Series in August.

   What city am I? _____

8. I was the nation's leading producer of glassware, iron and steel.

   What city am I? _____

Challenge Questions

1. Ben Franklin wanted the wild turkey for our national bird. He said the turkey was a true American bird, more respectable than the bald eagle. What if Ben Franklin had gotten his way and the wild turkey had been declared our national bird?

2. Pennsylvania has no official state song. Write a poem or song in honor of Pennsylvania.

Just for Fun

Which side of a cat in eastern Pennsylvania has the most fur?

What Can You Find in *Pennsylvania?*

How many words can you make using the letters in the word PENNSYLVANIA? Try to make at least 32 words. Words must be three or more letters. Words formed by adding *S* at the end do not count.

_____   _____   _____   _____

_____   _____   _____   _____

_____   _____   _____   _____

_____   _____   _____   _____

_____   _____   _____   _____

_____   _____   _____   _____

_____   _____   _____   _____

_____   _____   _____   _____

Look at the items related to Pennsylvania. Study the pictures for one minute. Turn the page over and list as many of the items as you can remember.

Rhode Island

Nickname: Little Rhody • State Bird: Rhode Island Red Chicken • Capital: Providence

■ Although it was the first to declare its independence from England, Rhode Island was the last of the 13 colonies to approve the new U.S. Constitution. Many feared they would lose their liberties. Others demanded a bill of rights and the abolishment of slavery. Finally, the state constitutional convention agreed to the Constitution by close vote: 34 to 32.

■ When the First Continental Congress met in Philadelphia, the smallest state was first to elect delegates. A Rhode Islander, Esek Hopkins, became commander in chief of the Continental navy. Rhode Island was the first state to declare independence from England on May 4, 1776.

■ Roger Williams left England seeking religious freedom in Massachusetts. He found that although the Puritans wanted religious freedom for themselves, they did not allow the same rights to anyone who disagreed with them.

■ Known as a safe haven, Quakers, Catholics, French Huguenots (Protestants) and people of many other religious beliefs started their own towns. Spaniards and Portuguese from the Caribbean Islands formed the first Jewish synagogue in Newport in 1763.

■ Roger Williams, honored as the founder of Rhode Island, was not the first European to venture into this area. Explorers from Spain, the Netherlands and Italy visited the state long before Williams founded the first settlement in 1636.

■ The governor of Massachusetts ordered Williams to return to England, but he and a few friends fled. With the help of Chief Massasoit, the group survived and eventually settled in a new area they named Providence. Here colonists were allowed political and religious freedom, liberties available in few places at that time.

■ Rhode Island is home to the oldest Baptist Church established in Providence in 1775 and the oldest Quaker Meeting House built in 1669 in Newport.

■ The origin of the Old Stone Mill in Newport is uncertain. Some say it was built by Norsemen in the eleventh century.

■ Rhode Island is the smallest state. From east to west, the Ocean State is only 37 miles wide. From north to south, the total distance is only about 48 miles. Many people commute to work farther than that every day.

Providence

■ The first indoor shopping center in America was the Arcade, built in 1828 in Providence.

■ The official name of this little state is Rhode Island and Providence Plantations.

Newport

■ Rhode Island was the first colony to prohibit the importing of slaves from Africa in 1774.

■ Thirty-five islands in Narragansett Bay are part of Rhode Island. Many are only small clumps of rocks, dangerous to ships.

Rhode Island Tic-Tac-Toe

To play Rhode Island Tic-Tac-Toe, correctly answer three questions in a row: up and down, across or diagonally.

1. Some people believe the Old Stone Mill in Newport was built by _____ in the eleventh century.	2. Two nicknames for Rhode Island: _____ _____	3. Rhode Island's state motto: _____ _____
4. Man honored as the founder of Rhode Island: _____	5. What did colonists enjoy in Rhode Island that was forbidden in most places? _____	6. The nation's first indoor shopping center was called the _____
7. Rhode Island's state bird: _____	8. Official name of Rhode Island: _____	9. Rhode Islander who became commander in chief of the first Continental navy: _____

What Can You Find in Rhode Island?

Rhode Island may be the smallest state, but there's lots to see and do in Little Rhody. How many words can you make using the letters in *Rhode Island*? Words must be three or more letters. Words formed by adding *S* at the end do not count. Can you find 36 or more words?

_____   _____   _____   _____
_____   _____   _____   _____
_____   _____   _____   _____
_____   _____   _____   _____
_____   _____   _____   _____
_____   _____   _____   _____
_____   _____   _____   _____
_____   _____   _____   _____

Number, Please

Match the numbers on the left with the correct answer in the box.

1. ___ 35		
2. ___ 37	A.	Distance, east to west, across Rhode Island
3. ___ 48	B.	Distance, north to south, across Rhode Island
4. ___ 1636	C.	First shopping center in America
5. ___ 1669	D.	First Jewish synagogue
6. ___ 1763	E.	Islands in Narragansett Bay
7. ___ 1774	F.	Oldest Baptist Church established
8. ___ 1775	G.	Oldest Quaker Meeting House built
9. ___ 1776	H.	Prohibited importing slaves from Africa
10. ___ 1828	I.	Rhode Island declared independence
	J.	Roger Williams founded the first settlement in Rhode Island

Challenge Questions

1. Rhode Island isn't an island. One island that is part of the state is officially known as the Island of Rhode Island. What is the other name of that island?

2. You'll find the Sakonnet, Seekonk, Pawtucket, Chepachet, Pettaquamscutt, Potowomut, Woonasquatucket, Ponaganset and Moshassuck in Rhode Island. What are they?

Just for Fun

Why did the chicken in Rhode Island cross the road?

TLC10029 Copyright © Teaching & Learning Company, Carthage, IL 62321

South Carolina

Nickname: Palmetto State • State Bird: Carolina Wren • Capital: Columbia

■ The Carolina parakeet, hunted for its beautiful green, orange and yellow feathers became extinct in the early 1900s.

■ The first known explorer of the South Carolina coast was the Spaniard, Francisco Gordillo in 1521.

■ King Charles I granted land to eight men who became landlords of Carolana. Over 100 people arrived in 1670 and began building the first settlement called Charles Towne. Although they had to pay rent to the landlords, the promise of religious freedom encouraged many French Huguenots, Quakers, Puritans and Baptists to settle in the area.

■ South Carolina was one of the 13 original colonies and the eighth state to ratify the Constitution on May 23, 1788. In 1990 the state ranked 40th in area and 25th in population.

■ North and South Carolina were named in honor of King Charles I of England. The original spelling was *Carolana*, meaning "land of Charles."

✪
Columbia

■ Milk is South Carolina's official state beverage.

■ South Carolina was the first state to secede from the Union in 1860. Ten other states joined with South Carolina to form the Confederate States of America.

■ The first submarine to sink a ship was the Confederate submarine, *Huntley* which sank the Union ship, *Housatonic* in 1864 in Charleston Harbor.

■ A dance called the Charleston was named for Charleston, South Carolina, but a different dance, the shag became the state's official dance in 1984.

Charleston

Beaufort

■ Penn School, founded in 1862 in Beaufort, was the first Southern school for freed slaves.

■ Poinsettias were named for Joel Poinsett of Charleston, who first brought the plant to the U.S. from Mexico.

■ At one time, much of South Carolina was covered with water. A life-size model of a 43-foot prehistoric shark is on display at the South Carolina State Museum. Fossils of camels and mammoths have also been found in the state.

■ During the Revolutionary War, English soldiers attacked Fort Moultrie in Charleston Harbor. Made of palmetto logs, the fort held even against cannon fire. The South Carolinians won the battle and the state received its nickname, the Palmetto State.

131

Number, Please

Fill in the blanks below with the correct number.

1. South Carolina was the ____th state to ratify the Constitution.

2. How many states joined the Confederate States of America? _____

3. North and South Carolina were named for King Charles ____ of England.

4. Penn School, founded in _____, was the first school in the South for freed slaves.

5. The shag became South Carolina's official state dance in _____.

6. Francisco Gordillo explored the South Carolina coast in _____.

7. South Carolina ranked ____th in size in 1990.

8. South Carolina ranked ____th in population in 1990.

9. A life-size model of a ____-foot prehistoric shark is on display at the South Carolina State Museum.

10. Colonists began building Charles Towne in _____.

Challenge Questions

1. Eliza Pinchkey discovered a blue dye made from a plant that grew well in South Carolina. The dye was very popular in England, and this plant became the second major cash crop in South Carolina. What plant produces this popular blue dye?

2. Columbia became the capital of South Carolina in 1790. What city was the first state capital?

Just for Fun

Why did the spaniel in South Carolina wag its tail?

A Visit to South Carolina

Look up and down, backwards, forwards and diagonally to find 32 interesting places to visit in South Carolina. Words in CAPITAL letters can be found in the puzzle.

W	M	O	U	L	T	R	I	E	R	Y	E	H	M
C	O	W	P	E	N	S	H	E	R	N	R	Y	A
Y	Y	O	O	O	G	N	S	N	E	D	R	A	G
P	O	W	D	E	R	U	E	H	U	T	M	A	N
R	R	L	O	R	Y	H	F	P	L	E	A	E	O
E	E	I	H	R	O	A	A	E	B	W	N	F	L
S	N	K	C	I	M	W	R	N	R	W	S	L	I
S	O	I	R	E	L	S	O	O	O	Y	I	O	A
E	O	N	W	E	I	T	M	T	A	H	O	R	D
B	B	G	Y	R	T	A	O	R	S	M	N	E	N
B	I	S	R	O	I	M	R	N	A	I	R	N	A
I	N	A	R	N	R	U	U	R	A	E	D	C	R
G	P	E	E	D	M	K	A	S	T	A	T	E	G

BLUE Ridge Mountains
BOONE Hall Plantation
Brookgreen GARDENS
Cape ROMAINE
Carolina Sandhills Wildlife REFUGE
Charles TOWNE Landing
COWPENS National Battlefield
CYPRESS Gardens
EDISTO Memorial Gardens
FLORENCE Air and Missile Museum
Fort HILL
Fort MOULTRIE
Fort SUMTER
GIBBES Art Gallery
Governor's MANSION
GRAND Strand

HENRY Timrod Park
HILTON Head Island
KINGS Mountain
Lake MURRAY
MAGNOLIA Plantation
MYRTLE Beach
Old POWDER Magazine
PARRIS Island Museum
PAWLEYS Island
PENN School Museum
PRICE House
SELDON Church Ruins
South Carolina Hall of FAME
STATE House
WOODROW Wilson Home
YORK W. Baily Museum

South Dakota

Nickname: Sunshine State • State Bird: Ring-Necked Pheasant • Capital: Pierre

■ One tall tale about Paul Bunyan, the legendary lumberjack, says that Paul wanted some ponds for his sawmills, so he dug out the Great Lakes and filled them with water from the Ocean. Not wanting to dump the rubble on the forests of Minnesota, he tossed it into South Dakota. That's how the Black Hills were formed.

■ The cemetery in Deadwood is the final resting place of "Wild Bill" Hickok and Calamity Jane. Their real names were James Butler Hickok and Martha Jane Burke.

■ In 1743, Francois La Verendryne buried an inscribed lead plate claiming the area for France. School children discovered the plate in 1913.

■ The Badlands are a barren region in South Dakota filled with strange and beautiful rock formations formed by wind and water over millions of years.

■ Near Lemmon, a small town on the border between North and South Dakota, visitors can view gigantic petrified wood logs at the Petrified Wood Park.

■ At Keystone, near Mount Rushmore, visitors pan for gold and take a guided underground tour through Big Thunder Gold Mine.

■ The first gold in South Dakota was discovered near Custer in 1874. Two years later, another vein of gold was discovered near Lead. This proved to be the largest gold mine in North America.

- Lemmon
- Sturgis
- Deadwood
- Lead
- Rapid City
- Keystone
- ★ Pierre

■ Joseph La Framboise, a French fur trader, started the first permanent settlement in South Dakota in 1831. Located at the mouth of the Bad River, Pierre served as the region's headquarters for fur traders and trappers.

■ Dinosaur Park in Rapid City contains life-size sculptures of prehistoric dinosaurs that once lived in South Dakota.

■ The city of Sturgis began as a stop for wagon trains on their way to Fort Meade.

■ When gold was discovered in the Black Hills in 1874, thousands of white settlers poured into the area. Sitting Bull refused to sell the land or mining rights. The Sioux believed the Black Hills region was sacred—the resting place of the souls of their ancestors.

■ The pasqueflower was used as medicine by Native Americans. They treated rheumatism with its crushed leaves and used its flowers to stop nose bleeds.

■ Angered at the government's broken promises, Sitting Bull declared war on white settlers in 1865. After many battles, he agreed to a peace treaty which promised to keep white settlers from the Black Hills "as long as the sun shall shine . . . and the grass shall grow." Within a year, whites had broken the treaty.

■ *Dakota* is a Sioux word meaning "alliance of friends."

■ Chief Sitting Bull, born about 1830, spent his life as a warrior and leader of his people, the Hunkpapa Lokota Sioux. He refused a government order to live on a reservation and joined with the Cheyenne and Arapaho to defeat General Custer at Little Bighorn in 1876.

Mount Rushmore

Mount Rushmore is a national monument carved into a 6,000-foot mountain in the Black Hills. The work on Mount Rushmore was designed and done by Gutzon Borglum, an American sculptor and painter.

The original design for Mount Rushmore included sculpting four Presidents from the waist up. Difficulties forced Borglum to change and revise his plans several times. In the final design, the four presidential faces on Mount Rushmore are 60 to 70 feet tall.

Borglum began work on Mount Rushmore in 1927 at the age of 60. At his death in March 1941, the project had not been completed. His son, Lincoln Borglum, completed the final work on Mount Rushmore in November 1941.

The Presidents on Mount Rushmore are George Washington, Thomas Jefferson and Theodore Roosevelt. Who is the fourth one?

$$\overline{27} \ \overline{7} \ \overline{17} \ \overline{27} \ \overline{30} \ \overline{27} \ \overline{13} \qquad \overline{26} \ \overline{31} \ \overline{6} \ \overline{21} \ \overline{15} \ \overline{23} \ \overline{20}$$

To find the answer, fill in the blanks below. Write the letter that corresponds with the number below each blank.

1. Who designed and did most of the work on the Mount Rushmore monument?

$$\overline{1} \ \overline{2} \ \overline{3} \ \overline{4} \ \overline{5} \ \overline{6} \qquad \overline{7} \ \overline{8} \ \overline{9} \ \overline{10} \ \overline{11} \ \overline{12} \ \overline{13}$$

2. How many Presidents were planned in the original design for Mount Rushmore? $\overline{14} \ \overline{15} \ \overline{16} \ \overline{17}$

3. What was the first name of the man who completed the project after his father died?

$$\overline{18} \ \overline{19} \ \overline{20} \ \overline{21} \ \overline{22} \ \overline{23} \ \overline{24}$$

4. Mount Rushmore is a national monument in the

$$\overline{25} \ \overline{26} \ \overline{27} \ \overline{28} \ \overline{29} \qquad \overline{30} \ \overline{31} \ \overline{32} \ \overline{33} \ \overline{34} \quad \text{of South Dakota.}$$

South Dakota Question Game

To play South Dakota Question Game, read the answers, then finish the questions.

1. This nickname for South Dakota came from the name of the state animal.

   What is the _____?

2. It began as a stop for wagon trains on their way to Fort Meade.

   What is the city of _____?

3. Visitors to this small border town can see gigantic petrified wood logs.

   What is _____?

4. He led the Sioux and other tribes against General Custer at the Battle of Little Big Horn.

   Who was _____?

5. It is the final resting place of "Wild Bill" Hickok and Calamity Jane.

   What is the _____?

6. It is South Dakota's state bird.

   What is the _____?

7. It is a Sioux word meaning "alliance of friends."

   What is _____?

8. It is South Dakota's state insect.

   What is the _____?

Challenge Questions

1. A monument to the Sioux leader, Crazy Horse, is being carved in another granite mountain near Mount Rushmore. Who planned the Crazy Horse monument, and when was the work started?

2. The Corn Palace in Mitchell displays elaborate murals created from corn and other grains. Describe the inside and outside of the Corn Palace.

Just for Fun

When do buffalo charge?

Tennessee

Nickname: Volunteer State • State Bird: Mockingbird • Capital: Nashville

■ Millions of years ago, Tennessee was covered by water. Fossils of seashells as well as mammoths, mastodons, saber-toothed tigers and other animals now extinct have been discovered.

■ Tennessee was named for Tanasie, an early Cherokee village. The Cherokee Chief Sequoyah developed a written alphabet of 86 characters for the Cherokee language. Born in the late 1700s, Sequoyah became a silversmith, painter, warrior and scholar. He taught many of his people to read and write. The Cherokee formed their own schools and printed their own books. The huge sequoia trees of California were named for this remarkable man.

■ In western Tennessee, slaves sang as they worked on the cotton plantations. Their songs had a strong beat that helped establish a rhythm for the repetitive tasks they did. Many of the melodies were in a minor key which gave the music a sad sound.

■ The fiddle, banjo, guitar and harmonica were the instruments played most often in Tennessee. In the eastern mountains, settlers from England and Scotland sang traditional folk ballads.

■ String bands in Tennessee and Kentucky developed the style of music called bluegrass. Bluegrass is characterized by banjo or fiddle music played rapidly, combined with the vocal sounds of early ballads. Another type of music popular in Tennessee was gospel music.

■ In Memphis, W.C. Handy, a composer and performer, combined the sounds of ragtime and honky tonk with the mournful songs of the slaves to write "Beale Street Blues," "Memphis Blues" and St. Louis Blues."

■ Nashville is also known as the "Athens of the South" because many buildings look like ones from the ancient city of Athens in Greece. The Parthenon in Nashville houses an art collection and looks like the ancient Greek temple with the same name.

Nashville ✪

Memphis ●

● **Chattanooga**

■ In the 1950s, a young man from Mississippi began making records in Memphis. Elvis Presley's music combined country and western with rhythm and blues. From this combination, a new style of music was formed. We know it as rock and roll.

■ Lost Sea Caverns near Chattanooga has one of the world's largest underground lakes, called the Lost Sea.

■ A Civil War battle fought at Lookout Mountain in 1863 is known as the "Battle Above the Clouds."

■ When radio began broadcasting nationally in the 1920s, the music of the Tennessee and Kentucky hills was heard all over the country. The first recordings of country music were made in 1927 and the Grand Ole Opry made its debut. Nashville, became "Music City, USA."

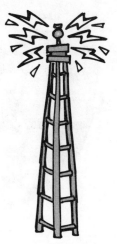

■ The people of Tennessee enjoy music so much, the state has five official state songs: "My Homeland, Tennessee"; "When It's Iris Time in Tennessee"; "My Tennessee"; "The Tennessee Waltz" and "Rocky Top."

137

The State of What?

After the Revolutionary War, Tennessee was part of the state of North Carolina. In 1784, people in eastern Tennessee elected a governor and formed a separate state. The new state lasted four years before becoming part of North Carolina again. In 1789, Tennessee was made a U.S. territory, but it was not admitted to the Union as a state until 1796. What was the name of the state that separated from North Carolina?

$$\overline{}_{23} \ \overline{}_{5} \ \overline{}_{2} \ \overline{}_{14} \ \overline{}_{11} \ \overline{}_{20} \ \overline{}_{19} \ \overline{}_{14}$$

To find the answer, fill in the blanks below. Write the letter that corresponds with the number below each blank.

1. Millions of years ago, Tennessee was covered with $\underset{1}{\underline{}} \ \underset{2}{\underline{}} \ \underset{3}{\underline{}} \ \underset{4}{\underline{}} \ \underset{5}{\underline{}}$.

2. Chief Sequoyah invented an alphabet for what language? $\underset{6}{\underline{}} \ \underset{7}{\underline{}} \ \underset{8}{\underline{}} \ \underset{9}{\underline{}} \ \underset{10}{\underline{}} \ \underset{11}{\underline{}} \ \underset{12}{\underline{}} \ \underset{13}{\underline{}}$

3. What city is nicknamed "Music City, USA"? $\underset{14}{\underline{}} \ \underset{15}{\underline{}} \ \underset{16}{\underline{}} \ \underset{17}{\underline{}} \ \underset{18}{\underline{}} \ \underset{19}{\underline{}} \ \underset{20}{\underline{}} \ \underset{21}{\underline{}} \ \underset{22}{\underline{}}$

4. How many official state songs does Tennessee have? $\underset{23}{\underline{}} \ \underset{24}{\underline{}} \ \underset{25}{\underline{}} \ \underset{26}{\underline{}}$

TLC10029 Copyright © Teaching & Learning Company, Carthage, IL 62321

Matchmaker

Match the items in the box by writing the correct letter in each blank. Watch out; some may have more than one answer and not all the answers may be used.

1. ____ Tennessee nickname
2. ____ State motto
3. ____ State slogan
4. ____ State flower
5. ____ State wildflower
6. ____ State tree
7. ____ State bird
8. ____ State animal
9. ____ State gem
10. ____ State rock
11. ____ State song
12. ____ State horse
13. ____ State insect
14. ____ Capital of Tennessee

A. Agate
B. Agriculture and Commerce
C. Big Bend State
D. Dandelion
E. Firefly
F. Honeybee
G. Iris
H. Ladybug
I. Limestone
J. Memphis
K. Mockingbird
L. "My Homeland, Tennessee"
M. Music State
N. Nashville
O. Passionflower
P. Raccoon
Q. Robin
R. "Rocky Top"
S. Sunflower
T. Tennessee—America at Its Best
U. Tennessee River pearl
V. Tennessee walking horse
W. "The Tennessee Waltz"
X. Tulip poplar
Y. Volunteer State
Z. White-tailed deer

Challenge Questions

1. How was Reelfoot Lake, the largest natural lake in Tennessee formed?

2. The first people to settle in Tennessee arrived about 15,000 years ago. They were known as the Mound Builders because they supported their homes and temples with huge earthen mounds. What types of items have been discovered in these mounds?

Just for Fun

Tammy Tucker taught two turtles to toot tuba tunes under two tall trees in Tennessee. How many *T*s are there in that?

Texas

Nickname: Lone Star State • State Bird: Mockingbird • Capital: Austin

■ Millions of years ago, dinosaurs roamed across Texas. Saber-toothed tigers, small horses, camels, mammoths, mastodons and other animals now extinct made their homes in the Lone Star State.

■ Texas became part of Mexico after Mexico won its independence from Spain in 1821. Texas remained part of Mexico until 1836. Then it became the Republic of Texas, an independent country, for nine years before joining the United States. It had its own flag and issued its own paper money.

■ In 1856, Jefferson Davis, U.S. Secretary of War, sent camels to Texas to carry supplies to army posts in desert areas of the southwest. The experiment lasted only a short time before being discontinued.

■ The Texas oil boom began in 1901 after the Lucas well at Spindletop hit a gusher.

■ The first people to settle in Texas arrived between 13,000 and 10,000 B.C.

■ The Mission San Antonio de Valero, founded by Spain in 1718, later became known as the Alamo.

■ The city of Texarkana is partly in Texas and partly in Arkansas.

Texarkana

■ The nation's first domed stadium, the Houston Astrodome, opened in 1965.

Corsicana

El Paso

■ The Texas coast stretches for 367 miles (591 km) from Louisiana to Mexico. The Rio Grande River separates El Paso, Texas, from the Mexican city of Juarez.

■ Austin, the state capital, was named for Stephen Austin who led the movement for Texas independence.

Austin ✪

Houston

■ Every November, thousands of people travel to Terlingua, a ghost town in Texas, to sample the entries in the World Champion Chili Cookoff Contest.

San Antonio

■ At Bracken Cave near San Antonio, more than 20 million bats may be flying in the cave at once.

■ The last battle of the Civil War was fought at Palmito Hill near Brownsville, Texas, a month after General Robert E. Lee had surrendered at Appomattox.

■ While drilling for water at Corsicana in 1894, workers struck oil instead.

Brownsville

■ In the late 1800s, ⅓ of all Texas cowboys were of African American or Mexican descent.

■ Nearly 500 types of grasses and over 5,000 varieties of wildflowers bloom in Texas.

Texas Tic-Tac-Toe

To play Texas Tic-Tac-Toe, correctly answer three questions in a row: up and down, across or diagonally.

1. What do thousands sample every year in a Texas ghost town?	**2.** What river separates Texas from Mexico?	**3.** Where was the first domed stadium built?
4. What was the original name of the Alamo?	**5.** A Civil War battle was fought in Texas a month after the war had ended. True or false?	**6.** Saber-toothed tigers once lived in Texas. True or false?
7. Who was the capital of Texas named for?	**8.** Texarkana is a city in two states, Texas and	**9.** When did people first settle in Texas?

Challenge Questions

1. How is oil located? How is it brought to the surface?

2. Make up a recipe for a bowl of your famous hot chili.

Just for Fun

What's gray, has four legs, whiskers and weighs 214 pounds?

Blooming Texas

Thousands of varieties of trees, wildflowers and grasses bloom in Texas. Fill in the missing letters to correctly name 26 types of plants found in Texas. Use each letter of the alphabet only once. Cross off the letters in the box below as you use them.

> A B C D E F G H I J K L M N O P Q R S T U V W X Y Z

1. A S T E ___
2. A ___ A L E A
3. B L U E ___ O N N E T
4. C E ___ A R
5. C H A P A R R A ___
6. C O ___ T O N W O O D
7. C Y P R ___ S S
8. D O G ___ O O D
9. G O L D E ___ R O D
10. G R E A S E W O ___ D
11. ___ U M
12. ___ I C K O R Y
13. I N D ___ A N P A I N T B R U S H
14. ___ U N I P E R
15. ___ A G N O L I A
16. M E S ___ U I T E
17. O A ___
18. O L I ___ E
19. P E ___ A N
20. P H L O ___
21. ___ I N E
22. P U R P L E ___ A G E
23. S ___ G E B R U S H
24. S U N ___ L O W E R
25. W A L N ___ T
26. ___ U C C A

Utah

Nickname: Beehive State • State Bird: Sea Gull • Capital: Salt Lake City

■ Utah could well be nicknamed the "Dinosaur State." Scientists have discovered the remains of many types of dinosaurs in northeastern Utah. Today, high mountains and red-walled canyons cover Dinosaur National Monument. More than 140 million years ago this area was flat swampland.

■ More than 10,000 Mormons marched west in 1846 to the place that became Salt Lake City. They called their new homeland Deseret, meaning "honeybee." Under the leadership of Brigham Young, the Mormons founded Salt Lake City in 1847.

■ Utah's state emblem is the beehive, and the honeybee is the state insect.

Logan
●

■ How cold does it get in Utah? On February 1, 1985, a temperature of -69°F was recorded near Logan.

✪ **Salt Lake City**

Provo
●

■ Provo, another city founded by the Mormons, is the home of Brigham Young University.

■ Antelope Island is the largest of the seven islands found in the Great Salt Lake.

■ In spite of much hard work, the Mormons had little to eat the first year. Many survived by eating sego lily bulbs. The sego lily was later named Utah's state flower. The second year wasn't much better for the settlers. Millions of grasshoppers attacked the crops and all would have been lost if thousands of sea gulls hadn't arrived to eat the grasshoppers. The sea gull later became Utah's state bird.

■ Did you know that the state rock of Utah is coal?

■ Over 2,000 dinosaur bones are exposed on a wall inside the park building at Dinosaur National Monument.

■ "Utah, We Love Thee" is the official state song of Utah.

Fillmore
●

■ The largest natural lake in Utah is also the largest natural lake west of the Mississippi River. Great Salt Lake covers more than 1,700 square miles. It is seven times as salty as the ocean. Many rivers flow into Great Salt Lake, but none flow out. When the water evaporates, salt deposits remain. Only the Dead Sea contains more salt than Great Salt Lake.

■ In 1896 Martha Hughes Cannon became the first woman elected as a state senator. The opponent she ran against? Her husband!

Beaver
●

■ He was known as the outlaw, "Butch Cassidy." Born in Beaver, Utah, his real name was George Leroy Parker.

■ Fillmore was the capital of Utah from 1851 to 1856.

■ Utah was named for the Utes who lived there. *Eutaw* means "dwellers in the tops of the mountains."

■ Although the Church of Jesus Christ of Latter-Day Saints was founded by Joseph Smith in Fayette, New York, the Mormons were not popular in New York. They were forced to move west to Ohio, then to Missouri. After Joseph Smith and his brother were murdered by a mob in 1844, Brigham Young became their new leader.

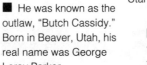

■ Utah averages only 21 people per square mile. Compare that to New Jersey where the average is 995 people per square mile.

Utah Question Game

To play Utah Question Game, read the answers, then finish the questions.

1. It is Utah's official state song.

   What is _____?

2. His real name was George Leroy Parker.

   Who was _____?

3. He led the Mormons to Utah.

   Who was _____?

4. It is seven times more salty than the ocean.

   What is _____?

5. Brigham Young University is located here.

   Where is _____?

6. He founded the Church of Jesus Christ of Latter-Day Saints.

   Who was _____?

7. It is Utah's state emblem.

   What is a _____?

8. Once a flat swampland, the remains of many types of dinosaurs were found in this mountainous area in northeastern Utah.

   What is _____?

9. It is Utah's state rock.

   What is _____?

10. It was the name of the Mormons' new homeland, meaning "honeybee."

    What was _____?

Challenge Questions

1. Golden Spike National Historic Site marks the place where the two parts of the nation's first transcontinental railroad joined in 1869. Where is Golden Spike National Historic Site?

2. Between 1800 and 1840, a few hundred fur trappers and traders roamed throughout Utah. Jim Bridger was one of the best known of these "Mountain Men." Learn more about how the Mountain Men lived.

Just for Fun

What goes buzz-a-choo, buzz-a-choo, buzz-a-choo?

Fun in Utah

The Beehive State has more national parks than any other state except Alaska. The state is home to five national parks, 48 state parks, six national monuments, two national recreation areas and thousands of acres of national forest.

Unscramble the groups of letters to discover 20 fun activities to do in Utah's many parks and recreation areas.

1. KBINGI _____
2. TOBANIG _____
3. GACPMIN _____
4. ACENOING _____
5. KOUTSCOO _____
6. PLEXREO _____
7. KINGHI _____
8. GOJGGNI _____
9. KKAANIGY _____
10. TOUMNINA BLIICMNG _____

11. CIPSCIN _____
12. TARIGNF _____
13. GINWOR _____
14. NIGAILS _____
15. SINKIG _____
16. MMINGISW _____
17. KATE HOTSOP _____
18. CATAVNOI _____
19. CHAWT RIBSD _____
20. TAWER IKS _____

Fill in the blanks with the words in CAPITAL letters to complete the puzzle.

ARCHES National Park
BRYCE CANYON National Park
CANYONLANDS National Park
CAPITOL REEF National Park
DINOSAUR National Monument

GLEN CANYON National Recreation Area
HOVENKEEP National Monument
LITTLE SAHARA Recreation Area
NATURAL BRIDGES National Monument
ZION National Park

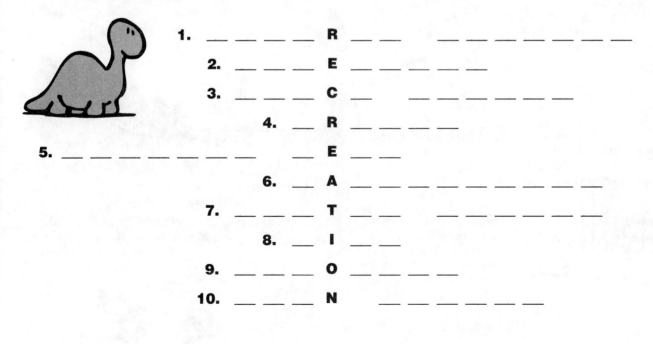

1. __ __ __ __ R __ __ __ __ __ __ __ __ __
2. __ __ __ E __ __ __ __ __
3. __ __ __ C __ __ __ __ __ __ __ __
4. __ R __ __ __ __
5. __ __ __ __ __ __ __ __ E __ __ __ __
6. __ A __ __ __ __ __ __ __ __
7. __ __ __ T __ __ __ __ __ __ __
8. __ I __ __
9. __ __ __ O __ __ __ __
10. __ __ __ N __ __ __ __ __ __

Vermont

Nickname: Green Mountain State • State Bird: Hermit Thrush • Capital: Montpelier

■ Samuel de Champlain explored Vermont in 1609 and claimed the area for France. Vermont comes from the French words *vert* and *mont* which mean "green mountains."

■ Ida M. Fuller of Ludlow received the first Social Security check ever issued in 1940. The check was for the amount of $22.54.

■ The honeybee is Vermont's state insect.

■ Horace Wells of White River Junction was the first person to use laughing gas as an anesthetic for pulling teeth in 1844.

■ Vermont's first constitution of 1777 outlawed slavery. The people elected their own president, coined their own money and had their own postal service. Unlike most states, all adult male citizens in Vermont had the right to vote whether they were property owners or not.

■ Vermont has over 100 covered bridges, more than any other state. The longest covered bridge still in use is a 450-foot bridge across the Connecticut River between Windsor, Vermont, and Cornish, New Hampshire.

Montpelier ★

■ The Vermont Dairyman's Association, the first of its kind, was formed in Montpelier in 1869.

■ The state leads the nation in the production of maple syrup, producing about 400,000 gallons a year. It takes 10 gallons of sap to make one gallon of maple syrup.

■ People in Vermont enjoy an old-fashioned treat called "sugar on snow." When hot maple syrup is poured over a dish of clean snow, it turns into a delicious, soft taffy.

■ The first ski tow in the U.S. opened in Woodstock in 1934. The first chairlift was used on Mount Mansfield in 1940.

● **Bennington**

■ Horses known as Morgans were bred and raised in Vermont in the 1790s to plow the hilly fields of that state.

■ Vermont has the third fewest people of any state. Only Wyoming and Alaska have less people. Montpelier is the smallest capital city in the U.S.

White River Junction
●

■ Seventy-five percent of Vermont is covered with forest. People began making paper in Bennington as early as 1784. Vermont continues to be a leading producer of paper and wood products.

■ Between 1750 and 1764 the royal governor of Vermont sold about 3 million acres of land at one-half cent per acre. At the same time, the governor of New York claimed the same land. He informed the people who had bought the land that they would have to pay for it a second time. People from New Hampshire sent a petition to King George III. The king told the New York governor to leave the settlers in New Hampshire alone.

■ When the 13 colonies declared their independence from England, Vermont decided not to join them. The people of Vermont didn't want to be part of any other country or state. They declared their independence on January 15, 1777, and named their country New Connecticut. Six months later they changed the name to Vermont. Vermont remained an independent country for 14 years.

■ Dr. H. Nelson Jackson was the first person to drive across the United States. The trip took him 70 days in 1903 in a car called the Vermont.

Name _____

How Cold Was It?

In 1816, snow fell in June, July and August in Vermont. Crops failed. Livestock died. The cold spell lasted two years.

What was the year 1816 called in Vermont?

‾6‾ ‾8‾ ‾36‾   ‾34‾ ‾37‾ ‾21‾ ‾27‾   ‾13‾ ‾17‾ ‾7‾ ‾1‾ ‾15‾ ‾10‾ ‾6‾

‾21‾   ‾25‾ ‾28‾ ‾4‾ ‾16‾ ‾33‾ ‾3‾

To find the answer, fill in the blanks below. Write the letter that corresponds with the number below each blank.

1. Vermont's state bird is the

‾1‾ ‾2‾ ‾3‾ ‾4‾ ‾5‾ ‾6‾   ‾7‾ ‾8‾ ‾9‾ ‾10‾ ‾11‾ ‾12‾.

2. Only Alaska and ‾13‾ ‾14‾ ‾15‾ ‾16‾ ‾17‾ ‾18‾ ‾19‾ have less people than Vermont.

3. Vermont is the nation's leading producer of this sweet

treat: ‾20‾ ‾21‾ ‾22‾ ‾23‾ ‾24‾   ‾25‾ ‾26‾ ‾27‾ ‾28‾ ‾29‾.

4. Other sweet treats are produced by Vermont's state insect,

the ‾30‾ ‾31‾ ‾32‾ ‾33‾ ‾34‾ ‾35‾ ‾36‾ ‾37‾.

Challenge Questions

1. The country's first Boy Scout troop started in Vermont. When and where was the first troop organized?

2. Silos were first used on farms in Vermont. Why are silos round? What are they used for? Why are they tall?

Just for Fun

What happens to a duck that flies upside down in Vermont?

What Can You Find in Vermont?

Look at the items related to Vermont. Study the pictures for one minute. Turn the page over and list as many of the items as you can remember.

A Visit to Vermont

What would you like to do in Vermont? Eat lots of maple syrup on pancakes? Go skiing? Climb mountains? Play in the snow?

Draw a picture of yourself doing something in Vermont. Give your picture a caption.

Snowbody's Business

Look up and down, backwards, forwards and diagonally to find the 36 winter words.

1816 wasn't the only cold year in Vermont. A temperature of -50°F was recorded in Bloomfield on December 30, 1933. About 100 inches of snow falls on Vermont's mountains each year.

```
S  L  E  I  G  H  S  S  I  S  S  I  W  F
E  N  O  Z  S  N  Y  E  K  C  O  H  R  J
E  B  O  T  O  F  R  A  A  I  I  O  A  O
L  L  O  W  F  R  T  R  S  T  S  C  W  Y
I  O  Y  U  A  E  F  E  E  T  K  I  L  S
B  W  L  C  S  N  O  W  M  E  N  D  U  E
O  F  S  T  I  H  G  S  T  D  U  R  C  V
M  D  A  H  S  P  A  E  T  F  F  O  A  O
W  H  E  W  I  Z  E  A  L  F  L  N  P  L
O  W  O  L  E  V  O  H  S  D  I  A  S  G
N  N  S  R  S  N  E  T  T  I  M  R  K  W
S  N  O  W  S  T  O  R  M  S  L  I  D  E
```

BLOW	HOCKEY	SLEIGH
BOOTS	ICICLE	SLIDE
CAPS	ICY	SLIP
COLD	JACKET	SNOW ANGEL
DRIFTS	MITTENS	SNOWMEN
FLAKE	NORDIC	SNOWMOBILE
FLUFFY	SCARF	SNOWSHOES
FROST	SHIVER	SNOWSTORM
FROZE	SHOVEL	SNOWY
FUN	SKATES	WHITE
GLOVES	SKIS	WIND
HATS	SLED	ZERO

Virginia

Nickname: Mother of Presidents • State Bird: Cardinal • Capital: Richmond

■ Millions of years ago, dinosaurs lived in Virginia. Hundreds of their footprints were discovered at Culpeper in 1989.

■ The first major battle of the Civil War was fought near Bull Run Creek. Northerners called it the First Battle of Bull Run. Southerners refer to it as the First Battle of Manassas.

■ Although Virginia is considered an eastern state, the western corner of Virginia is farther west than Detroit, Michigan.

■ The nickname "Old Dominion" was given to Virginia by King Charles II of England. The Virginia colony was much larger than the state of Virginia is today. Eight states were carved from the original area.

■ One of the final major battles of the Revolutionary War occurred at Yorktown where George Washington's army defeated British troops under General Cornwallis.

■ England's first permanent settlement was founded at Jamestown in 1607, but Jamestown wasn't the first permanent European settlement. St. Augustine, Florida, was settled by Spaniards in 1565.

■ The Little River Turnpike, built in the 1780s, was the nation's first toll road.

■ Virginia's first public library was established in 1794 in Alexandria.

■ Virginia seceded from the Union on April 17, 1861. A month later Richmond became the Confederate capital.

■ A huge natural stone bridge, once owned by Thomas Jefferson stands near Lexington. Deep underground are the Caverns of Natural Bridge.

Alexandria
Culpeper
Lexington
Richmond
Williamsburg
Jamestown
Hampton

■ Eight men from Virginia have been elected President of the United States: Thomas Jefferson, James Madison, George Washington, James Monroe, William Harrison, John Tyler, Zachary Taylor and Woodrow Wilson.

■ William Harrison served the shortest term of any President. He caught a cold on Inauguration Day and died of pneumonia a month later.

■ The first free school in the United States opened in Hampton in 1634.

■ Williamsburg replaced Jamestown as the capital of Virginia in 1699. Richmond did not become the capital until 1780.

■ Virginia was named for Queen Elizabeth I of England, known as the "Virgin Queen" because she never married.

■ More than half of the battles of the Civil War were fought in Virginia. The Shenandoah Valley, called the "Granary of the Confederacy" was the site of many Civil War battles as the North fought to control the Confederates' food supply.

Medical Marvel

This Virginian, born in Belroi, served as a medical officer in the Army. His discovery of how typhoid and yellow fever were spread helped control these deadly diseases. What was his name?

$\overline{6}$ $\overline{30}$ $\overline{9}$ $\overline{34}$ $\overline{32}$ $\overline{21}$ $\overline{15}$ $\overline{1}$ $\overline{32}$ $\overline{28}$

To find the answer, fill in the blanks below. Write the letter that corresponds with the number below each blank.

1. How many men from Virginia have become President of the United States? $\overline{}$ $\overline{}$ $\overline{}$ $\overline{}$ $\overline{}$
    1   2   3   4   5

2. What man from Virginia served the shortest term of any President?

$\overline{6}$ $\overline{7}$ $\overline{8}$ $\overline{9}$ $\overline{10}$ $\overline{11}$ $\overline{12}$ $\overline{13}$ $\overline{14}$ $\overline{15}$ $\overline{16}$ $\overline{17}$ $\overline{18}$ $\overline{19}$ $\overline{20}$

3. Name the Virginia city that became the capital of the Confederate States of America.

$\overline{21}$ $\overline{22}$ $\overline{23}$ $\overline{24}$ $\overline{25}$ $\overline{26}$ $\overline{27}$ $\overline{28}$

4. What was the first permanent English settlement in Virginia?

$\overline{29}$ $\overline{30}$ $\overline{31}$ $\overline{32}$ $\overline{33}$ $\overline{34}$ $\overline{35}$ $\overline{36}$ $\overline{37}$

Challenge Questions

1. What did pioneers do at a quilting bee? What did they do at a corn-shucking bee? What were some other types of "bees" popular with the early colonists?

2. A Virginian received credit for writing the Declaration of Independence. Who was he?

Just for Fun

What did the Virginian get when he crossed an elephant with a kangaroo?

Virginia Bingo

To the Teacher: The master game sheet, rules and game suggestions are on pages 179 and 180.

Statements for Virginia Bingo

- Virginia was one of the 13 original colonies and the **tenth** state to ratify the Constitution.
- The **cardinal** is Virginia's state bird.
- **"Carry Me Back to Old Virginia"** is the official state song.
- The **American foxhound** is Virginia's state animal.
- The **flowering dogwood** is Virginia's official state tree and state flower.
- Virginia's first public library opened in 1794 in **Alexandria**.
- A small part of Virginia called the **Eastern Shore** is not connected to the rest of the state.
- In 1989, hundreds of dinosaur footprints were discovered at **Culpeper**.
- The nickname **"Old Dominion"** was given to Virginia by King Charles II of England.
- George Washington's home on the bank of the Potomac River was in **Mount Vernon**.
- Thomas Jefferson spent **40 years** completing his 35-room home called Monticello.
- Virginian **Woodrow Wilson**, the 28th President, received the 1919 Nobel Peace Prize.
- The nation's 4th President, **James Madison**, lived at Montpelier.
- John Tyler, the 10th President, named his home **Sherwood Forest**.
- **Coal** is the number one mining product in Virginia.
- The Tomb of the Unknown Soldier in **Arlington** National Cemetery honors dead American soldiers whose names are unknown.
- **Jamestown** was the first permanent English settlement in the New World.
- The abolitionist, John Brown, led a raid on the arsenal at **Harper's Ferry**.
- **Richmond** became the capital of the Confederacy.
- The Civil War ended when Robert E. Lee surrendered to General Grant at **Appomattox**.
- **Robert E. Lee** was the leader of the Confederate Army.
- Virginian **Patrick Henry** was famous for his speech, "Give me liberty or give me death."
- Born a slave in Virginia, **Booker T. Washington** founded Tuskegee Institute in Alabama to educate freed slaves.
- Virginian **Arthur Ashe** was the first African American to win the U.S. men's singles tennis title.

Washington

Nickname: Evergreen State • State Bird: Willow Goldfinch • Capital: Olympia

■ Mount Olympus was named for the mythical home of the Greek gods by John Meares in 1788.

■ Mount St. Helens, which erupted in 1980, is now protected as a national monument.

■ Native Americans called Mount Ranier *Tahoma*, meaning "the place where the gods live." On a clear day, the highest mountain in Washington, can be seen from Seattle, more than 60 miles away. Mount Ranier is 14,410 feet high.

■ National forests and parklands cover more than one-third of Washington.

■ A rare variety of quartz called Ellensburg Blue is found only in central Washington.

■ The San Juan Islands, 172 small islands that are part of Washington, are located in Puget Sound.

■ The Peace Arch in Blaine is a six-story arch that stretches across the U.S.-Canadian border.

■ The square dance is Washington's official state dance.

■ Washington was named for the first President, George Washington.

■ Seattle's monorail, built for the 1962 World's Fair, was the nation's first one-rail train. It links Seattle Center with the downtown area.

■ Olympia, the capital of Washington, began as a shipping port for logging companies.

■ The city of Tacoma started in 1852 at the site of a water-driven sawmill.

■ When the Northern Pacific Railroad bypassed Yakima, residents jacked up their houses, put them on wheels and rolled them closer to the tracks.

(Map labels: Blaine, Seattle, Olympia, Tacoma, Yakima)

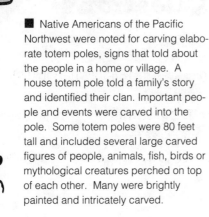

■ Native Americans of the Pacific Northwest were noted for carving elaborate totem poles, signs that told about the people in a home or village. A house totem pole told a family's story and identified their clan. Important people and events were carved into the pole. Some totem poles were 80 feet tall and included several large carved figures of people, animals, fish, birds or mythological creatures perched on top of each other. Many were brightly painted and intricately carved.

■ Washington is the nation's leading grower of apples. Red Delicious and Golden Delicious are two of the state's most famous apple varieties.

■ A mud slide destroyed part of a Makah village 500 years ago, covering everything in its path—people, houses, dogs, tools and totem poles. Much of the village was frozen in time. In 1970, a heavy storm washed away some of the mud. Scientists discovered thousands of items preserved under the mud.

Washington Question Game

To play Washington Question Game, read the answers, then finish the questions.

1. It was named for the mythical home of the Greek gods.

   What is _____?

2. It is Washington's nickname.

   What is the _____?

3. This rare variety of quartz is found only in central Washington.

   What is _____?

4. It became a national monument after it erupted in 1980.

   What is _____?

5. This Washington city started in 1852 at the site of a water-driven sawmill.

   What is _____?

6. It is Washington's state dance.

   What is _____?

7. This six-story structure commemorates the friendship between
   the U.S. and Canada.

   What is _____?

8. Scientists have learned much about village life of the Makah people
   500 years ago because of this.

   What was _____?

9. Native Americans of the Pacific Northwest carved these "signs" to
   commemorate important people and events.

   What are _____?

10. It is the capital of Washington.

    What is _____?

Challenge Questions

1. Spokane, Washington, was the site of the 1974 World's Fair. What name was this event known by?

2. "Fifty-Four-Forty or Fight" was James Polk's campaign slogan in 1844. What did this slogan mean?

Just for Fun

Tina: What are those holes in the wood?
Tim: They're knot holes.
Tina: Well, if they're not holes, what are they?

Washington Lakes

Washington has about 1,000 natural lakes. Many of these lakes were formed by the runoff from mountain glaciers.

Look up and down, backwards, forwards and diagonally to find the names of 39 lakes in Washington.

```
B  R  E  K  A  B  U  M  O  C  T  A  H  W
D  M  P  R  E  M  L  A  P  N  O  W  H  I
O  C  U  R  L  E  W  U  I  Z  E  I  N  L
W  E  N  A  T  C  H  E  E  M  T  D  O  L
N  A  L  E  H  C  D  T  S  E  O  N  L  I
S  G  S  S  Y  E  T  U  S  T  G  S  T  A
O  O  I  H  E  E  L  T  N  I  W  R  E  M
R  F  A  R  I  E  O  C  U  N  O  I  R  S
G  E  K  P  H  N  L  P  A  U  Y  O  N  N
B  A  V  C  E  C  G  U  T  T  S  A  O  E
A  I  E  L  O  W  A  T  T  S  C  O  L  V
N  E  S  P  I  R  I  T  O  F  L  E  I  E
K  A  C  H  E  S  S  C  O  N  A  K  P  T
S  H  A  N  N  O  N  A  V  I  L  L  U  S
```

The unused letters spell the names of three other Washington lakes:

__ __ __ __ __ __ __ __ ,   __ __ __ __ __   and __ __ __ __ __ __ __ __ __ .

ALDEN	MERWIN	STEVENS
BAKER	MOSES	SULLIVAN
BANKS	ONAK	TROUT
BLUE	OWHI	TULE
CHELAN	OZETTE	TWIN
CURLEW	PALMER	WASHINGTON
DEER	ROCK	WATTS
DOWNS	ROSS	WENATCHEE
FISH	SHANNON	WEST
KACHESS	SILVER	WHATCOM
KEECHELUS	SOAP	WHITESTONE
LONG	SPECTACLE	WILLIAMS
LOON	SPIRIT	YALE

West Virginia

Nickname: Mountain State • State Bird: Cardinal • Capital: Charleston

■ The first people in West Virginia were nomadic hunters who arrived about 15,000 B.C. Archaeologists have found tools and arrowheads of these people who hunted mammoths, mastodons, camels and other animals now extinct.

■ Europeans began exploring and mapping West Virginia in the 1670s, but few pioneers moved to the area until after 1725. Even then, the population grew slowly. Most early settlers lived in the Eastern Panhandle region called western Virginia.

■ West Virginia has been called the Switzerland of America. The Alleghenies, the Blue Ridge Mountains and the rugged Appalachian Plateau give West Virginia its nickname, the Mountain State.

★ **Charleston**

■ By the mid 1800s, coal became the major industry, providing jobs for thousands. Cotton may have been king in many neighboring states, but coal was king in West Virginia. In 1870, 600,000 tons of coal came from the state's mines.

■ After the Civil War, Virginia asked West Virginia to reunite and form one state again. When West Virginians refused, Virginia presented the state with a bill for millions of dollars to pay off the state debt incurred before the two states separated. It took the courts 45 years to settle the case. Eventually West Virginia paid $12.4 million to Virginia.

■ Salt was the first major industry in West Virginia. Commercial salt mines opened in Bulltown, Clarksburg and in the Great Kanawha Valley in the early 1800s. Salt was important as a seasoning and used to preserve meat.

■ West Virginia has a rather odd shape. The two parts that stick out are called panhandles. The Northern Panhandle is a narrow strip of land between Ohio and Pennsylvania. The Eastern Panhandle is bordered by Virginia and Maryland.

■ During the Civil War, Virginia joined the Confederate States and West Virginia remained with the Union, even though many in the Eastern Panhandle fought in the Confederate Army.

■ The first coal in West Virginia was discovered in 1742 on the Coal River. Although West Virginia had a lot of coal, wood remained the major fuel for heating until 1820.

■ The railroads helped West Virginia industrial growth. Coal could be sent to new markets on the Atlantic coast. Needing coal to fuel the steam-driven engines, the railroad became an important customer for West Virginia coal.

■ In 1763 King George III of England banned further settlements west of the Alleghenies, hoping to end conflicts between colonists and Native Americans. People from the Netherlands, Germany, Scotland and Ireland ignored the order. So did the English colonists.

■ Another early industry began at a large iron-making plant which opened in 1794. At its peak, the plant produced two tons of iron a day.

■ West Virginia was part of Virginia until 1861. By a large majority, voters of western Virginia favored becoming a separate state. Wheeling became the new capital. Political leaders considered several names for the new state including Kanawha, Allegheny and Augusta. On June 20, 1863, West Virginia became the 35th state.

The Nation's Capital in West Virginia?

At one time, George Washington proposed that Mecklenburg, West Virginia, be made the nation's capital city. By what name is the city of Mecklenburg known today?

$$\overline{22} \ \overline{15} \ \overline{6} \ \overline{12} \ \overline{15} \ \overline{20} \ \overline{7} \ \overline{18} \ \overline{21} \ \overline{25} \ \overline{27} \ \overline{2} \ \overline{10}$$

To find the answer, fill in the blanks below. Write the letter that corresponds with the number below each blank.

1. Because of its many mountains, West Virginia is sometimes

    called the $\overline{}_{1} \ \overline{}_{2} \ \overline{}_{3} \ \overline{}_{4} \ \overline{}_{5} \ \overline{}_{6} \ \overline{}_{7} \ \overline{}_{8} \ \overline{}_{9} \ \overline{}_{10} \ \overline{}_{11}$ of America.

2. The two strips of land that stick out from the northern and eastern

    parts of West Virginia are called $\overline{}_{12} \ \overline{}_{13} \ \overline{}_{14} \ \overline{}_{15} \ \overline{}_{16} \ \overline{}_{17} \ \overline{}_{18} \ \overline{}_{19} \ \overline{}_{20} \ \overline{}_{21}$.

3. $\overline{}_{22} \ \overline{}_{23} \ \overline{}_{24} \ \overline{}_{25}$ mining was the first major industry in West Virginia.

4. After it was discovered in 1742, this natural resource

    became "king" in West Virginia: $\overline{}_{26} \ \overline{}_{27} \ \overline{}_{28} \ \overline{}_{29}$

Challenge Questions

1. George Washington's youngest brother founded a town in West Virginia near the Virginia border. What was his youngest brother's first name and the name of the town he founded?

2. The people of West Virginia were dependent on coal for jobs and income. When the price of coal fell, thousands were out of work. What types of industries are becoming more important in West Virginia today?

Just for Fun

What has three feet but no toes in West Virginia?

Take Me Home to West Virginia

Use the clues to fill in the blanks below.

1. State song
2. West Virginia nickname
3. Capital of West Virginia
4. State fish
5. West Virginia was once part of this state

6. West Virginia nickname
7. State tree
8. State colors
9. State bird

10. State flower
11. First capital of West Virginia
12. State animal

1. "_ _ _ W _ _ _ _ _ _ _ _ _ _ _ _ _ _ _ _ _ _"
2. _ _ _ _ _ _ _ E _ _ _ _ _ _ _ _
3. _ _ _ _ _ S _ _ _
4. _ _ _ _ _ T _ _ _ _
5. _ _ _ _ _ V _ _ _ _ _ _
6. _ _ _ _ _ _ _ I _ _ _ _ _ _ _
7. _ _ _ _ _ R _ _ _ _ _
8. _ _ _ _ and G _ _ _ _
9. _ _ _ _ _ I _ _ _ _
10. _ _ _ _ _ _ _ _ N _ _ _ _ _
11. _ _ _ _ _ _ I _ _ _
12. _ _ A _ _ _ _ _

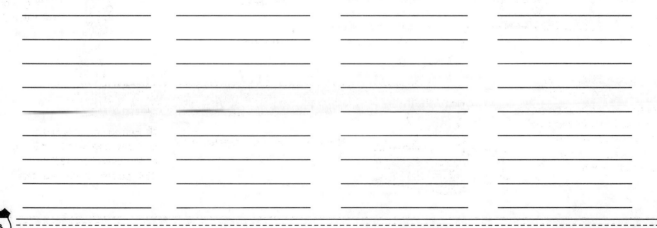

What Can You Find in *West Virginia*?

How many words can you make using the letters in the words *West Virginia*? Words must be three or more letters. Words made by adding *S* at the end do not count. Work with a partner. Write your list below. You should be able to make at least 36 words.

_____   _____   _____   _____

_____   _____   _____   _____

_____   _____   _____   _____

_____   _____   _____   _____

_____   _____   _____   _____

_____   _____   _____   _____

_____   _____   _____   _____

Wisconsin

Nickname: Badger State • State Bird: Robin • Capital: Madison

■ Glaciers covered much of Wisconsin during the last Ice Age. The enormous walls of ice moved south from Canada like a giant bulldozer, flattening mountains and forming valleys. When the ice melted and the glaciers retreated, thousands of lakes, streams and creeks remained.

■ Ninety-five percent of the ginseng grown in the U.S. is raised in Wisconsin. Ninety percent of Wisconsin's ginseng is raised in Marathon County. The U.S. is currently the third largest exporter of ginseng in the world.

■ One Wisconsin tale claims that Paul Bunyan, the giant lumberjack, scooped out Wisconsin's lakes with a shovel. When the holes filled with rainwater, Babe, the Blue Ox had enough to drink.

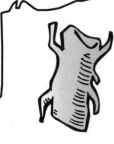

■ Ginseng is used in China, as a remedy for many diseases. Native Americans used the root for medicinal purposes. To the Cherokee, ginseng was known as "Little Man" because of its resemblance to the human form. The Chippewa, Creek, Pawnee, Iroquois and Sioux also used ginseng as a medicine.

■ The first cooperative store (co-op), a store owned by the people who shop there, opened in Black Earth in 1886.

■ Wisconsin has nearly 15,000 lakes, rivers, streams and creeks—so many that Wisconsin ran out of names for them. There are 51 named Beaver Creek and 74 named Long Lake. Lake Winnebago, the largest inland lake in Wisconsin, covers 215 square miles.

■ Although the prize was $10,000, only two cars entered the world's first auto race in 1878. The car from Oshkosh beat the car from Green Bay. The winning car averaged 6 miles per hour for the 200-mile race from Green Bay to Madison.

Green Bay

■ Harry Houdini, the famous magician and escape artist, was raised in Appleton.

■ Swiss immigrants in New Glarus were the first Wisconsin cheesemakers in 1845.

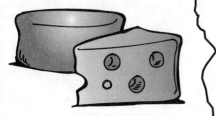

■ The nation's first hydroelectric plant opened in Appleton in 1882. Running water from the Fox River was used to create electricity to light homes and run the city's streetcars.

Appleton

Neenah

Black Earth

★ **Madison**

New Glarus

■ The word *Wisconsin* comes from the Chippewa word meaning "the gathering of waters."

■ Nomadic hunters arrived in Wisconsin 13,000 to 14,000 years ago. As the huge glaciers retreated, they followed the herds of mastodons, giant beavers, deer, caribou and elk which headed north.

■ Facial tissues were invented in Neenah in the early 1900s.

■ Burlington, a city in present-day Iowa, was the capital of Wisconsin from 1837 to 1838 before it became a state.

Matchmaker

Match the items in the box by writing the correct letter in each blank. Some may have more than one answer and not all the answers may be used.

1. ____ State bird
2. ____ State fish
3. ____ Means "the gathering of waters"
4. ____ State wildlife animal
5. ____ State animal
6. ____ State song
7. ____ State flower
8. ____ State tree
9. ____ State motto
10. ____ Capital of Wisconsin
11. ____ State insect
12. ____ State mineral
13. ____ State fossil
14. ____ State rock
15. ____ State dog
16. ____ State farm animal
17. ____ State drink
19. ____ Wisconsin nickname

A. America's Dairyland
B. Badger
C. Badger State
D. Cardinal
E. Dairy cow
F. Forward
G. Galena
H. Honeybee
I. Milk
J. Milk State
K. Madison
L. Muskellunge (muskie)
M. "On Wisconsin!"
N. Red granite
O. Robin
P. Sugar maple
Q. The Big Cheese
R. Trilobite
S. Water spaniel
T. White-tailed deer
U. Wisconsin
V. Wisconsin rose
W. Wood violet

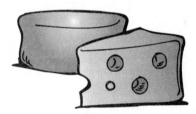

Challenge Questions

1. In 1884, Albert, Otto, Alfred, Charles and John Ringling began a circus in this Wisconsin city. Today, this city is home to the Circus World Museum. What is the name of the city?

2. Although badgers live in Wisconsin, that's not how Wisconsin got its nickname. Why is Wisconsin known as the Badger State?

Just for Fun

What do you call a cow in Wisconsin that won't give milk?

Name _____

Wisconsin

X Marks the Spot

Look at the Wisconsin map. Read the clues to find the name of this city in Wisconsin.

1. I have a French name.

2. Translated, my name means "foot of the lake."

3. A small town nearby has a name that sounds like Paradise.

4. You can reach me by driving north from Milwaukee.

5. If you go as far north as Green Bay, you went to far.

6. I'm at the foot of Lake Winnebago.

> **What's my name?**
>
> _____

Words of Wisdom

Here's an old saying heard in Wisconsin. Use the symbols at the bottom of the page to read the message.

{ [%   ¿ ^ ! + $ = ø   ÷ ^ @ !   ≠ ^ ¿ '

< @ {   ÷ ^ @   [* } %   { ^ $ ^

{ [%   & = + ? =] # .

```
*  <  ≠  $  %  #  [  =  ?  +  &  ]  ^  !  ø  {  @  }  ¿  ÷
A  B  C  D  E  G  H  I  K  L  M  N  O  R  S  T  U  V  W  Y
```

TLC10029 Copyright © Teaching & Learning Company, Carthage, IL 62321

Wyoming

Nickname: Equality State • State Bird: Meadowlark • Capital: Cheyenne

■ People first lived in Wyoming about 12,000 years ago. Some time between 1,000 and 10,000 years ago, these prehistoric people built Medicine Wheel in the Bighorn Mountains. Medicine Wheel is made of flat white stones in the shape of a huge wheel, 70 feet across. It may have been used as a giant calendar. By lining up the sun with certain rocks, they could tell the first day of each season.

■ Max Meyer, who ran a clothing store in Cheyenne, is credited with inventing the 10-gallon hat.

■ Although it is the ninth largest state in area, Wyoming has the smallest population of all fifty states. The Cowboy State averages only five people per square mile.

■ Women first served on juries in Wyoming in 1870, but that practice was discontinued a year later. Women were rarely called for jury duty, even in the Equality State, until 1950.

■ Mountain men used the word *hole* to mean "a valley surrounded by mountains." Jackson Hole in Grand Teton National Park is 50 miles long and 7 miles wide.

Jackson Hole
●

■ The area around the beautiful, rugged Teton Mountains in western Wyoming became a national park in 1929. The lakes at the base of the mountains are also part of the 500-square-mile park. Grand Teton National Park has something found in few other places in the U.S.—12 small glaciers. The highest peak is Grand Teton, 13,700 feet above sea level.

■ The word *Wyoming* means "large plains." It was named for Wyoming Valley in Pennsylvania.

Sundance ●

● **Gillette**

■ About 10,000 elk winter at the National Elk Refuge near Jackson. The nation's largest herd of pronghorn antelope, about 50,000 animals, can be found near Gillette.

■ Butch Cassidy and the Sundance Kid reportedly hid out in a place called Hole-in-the-Wall, south of Buffalo. Some people believe Cassidy hid $70,000 in Wyoming's Wind River Mountains, but the money has never been found.

■ In December 1869, long before it became a state, women received the right to vote and hold public office in Wyoming. Two months later, Esther Hobart Morris became the nation's first female judge when she was appointed as Justice of the Peace in South Pass City. Her statue stands before the main entrance to the state capitol building in Cheyenne.

☆ **Cheyenne**

■ Cheyenne was the first Union Pacific railroad station in Wyoming.

■ In 1870, Eliza Swain, a 70-year-old grandmother, became the first woman to cast a ballot in a general election. Other women from Wyoming made history as the first to be elected to public office and as first woman state senator.

■ Devil's Tower is a 1,280-foot tower-shaped cluster of volcanic rocks northwest of Sundance. It became the nation's first national monument in 1906.

Not So Inviting

Wyoming has much spectacular scenery, beautiful mountains and valleys, but one canyon in central Wyoming, doesn't sound like a very inviting place to visit. Part of it is called Devil's Kitchen. Coal deposits in the area caught fire in the 1800s and burned for many years. What is this place called?

$$\overline{\underset{8}{\quad}}\ \overline{\underset{4}{\quad}}\ \overline{\underset{23}{\quad}}\ \overline{\underset{40}{\quad}}\ \overline{\underset{46}{\quad}}\ {}^,\quad \overline{\underset{32}{\quad}}\ \overline{\underset{41}{\quad}}\ \overline{\underset{13}{\quad}}\ \overline{\underset{27}{\quad}}\quad \overline{\underset{15}{\quad}}\ \overline{\underset{31}{\quad}}\ \overline{\underset{45}{\quad}}\ \overline{\underset{38}{\quad}}$$

To find the answer, fill in the blanks below. Write the letter that corresponds with the number below each blank.

1. Butch Cassidy and the Sundance Kid reportedly hid out at a

    place called $\overline{\underset{1}{\quad}}\ \overline{\underset{2}{\quad}}\ \overline{\underset{3}{\quad}}\ \overline{\underset{4}{\quad}}\ \overline{\quad}\ \overline{\underset{5}{\quad}}\ \overline{\underset{6}{\quad}}\ \overline{\quad}\ \overline{\underset{7}{\quad}}\ \overline{\underset{8}{\quad}}\ \overline{\underset{9}{\quad}}\ \overline{\quad}\ \overline{\underset{10}{\quad}}\ \overline{\underset{11}{\quad}}\ \overline{\underset{12}{\quad}}\ \overline{\underset{13}{\quad}}$.

2. About 10,000 elk winter at the $\overline{\underset{14}{\quad}}\ \overline{\underset{15}{\quad}}\ \overline{\underset{16}{\quad}}\ \overline{\underset{17}{\quad}}\ \overline{\underset{18}{\quad}}\ \overline{\underset{19}{\quad}}\ \overline{\underset{20}{\quad}}\ \overline{\underset{21}{\quad}}$

    $\overline{\underset{22}{\quad}}\ \overline{\underset{23}{\quad}}\ \overline{\underset{24}{\quad}}\quad \overline{\underset{25}{\quad}}\ \overline{\underset{26}{\quad}}\ \overline{\underset{27}{\quad}}\ \overline{\underset{28}{\quad}}\ \overline{\underset{29}{\quad}}\ \overline{\underset{30}{\quad}}$ in Wyoming.

3. Which city was the first Union Pacific railroad station in

    Wyoming? $\overline{\underset{31}{\quad}}\ \overline{\underset{32}{\quad}}\ \overline{\underset{33}{\quad}}\ \overline{\underset{34}{\quad}}\ \overline{\underset{35}{\quad}}\ \overline{\underset{36}{\quad}}\ \overline{\underset{37}{\quad}}\ \overline{\underset{38}{\quad}}$

4. Grand Teton National Park has something found in few other

    parks—12 small $\overline{\underset{39}{\quad}}\ \overline{\underset{40}{\quad}}\ \overline{\underset{41}{\quad}}\ \overline{\underset{42}{\quad}}\ \overline{\underset{43}{\quad}}\ \overline{\underset{44}{\quad}}\ \overline{\underset{45}{\quad}}\ \overline{\underset{46}{\quad}}$.

Challenge Questions

1. Buffalo Bill gave cowboys an exciting, romantic image. His traveling show thrilled audiences in the United States and Europe. What was Buffalo Bill's real name? What was the name of his wild west show?

2. Women in Wyoming could vote in 1869, long before women in any other state had that right. Which amendment to the Constitution granted women the right to vote? When was it passed?

Just for Fun

Stories are told about the jackalope, an imaginary animal found in Wyoming. It has the body of a rabbit and the antlers of an antelope. Some people take the stories seriously. A huge statue of a jackalope stands in Douglas, Wyoming.

Old Faithful

As you read about the wonders of Yellowstone National Park, circle the words that appear in CAPITAL letters. These words are hidden in the puzzle. Look up and down, backwards, forwards and diagonally to find the hidden words.

```
S  T  O  O  H  S  P  R  I  N  G  S  R  O
F  B  L  U  R  P  S  O  F  T  T  E  G  Y
A  U  N  I  Q  U  E  A  T  O  H  E  R  L
I  B  M  P  A  R  K  L  V  S  U  E  E  U
T  B  U  A  U  H  A  E  U  A  E  R  A  R
H  L  U  P  R  M  A  G  M  A  L  L  T  T
F  E  T  R  R  O  O  T  G  P  C  O  O  S
U  S  N  E  P  M  L  L  E  F  S  H  N  H
L  T  H  O  E  S  A  E  T  E  A  R  R  G
O  T  O  N  E  V  T  E  S  E  U  E  O  R
O  L  J  L  D  S  I  A  T  T  N  T  C  E
S  O  D  U  D  E  G  L  A  S  M  A  K  E
Y  E  L  L  O  W  S  T  O  N  E  W  I  N
```

People would ENJOY visiting Yellowstone National Park simply to see the beautiful ROCK formations, DEEP canyons, roaring waterfalls, STEEP mountains and abundant wildlife. These sights are GREAT, but they are not why the PARK is so special. The many THERMAL wonders MAKE Yellowstone TRULY UNIQUE. *Thermal* means "caused by HEAT."

When JOHN Colter and other early explorers TOLD of seeing STEAM coming from the Earth, of brightly colored POOLS of boiling WATER and mud, of hot SPRINGS and geysers that spouted fountains of HOT water, people thought they were making up stories.

LONG ago, volcanoes erupted in Yellowstone. Deep in the Earth, is a layer of MOLTEN rock called MAGMA. When a volcano ERUPTS, magma (LAVA) is pushed to the surface. When lava cools, it hardens into rock. Huge cone-shaped mountains may form from the lava. Flowing lava created many of the landscape features in YELLOWSTONE.

The volcanoes are no longer active, but the Earth below the surface remains very hot. When water trapped below ground is heated, it expands and TURNS to steam. As water expands, pressure causes the water to find a way out. Water that BUBBLES to the surface becomes a hot spring. Bacteria and ALGAE that LIVE in hot springs may cause the water to look brown, yellow, orange or GREEN.

Mud POTS form when steam rises through puddles of mud. The mud bubbles, BURPS and BLURPS like pudding boiling in a pot on the STOVE. Another thermal oddity in Yellowstone are FUMAROLES which shoot out hot GASES and steam from HOLES in the Earth.

The best-known thermal feature of Yellowstone is Old FAITHFUL, a geyser that "blows its top" every 40 to 100 minutes. *Geyser* comes from an Icelandic word meaning "GUSHER." A geyser is a fountain of hot water that shoots into the air. Each time OLD Faithful erupts, water SHOOTS up 100 to 184 FEET. The eruption lasts about FOUR minutes.

(*TOLD and OLD are in separate locations.)

Washington, D.C.

Nickname: Capital City • District Bird: Wood Thrush • District Motto: Justice for All

■ Washington, D.C.'s earliest inhabitant may have been an 80-foot brachiosaurus or a triceratops. One hundred fifty million years ago, dinosaurs lived in the cypress swamp that is now our nation's capital.

■ The *D.C.* in *Washington, D.C.* stands for *District of Columbia*, named in honor of Christopher Columbus.

■ More than a million visitors enjoy the breathtaking view of the city from the top of the 555-foot tall Washington Monument. The climb can be pretty breathtaking, too, for anyone willing to walk up the 898 steps to the top. Most visitors prefer to take the elevator.

■ By 1790, the newly formed United States already had eight temporary capitals. George Washington knew the country needed a permanent center of government. He selected the site of the capital for its central location. The land was donated by Maryland.

■ During the early years, the city looked more like a country village than a great center of government. Only a few hundred wooden houses stood along the streets. The unpaved roads were dusty in dry weather and muddy when it rained. Cows and pigs wandered through the streets. Corn grew on Pennsylvania Avenue. The city did not grow very fast. For the first 10 years, only one police officer was needed for the whole city.

■ A contest was held to determine the design for the President's home. James Hoban, an Irishman, won the contest with a plan that resembled a grand Irish manor house. The first foundation block was laid on October 12, 1792, on the 300th anniversary of the day Columbus landed in the New World.

■ During the Civil War, Union soldiers camped in the White House ballroom and on the lawn. The basement of the Capitol became the army bakery. A slaughterhouse was set up near the Washington Monument.

■ George Washington was the only President never to live in the White House. It wasn't called the White House until it was painted and restored after being burned by the British during the War of 1812.

■ When John and Abigail Adams moved in, their home wasn't finished. The place was drafty, the roof leaked and the walls weren't plastered. There was no place to hang laundry so the First Lady had it hung in the East Room to dry.

■ Philadelphia, Pennsylvania was the nation's capital before it was moved to Washington, D.C. in 1800.

■ In 1800 when the center of government moved from Philadelphia to Washington, D.C., there were 126 clerks on the government payroll. Today, about 400,000 people in the Washington area work for the federal government.

■ The original Declaration of Independence, the Constitution and other important government documents are stored at the National Archives.

■ Today the White House has 132 rooms. Besides the first family's private quarters, the Oval Office and staff rooms, there are kitchens and supply rooms; a dentist's office and medical clinic; rooms for a barber and a florist; a movie theater; carpentry, paint and upholstery shops and an electrical center.

■ Jenkin's Hill was chosen as the site for the nation's capitol building. Dr. William Thornton won $500 in a contest for the best plan. His design featured two identical wings, one for the House of Representatives and one for the Senate, joined by a round, domed center room called a rotunda.

■ George Washington laid the cornerstone for the capitol with a silver trowel on September 18, 1793. Lack of workers, money and materials caused many delays. Seven years later when Congress was scheduled to move in, only the north wing was ready. In summer it was so hot, people called it "The Oven."

■ When the capitol was enlarged in 1959, President Dwight D. Eisenhower laid the new cornerstone with the same silver trowel George Washington had used for the original building. Today the capitol contains 540 rooms.

■ About 30 million dollars is printed every day at the Bureau of Engraving and Printing.

■ The White House is pictured on the back of $20 bills.

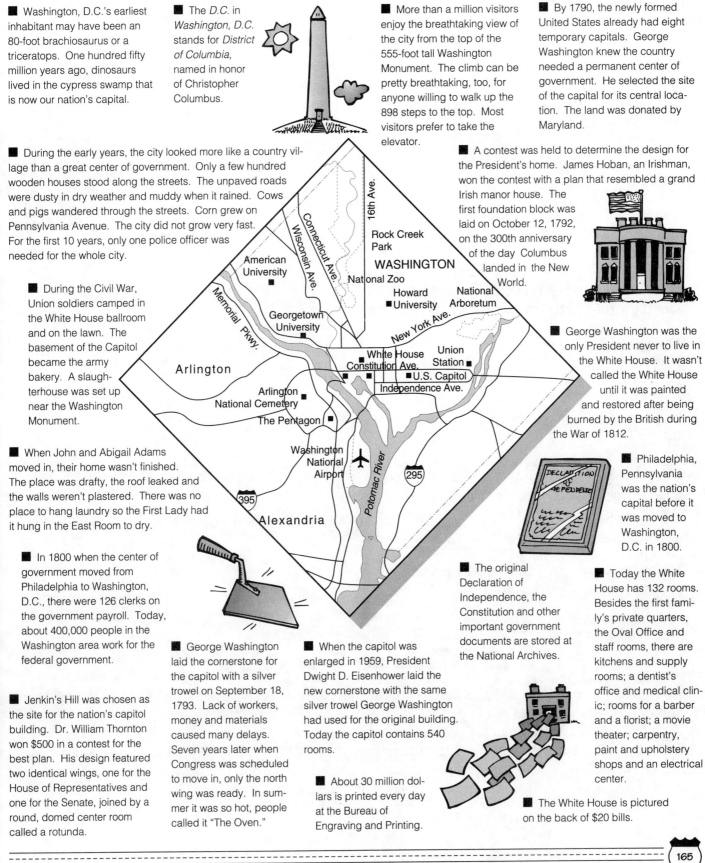

Map labels: 16th Ave., Connecticut Ave., Wisconsin Ave., Rock Creek Park, WASHINGTON, American University, National Zoo, Memorial Pkwy., Georgetown University, Howard University, National Arboretum, New York Ave., White House, Union Station, Constitution Ave., U.S. Capitol, Independence Ave., Arlington, Arlington National Cemetery, The Pentagon, Washington National Airport, Potomac River, 295, 395, Alexandria

The Nation's Attic

The Smithsonian Institution began with a $500,000 gift to the American people, from an Englishman, James Smithson in his will in 1829. The money was to be used for "an establishment for the increase and diffusion of knowledge among men." Smithson had never visited the United States. The first Smithsonian building, called the Castle, opened in 1852.

Today the Smithsonian Institution owns about 140 million objects and includes 14 museums and galleries, five research centers and a zoo. Eighty million people visit the Smithsonian every year.

Which popular Smithsonian museum building displays the Wright brothers' first airplane and the command module from *Apollo 11*?

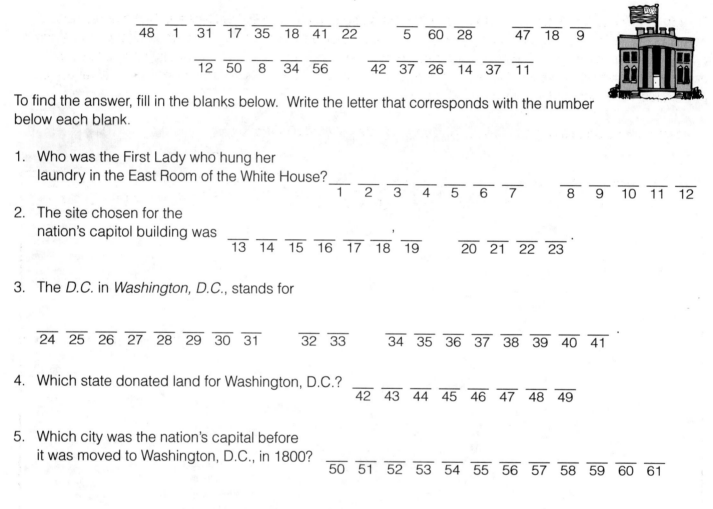

$\overline{48}$ $\overline{1}$ $\overline{31}$ $\overline{17}$ $\overline{35}$ $\overline{18}$ $\overline{41}$ $\overline{22}$ $\overline{5}$ $\overline{60}$ $\overline{28}$ $\overline{47}$ $\overline{18}$ $\overline{9}$

$\overline{12}$ $\overline{50}$ $\overline{8}$ $\overline{34}$ $\overline{56}$ $\overline{42}$ $\overline{37}$ $\overline{26}$ $\overline{14}$ $\overline{37}$ $\overline{11}$

To find the answer, fill in the blanks below. Write the letter that corresponds with the number below each blank.

1. Who was the First Lady who hung her laundry in the East Room of the White House? $\overline{}$ $\overline{}$ $\overline{}$ $\overline{}$ $\overline{}$ $\overline{}$ $\overline{}$ $\overline{}$ $\overline{}$ $\overline{}$ $\overline{}$ $\overline{}$
                                                   1   2   3   4   5   6   7   8   9 10 11 12

2. The site chosen for the nation's capitol building was $\overline{}$ $\overline{}$ $\overline{}$ $\overline{}$ $\overline{}$ $\overline{}$ $\overline{}$, $\overline{}$ $\overline{}$ $\overline{}$ $\overline{}$.
                      13 14 15 16 17 18 19   20 21 22 23

3. The *D.C.* in *Washington, D.C.*, stands for

   $\overline{24}$ $\overline{25}$ $\overline{26}$ $\overline{27}$ $\overline{28}$ $\overline{29}$ $\overline{30}$ $\overline{31}$ $\overline{32}$ $\overline{33}$ $\overline{34}$ $\overline{35}$ $\overline{36}$ $\overline{37}$ $\overline{38}$ $\overline{39}$ $\overline{40}$ $\overline{41}$.

4. Which state donated land for Washington, D.C.? $\overline{}$ $\overline{}$ $\overline{}$ $\overline{}$ $\overline{}$ $\overline{}$ $\overline{}$ $\overline{}$
                                           42 43 44 45 46 47 48 49

5. Which city was the nation's capital before it was moved to Washington, D.C., in 1800? $\overline{}$ $\overline{}$ $\overline{}$ $\overline{}$ $\overline{}$ $\overline{}$ $\overline{}$ $\overline{}$ $\overline{}$ $\overline{}$ $\overline{}$ $\overline{}$
                          50 51 52 53 54 55 56 57 58 59 60 61

Challenge Questions

1. The sculpture on top of the capitol dome was put in place in 1830. What is the name of this statue? Who designed it?

2. Building of this monument began in 1848, but money ran out when it was only 160 feet tall. Mark Twain said it looked like "a factory chimney with the top broken off." The 555-foot tall structure wasn't finished until 1885. What is the name of this monument that took so long to build?

Design a Capital

President Washington selected Pierre Charles L'Enfant, a French soldier, engineer and architect, to draw up the plans for the new city. He laid out the city in the shape of a wheel with streets as spokes of the wheel and the capitol in the center. His plans were grand, with magnificent wide avenues. If a house, a store or even a tree stood in the way of a planned street, L'Enfant wanted it torn down.

Many people felt he was too rigid with his plans, and the city would cost far too much to build. He was finally fired. When he left, he took his detailed plans for the city with him. The task of completing the city fell to his assistant, Andrew Ellicott.

Design a new city for a capital. Before you start, list some of the buildings you'll need. Make notes about where people will live, shop, play and work. Where will hospitals, libraries, schools, churches, police stations and fire stations be needed? How will the people get from place to place? Will your city have a subway? An airport? What about garbage disposal? Where will you put it? How will you control pollution? What about population increases and expansion for the city?

Write your ideas on this page. Do your design on another, large piece of paper.

United States

Nickname: Uncle Sam • Capital: Washington, D.C.
National Anthem: "The Star-Spangled Banner"
National Bird: Bald Eagle • National Flower: Rose

■ The highest annual unemployment average in the U.S. occurred in 1933, at the height of the Great Depression. 12,830,000 people were out of work.

■ Yellowstone, the world's first national park, was formed when 3,473 square miles of land, mostly in Wyoming were set aside in 1872. This area of beautiful rock formations, steep mountains, deep canyons and roaring waterfalls includes hot springs, mud pots, fumaroles and geysers. When Old Faithful erupts, it shoots water 100 to 184 feet in the air and lasts about four minutes.

■ When the bald eagle was chosen as the national bird, Benjamin Franklin objected: ". . . I wish the bald eagle had not been chosen as the representative of our country; he is a bird of bad moral character; he does not get his living honestly . . ." because he steals the catch made by other birds. What was Franklin's choice for a national bird? The turkey.

■ By 1990, 74% of the population lived in urban areas. It took a staff of over 315,000 to take the 1990 census at a cost of 2.6 billion dollars. The population of the United States in 1990: 248,700,000.

■ California is home to the world's oldest trees called bristlecone pines. One tree, named Methuselah, is over 4,000 years old. The world's tallest trees, the redwoods, also grow in California. The General Sherman Tree is 275 fee tall and measures 103 feet around the trunk.

■ The oldest fossil of a flowering plant found in the United States was discovered in Colorado in 1953. It dates back about 65 million years.

■ The first U.S. census was taken in 1790 by 17 U.S. marshals and a support staff of less than 600. The (white) population in 1790: 3,900,000. Ninety-five percent of the population lived in rural areas. It wasn't until the 1920 census that the population shifted and more people lived in cities than in rural areas.

■ Millions of years before anyone lived on the North American continent, nature shaped the land. Volcanos, earthquakes and glaciers built mountains and formed valleys, lakes and rivers. The Colorado River cut the deep gorge known as the Grand Canyon. Inland seas changed to deserts; forests grew; dinosaurs, mammoths and mastodons flourished and became extinct as time marched across the land.

■ By 1800 there were about 50 libraries in the U.S. containing about 80,000 volumes. Most of these libraries required membership dues or payment of fees to borrow books.

■ The first Americans were nomadic hunters who followed herds of animals from Asia to North America across a land bridge called Beringia 20,000 to 50,000 years ago. When the last Ice Age ended, the water levels rose and the Bering Sea separated the two continents. From the north, people traveled south and east over thousands of years across the area that would become the United States.

■ The Hawaiian Islands, Guam, the Philippines and Puerto Rico became U.S. territories in 1898.

Highest Point: Mount McKinley—20,320 feet above sea level
Lowest Point: Death Valley—282 feet below sea level
Area: 3,618,770 square miles. The United States is the fourth largest country in the world.
Only Canada, Russia and China are larger.

■ In 1879, Charles F. Brush installed the first public electrical street lights in Cleveland, Ohio. On March 31, 1880, Wabash, Indiana, became the first city in the United States to be completely lighted by electricity.

■ President Roosevelt signed the Wage and Hours Act in 1938 raising the minimum wage for workers in interstate commerce from 25 to 40 cents an hour. President Truman raised the minimum wage again in 1949 to 75 cents an hour for workers in certain industries.

■ By 1905, 77,988 automobiles were registered in the U.S., but most people still considered automobiles as useless toys. In 1909, a Model T Ford sold for $950. Henry Ford set up his automobile assembly line in 1913. By 1924, the price of a new Model T had been reduced to $290.

■ The shoemakers and coopers of Boston, Massachusetts, formed the first officially recognized labor organization in the United States in 1648. They received a three-year charter from King Charles II.

■ Chicago's O'Hare Airport is the busiest in the world. About 56 million passengers land and take off from there each year.

■ The Sears Tower in Chicago, Illinois, is 110 stories high (1,454 feet). The World Trade Center in New York City is also 110 stories high but only 1,377 feet tall.

■ In 1800, the nation's capital was moved to Washington, D.C. One hundred fifty million years ago, dinosaurs lived in a cypress swamp on this same site.

■ The highest annual unemployment average in the U.S. occurred in 1933, at the height of the Great Depression. 12,830,000 people were out of work.

■ Before the Louisiana Purchase in 1803, the United States controlled about 891,364 square miles of territory in North America. For the sum of $11,250,000 plus the assumption of $3,750,000 in debts, the U.S. nearly doubled its territory when the 831,321 square miles of the Louisiana Territory was purchased from France.

■ Only 63 years passed from the time the Wright brothers made their first successful flight in a self-propelled, heavier-than-air craft at Kitty Hawk, North Carolina, in 1903 until the first manned space flight landed on the moon in 1969.

■ The first major public education law was passed in Massachusetts in 1647. It required every community of 50 or more homeowners to provide free elementary education. In communities of more than 100 home owners, free secondary education also had to be provided.

■ In 1842, the governor of Massachusetts signed a law regulating child labor making it illegal for children under 12 to work more than 10 hours a day in manufacturing establishments.

■ Massachusetts also took the lead in requiring compulsory education for children. In 1852 a school attendance law required all children in the state between the ages of 8 and 14 to attend school at least 12 weeks a year. Six of the weeks had to be consecutive. The last state to pass a compulsory school attendance law was Mississippi, in 1918.

169

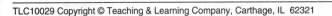

Her Real Name

For more than 100 years, she has been a symbol of freedom and hope for the people of the United States and for new citizens as they arrive. Most people call her the Statue of Liberty. What is her correct, original name?

$\overline{31}$ $\overline{36}$ $\overline{1}$ $\overline{21}$ $\overline{13}$ $\overline{27}$ $\overline{20}$ $\overline{11}$ $\overline{29}$ $\overline{3}$ $\overline{36}$ $\overline{7}$ $\overline{41}$ $\overline{27}$ $\overline{18}$ $\overline{38}$ $\overline{34}$ $\overline{29}$ $\overline{7}$

$\overline{15}$ $\overline{41}$ $\overline{30}$ $\overline{17}$ $\overline{24}$ $\overline{19}$ $\overline{8}$ $\overline{4}$

To find the answer, fill in the blanks below. Write the letter that corresponds with the number below each blank.

1. What is the national bird of the United States? $\overline{}$ $\overline{}$ $\overline{}$ $\overline{}$ $\overline{}$ $\overline{}$ $\overline{}$ $\overline{}$ $\overline{}$
 1 2 3 4   5 6 7 8 9

2. The World Trade Center and the $\overline{}$ $\overline{}$ $\overline{}$ $\overline{}$ $\overline{}$ $\overline{}$ $\overline{}$ $\overline{}$ $\overline{}$ $\overline{}$
 10 11 12 13 14   15 16 17 18 19

are both 110 stories high.

3. $\overline{}$ $\overline{}$ $\overline{}$ $\overline{}$ $\overline{}$ $\overline{}$ $\overline{}$ $\overline{}$ $\overline{}$ $\overline{}$ $\overline{}$ became the first national
 20 21 22 23 24 25 26 27 28 29 30

park in the United States in 1872.

4. The $\overline{}$ $\overline{}$ $\overline{}$ $\overline{}$ $\overline{}$ $\overline{}$ $\overline{}$ $\overline{}$ $\overline{}$ Purchase of 1803
 31 32 33 34 35 36 37 38 39

nearly doubled the size of the United States.

5. Chicago's $\overline{}$'$\overline{}$ $\overline{}$ $\overline{}$ $\overline{}$ Airport is the busiest in the world.
 40 41 42 43 44

Challenge Questions

1. The Statue of Liberty was a gift from the people of France to the people of the United States. Why? Who paid for the statue and the base? Who designed the statue? How tall is it? Where can this symbol of the United States be found? Who wrote the poem inscribed on the statue's base?

2. The United States has a national bird, anthem and flower. Choose national symbols for two of the items listed below. Explain why you made your choice.

National tree	National fossil	National domestic animal	National insect
National mammal	National mineral	National farm animal	National candy bar
National fish	National rock	National soft drink	National toy or game
National beverage	National hero	National food	National wild animal
National dance	National sport	National reptile	

U.S. Tic-Tac-Toe

To play U.S. Tic-Tac-Toe, correctly answer three questions in a row: up and down, across or diagonally.

1. Name the land bridge that once connected Asia with North America.	**2.** What is the national anthem?	**3.** What was the population of the U.S. in 1790 and 1990?
4. What was the minimum wage before President Roosevelt increased it in 1938?	**5.** What are the highest and lowest points in the United States?	**6.** What type of trees are the oldest in the world?
7. What bird did Benjamin Franklin want as the national bird?	**8.** How much did a Model T Ford cost in 1924?	**9.** When did Washington, D.C., become the nation's capital?

Time Line

ORIGINAL THIRTEEN COLONIES 1776

AREA GAINED BY TREATY OF 1783

ORIGINAL THIRTEEN COLONIES 1776

The Original 13 Colonies

Men and women braved the dangers of the Atlantic to seek a new life in the New World. Some, like the Pilgrims, the Quakers, and the colonists of Rhode Island and Maryland, sought religious freedom. Others came searching for wealth and adventure. Some were lured by the promise of free land.

For over 150 years, England had left the colonists pretty much on their own until the war between France and England, known as the French and Indian War (1756-1763), changed that. Great Britain found herself the victor, but victory came with a high price tag. To help rebuild her treasury, Britain passed the Stamp Act which required colonists to purchase official stamps for legal documents and newspapers. The colonists rebelled. Although Britain repealed the Stamp Act, new forms of taxation were enacted.

On July 4, 1776, the colonists issued the Declaration of Independence, an act which led directly to the Revolutionary War. With the final battle at Yorktown, Virginia, in 1781, the American colonists had won their freedom.

Thirteen colonies ratified (approved) the Constitution, becoming the core of a new nation, the United States of America.

West to the Mississippi River

Once the new nation was formed, people began looking west for new lands to explore and settle. New territories were formed and added to the area claimed by the United States.

Although much of the land was unexplored and uninhabited, by 1783 the United States claimed all of the territory east of the Mississippi River except the Spanish colony of Florida. Spanish Florida included the present state of Florida and a small portion of southern Mississippi and southern Alabama.

In the late 1700s and early 1800s, areas like Kentucky, Tennessee and Ohio were considered the far western frontier. Daniel Boone was one of the adventurous men who led the way through the Appalachian Mountains and on to Kentucky.

The Northwest Ordinance of 1787 established rules covering how territories could become states and guaranteeing that the new states would be equal to the original 13.

By 1837, all states east of the Mississippi, except Wisconsin, had joined the Union.

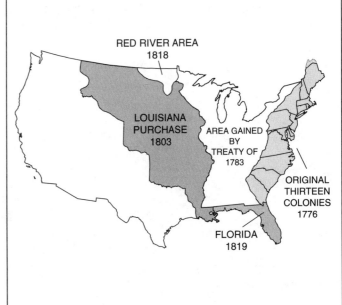

The Louisiana Purchase

In 1671 Louis Joliet and Father Marquette, a Jesuit priest, traveled from the French colony in Canada down the Fox and Wisconsin Rivers, then down the Mississippi River, claiming this vast territory for France.

When the Treaty of Paris was signed in 1763 after the French and Indian War, France ceded all claims to land west of the Mississippi to Spain, her ally in the war. France never lost interest in the New World and made repeated efforts to regain the lost territory. In 1800, Spain agreed to exchange Louisiana for a kingdom in Italy and Louisiana once more became French.

President Jefferson began negotiations to purchase a small part of the Louisiana territory that included New Orleans. Napoleon, threatened by rebellions in Haiti and impending war in Europe, needed cash. He offered to sell all of the Louisiana Territory.

In 1803, President Jefferson was able to complete the "biggest real estate deal in history." For $15 million, the U.S. received 831,321 square miles of land from Napoleon in the Louisiana Purchase. This acquisition nearly doubled the size of the U.S.

Jefferson sent William Clark and Meriwether Lewis to explore the new territory, a journey that continued all the way to the Pacific coast. With the opening of this new land, the movement west gained even more momentum.

The Acquisition of Florida

Florida was first explored and colonized by the Spanish. The first permanent European settlement, St. Augustine, began in 1565 on the eastern coast of the Florida peninsula.

When the United States acquired Louisiana, many thought the area known as West Florida was part of the deal. West Florida covered the southern parts of Mississippi and Alabama, a section of land that stretched Florida's panhandle west to the Mississippi River.

As American settlers poured into the area, parts of West Florida were incorporated into the United States between 1810 and 1819, but Spain continued to claim Florida. This presented problems for the U.S.

Florida had become a refuge for runaway slaves, buccaneers and pirates. Jackson invaded Florida in 1814 and again in 1818. His actions convinced Spain to sell before the area was taken by force. In the Treaty of 1819, Spain ceded all land east of Mississippi and all claims to the Oregon Territory in exchange for $5 million and the promise that the United States would relinquish claims to the part of Texas acquired in the Louisiana Purchase.

The Red River Area: The United States acquired additional land from Great Britain in 1818 when the 49th parallel was established as the border between Canada and the United States from the Lake of the Woods to the Rocky Mountains. The area included a small part of South Dakota, parts of northern and western Minnesota and the eastern and northern parts of North Dakota.

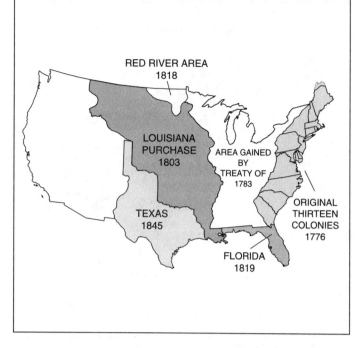

Texas Joins the Union

When Mexico won independence from Spain, Texas and the other former Spanish claims in the southwest became part of Mexico. This included the present states of California, Nevada, Utah, Arizona, New Mexico and parts of Colorado and Oklahoma.

Although the United States had agreed to relinquish claims to Texas in the treaty of 1819, thousands of American ranchers, farmers and adventurers moved into the area. Many, like Moses Austin, received permission to establish American settlements with the understanding that the settlers would become Mexican citizens.

Controversy soon arose with the unstable Mexican government over taxation and political representation. Santa Anna, president of Mexico, was determined to put down the revolution in Texas. After winning the Battle at the Alamo, Santa Anna lost the battle at San Jacinto and was captured in 1836.

The Texans ratified their own constitution and elected Sam Houston as president. He sent an envoy to Washington, D.C., demanding either annexation as a new state or recognition as an independent republic. Because of the slavery issue, Texas became an independent republic.

Although Mexico had never recognized the independence of Texas, the republic joined the Union as a state in 1845. War between Mexico and the United States broke out a year later.

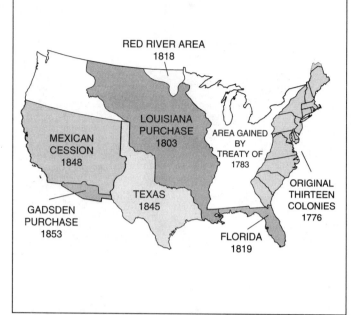

The Mexican Cession of 1848

Although Texas had declared its independence and become a state in 1845, Mexico continued to claim Texas and the rest of the southwest, places that the United States also had a strong interest in acquiring.

The war with Mexico took place on three fronts: the campaign in northern Mexico under Zachary Taylor, the invasion from Vera Cruz to Mexico City under General Scott and Colonel Kearney's expedition against California.

After Taylor defeated Santa Anna at Buena Vista, Scott continued the campaign against Mexico City until the city was captured in 1847. In the meantime, Colonel Kearney pushed west through New Mexico and on to California where he was joined by American settlers who revolted against Mexican rule and secured the area.

By then Mexico had no choice but to accept peace on American terms. By the Treaty of Guadalope-Hidalgo, Mexico gave up claims to Texas, the New Mexico Territory and upper California. This included most of New Mexico and Arizona, all of Nevada and Utah, and parts of Idaho, Wyoming and Colorado.

Boundary line disputes between the U.S. and Mexico continued to be a problem. In 1853, James Gadsden purchased land south of the Gila River (southern Arizona and New Mexico) from Mexico for $10 million.

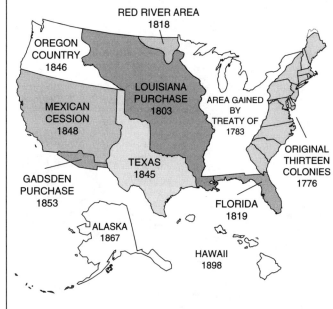

The Oregon Territory (1846)

The exact boundaries between the United States and Canada were not determined at the end of the Revolutionary War. By 1817, agreement had been reached in all but three areas: the boundary between Maine and New Brunswick, between Lake Huron and the Lake of the Woods and the Oregon boundary. The first two areas of dispute were settled by the Webster-Ashburton treaty of 1842.

Both Britain and the United States claimed areas north and west of the Louisiana Purchase (present-day Oregon; Washington; Idaho and parts of Montana, Wyoming and Canada) based on trading posts and settlements established and exploration by both Americans and British.

The United States wanted all land south of a line 54°40'. "Fifty-Four-Forty or Fight," Polk's 1844 campaign slogan, was largely a bluff. The United States was close to a war with Mexico and two wars at the same time were out of the question. Britain had enough other problems in Ireland and Scotland, and they too could not handle another war.

Agreement was finally reached without war. The United States received all land south of the 49th parallel except Vancouver Island.

Alaska and Hawaii Join the Union

The fever for expansion that compelled the U.S. to stretch its boundaries from the Atlantic to the Pacific had not died away by the 1860s even though Civil War was taking its toll on the nation.

Russia felt that her Alaskan possessions were worth little and if war began with England, the area would be lost anyway. When the Czar agreed to sell Alaska for $7.2 million, Secretary of State Seward jumped at the chance to acquire more territory. At the time, many Americans felt the purchase of "icebergs and walruses" was a waste of money.

The purchase later turned out to be one of the best land deals the U.S. ever made. In 1959 Alaska became the 49th and largest state of the Union.

By 1875 Hawaii had long been a port of call for American ships in the Pacific. Friendly relations had been established with the island government. Americans gradually came to control the sugar industry and assume more power over the government. When a member of the Hawaiian royalty tried to regain control, Americans overthrew the government (1893) and presented a treaty of annexation to the United States. President Cleveland initially refused the treaty and the country became a republic until 1898 when the Hawaiian Islands became a U.S. territory.

The Aloha State, Hawaii, became the 50th state on August 21, 1959.

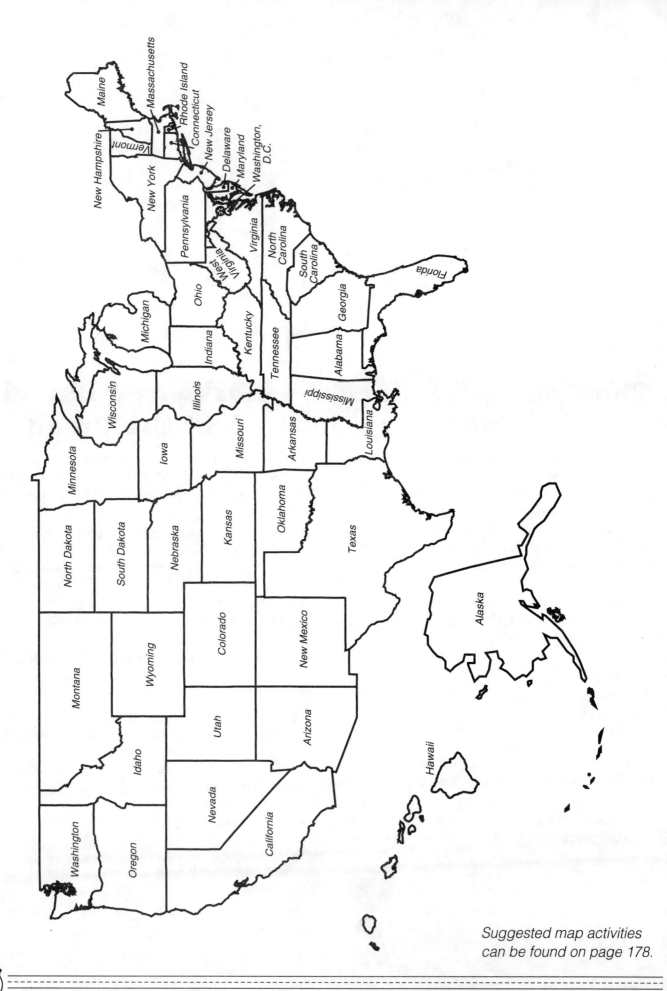

Suggested map activities can be found on page 178.

Suggested map activities can be found on page 178.

Student Map Activity Ideas

Two reproducible maps of the United States are provided. On one map, the states are labeled. The other map contains only the outlines of the states. Make copies of the maps for students to complete the suggested activities suitable for your class.

On the unlabeled U.S. map, students could . . .

- Label the states.
- Trace the route of the Oregon Trail or Santa Fe Trail.
- Trace the route taken by the Mormons from New York to Salt Lake City.
- Trace the route of various explorers, like Coronado, Marquette and Joliet, Lewis and Clark.
- Color in and label the following areas:

> the original 13 colonies
> land claimed by various countries: Spain, France, England, the Netherlands, Sweden
> the states acquired by the Florida Purchase in 1819
> the area added by the Texas annexation of 1845
> the area known as the Oregon Territory
> the states acquired in the Mexican cession of 1848
> the states acquired by the Gadsden Purchase of 1853

On the map with the states labeled, students could . . .

- Locate all states beginning with a given letter.
- Label the state capitals.
- Draw a symbol for each state (potatoes for Idaho, cheese for Wisconsin . . .).
- Label the Great Lakes, Atlantic and Pacific Oceans.
- Draw in and label major rivers.
- Label major mountain chains: the Rockies, Appalachians, etc.
- Locate national parks, forests and monuments.
- Draw in time zones. Compare times in different states.
- Identify the neighbors of a given state.
- Indicate the direction from one state to another.
- Identify the states one would drive through when traveling from one state to another.

I'm Thinking of a State

To play I'm Thinking of a State, give students clues about a specific state and see who can identify the state you are thinking of.
Example: "I'm thinking of a state that is north of Nebraska. The state is nicknamed the Coyote State. The capital is Pierre. People visiting this state can see Mount Rushmore."

The first student to correctly guess the state could give clues for the next state. For younger students, you could write the clues in advance and let them take turns reading them.

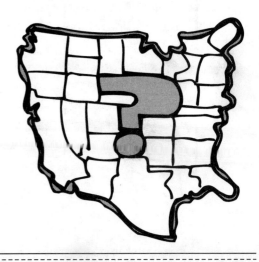

Play Geography Bingo with Your Class

Make copies of the bingo card on the following page for each student. Younger students could work in pairs. Use buttons, bottle caps, small squares of colored paper or other small items for markers. Each student will need 10 to 15 markers.

Several states include bingo game activities. (See Alabama for an example.) Read each statement to the class. When you finish reading the statement, repeat the key word(s) (the word[s] in bold letters), and ask students to write it on any square on their bingo card. You may want to write the key words on the board for younger students.

Make a copy of the statement sheet. Cut apart on the sentences and put the slips in a box. Select one statement at random.

Options

- Read the entire statement, stressing the key word as you read. Students place a marker on that word on their cards. The first student to get five in a row up, down or diagonally, is the winner. Instead of "bingo," they should call out the name of the state.
- For older students, substitute the word *blank* for the key word when you read the statements during the game.
- Ask students to write the names of any 24 states on their cards. To play, name the capitals of states. Students cover the space with the correct state.

For variety, select one of these ways to win:

- Four corners
- Postage stamp (top four squares in the upper right-hand corner)
- Letter *T* (all squares in the top row and all squares in the middle row)
- Letter *X* (two corner-to-corner diagonals)

Use the Blank Bingo Cards with Other Subjects

- Give students a list of vocabulary words, science terms, history dates, etc., to write on their cards. You could read only the definition during the game.
- **Language Arts:** Give students a list of five nouns, five verbs, five adjectives, five adverbs and five prepositions to write on their cards in random order. Older students could be asked to write their own list of words. To play the game, simply say the type of word (noun, verb, etc.). Students cover one square with that type of word.
- **Math:** Have students write the numbers from 2 through 25 randomly on their cards. Give them math problems suitable for their age—addition, subtraction, multiplication, division. As they solve the math problems, they will cover the correct answers on their cards.

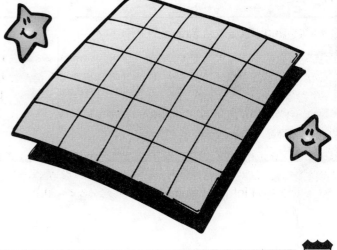

Geography Bingo

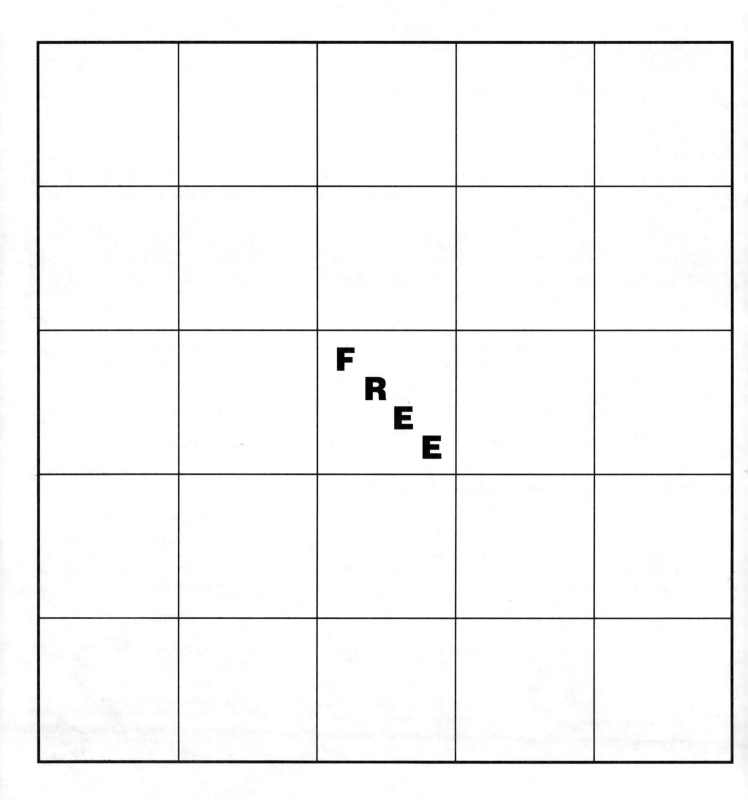

FREE

Alabama

Hooray for Peanuts! page 2
George Washington Carver—1. Montgomery, 2. boll weevils, 3. yellowhammer, 4. thicket clearers or vegetation gatherers

Just for Fun page 2
Enough drumsticks for a family of eight.

Alabama Puzzler page 4

Alaska

Look Along the Coast page 6
Whales—1. Seward, 2. gold rushes, 3. Denali,
4. Barrow, 5. Sitka

Challenge Question 1 page 6
Alaska has more than 3 million lakes and 3,000 rivers. The largest lake, Iliamna Lake, covers over 1,000 square miles. More than 1,800 islands are part of Alaska.

Challenge Question 2 page 6
The word *Alaska* came from an Aleut word meaning "great land" or "mainland."

Let It Snow! Let It Snow!
Let It Snow! page 7
i. and m. are exactly alike.

Mixed-Up Nature page 8
1. KODIAK BEARS
2. BLACK BEARS
3. POLAR BEARS
4. GRIZZLY BEARS
5. MOOSE
6. ELK
7. CARIBOU
8. WOLVES
9. MOUNTAIN GOATS
10. BEAVERS
11. PORCUPINES
12. FOXES
13. WOLVERINES
14. WEASELS
15. PTARMIGANS
16. TERNS
17. PUFFINS
18. LOONS
19. GEESE
20. BALD EAGLES
21. WHALES
22. DOLPHINS
23. SEALS
24. SALMON
25. HALIBUT
26. CLAMS
27. COD
28. CRABS
29. SHRIMP
30. HERRING

Arizona

Natural Wonders page 11
Painted Desert and Petrified Forest—1. Phoenix,
2. Apaches, 3. Casa Grande, 4. bola ties, 5. London Bridge, 6. fly, 7. Gila monster

Challenge Question 1 page 11
Colorado, Arizona, Utah and New Mexico

Just for Fun page 11
Because her children have to play inside all day.

Arkansas

Finders, Keepers page 14
Crater of Diamonds State Park—1. Mosasaurs,
2. Louisiana Purchase, 3. dulcimers,
4. mockingbird, 5. Fort Smith

Challenge Question 1 page 14
Arkansas Post

Challenge Question 2 page 14
Part of North Dakota, Minnesota, Montana, Wyoming and Colorado; most of Oklahoma, Kansas and Louisiana; and all of Arkansas, Missouri, Iowa, Nebraska and South Dakota were part of the Louisiana Purchase.

Just for Fun page 14
For the same reason nobody else likes turnips.

Musical Words page 15
1. BAD
2. FED
3. BAG
4. BEEF
5. CAGE
6. FEED
7. BEG
8. FACED
9. BED
10. CABBAGE
11. BAGGAGE
12. DEED
13. BEAD
14. FADED

California

Birds and Bees page 17
San Diego Zoo
1. King's Highway, 2. Sacramento, 3. gold,
4. Lombard, 5. Alcatraz

Challenge Question 1 page 17
Mann's (formerly Grauman's) Chinese Theater

Just for Fun page17
Because he'd make 10 times as much money

All Mixed Up page 18
1. Anaheim
2. Beverly Hills
3. Burbank
4. Carmel
5. Encino
6. Fresno
7. Glendale
8. Hollywood
9. Ingelwood
10. Los Angeles
11. Long Beach
12. Malibu
13. Newport Beach
14. Oakland
15. Pasadena
16. Palm Springs
17. Sacramento
18. Salinas
19. San Bernadino
20. San Diego
21. San Francisco
22. San Jose
23. Santa Barbara
24. Sunnyvale
25. Van Nuys

Places to Visit,
Things to See page 19

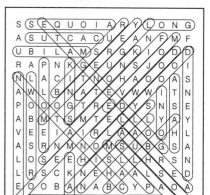

Unused letters: San Francisco Bay

Colorado

The Source page 22
Grand Lake—1. Cliff Palace, 2. Centennial, 3. Garden,
4. Pike's Peak

Challenge Question 1 page 22
Wyoming, Nebraska, Kansas, Oklahoma, New Mexico, Arizona and Utah

Just for Fun page 22
Nine dollars

Connecticut

Connecticut Connections page 26
1. B., 2. G., 3. E., 4. A., 5. N., 6. I., 7. D., 8. K., 9. L.,
10. H., 11. J., 12. C., 13. M., 14. F., 15. O.

Challenge Question 1 page 26
The church is shaped like a fish.

Challenge Question 2 page 26
They are major rivers in Connecticut.

Just for Fun page 26
Airline tickets are too expensive.

Delaware

Let There Be Light page 29
Fenwick Island—1. Fort Christina, 2. Netherlands,
3. Newark, 4. First

Challenge Question 1 page 29
Johan Printz

Challenge Question 2 page 29
Pea Patch Island

Just for Fun page 29
Leap year

What Can You
Find in *Delaware*? page 29

ADE	DEER	EWER	REEL
ALE	DEW	LAD	WAD
ARE	DRAW	LAW	WADE
AREA	DRAWL	LEAD	WADER
AWARD	DREW	LEADER	WARD
AWE	EAR	LED	WARE
AWL	EEL	RAW	WEAL
DEAL	ERA	REAL	WEAR
DEALER	EWE	REDEAL	WED
DEAR			

Florida

Florida Tic-Tac-Toe page 32

1. old town, 2. false, 3. St. Augustine, 4. 1821,
5. England, 6. full of flowers, 7. Ponce de Leon, 8. small islands off the southern tip of Florida, 9. because it is surrounded by water on three sides

Just for Fun page 32

A mouse on vacation

Enjoy the Wildlife in Florida page 33

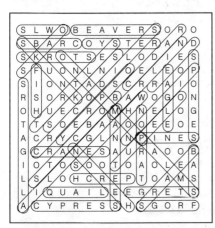

Georgia

Who Took the Vowels? page 35

1. Albany
2. Atlanta
3. Columbus
4. Athens
5. Augusta
6. Cairo
7. Macon
8. Santa Claus
9. Savannah
10. New Echota
11. Dahlonega
12. Louisville
13. Milledgeville
14. Commerce
15. Cordele

Challenge Question 2 page 35

Alexander H. Stephens

Just for Fun page 35

An elephant that sticks to the roof of your mouth.

Hawaii

Tasty Treats page 39

Macadamia nuts—1. O'ahu, 2. Sandwich, 3. dormant, 4. Big Island

Just for Fun page 39

Kittens

Idaho

Out of This World page 42

Craters of the Moon—1. French, 2. Potatoes, 3. Emerald Creek, 4. Boise

Challenge Question 2 page 42

Shoshone Falls

Just for Fun page 42

A potato

Idaho Is a Five-Letter Word page 43

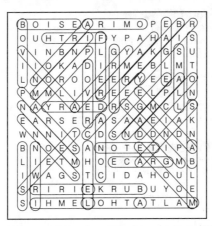

2. The second thing they all have in common is that they are all five-letter words.

Illinois

Matchmaker page 45

1. G, K and Q; 2. O; 3. P; 4. S; 5. T; 6. B; 7. U; 8. A; 9. I; 10. D; 11. F; 12. N; 13. C.

Challenge Question 1 page 45

There are two U.S. cities larger than Chicago: New York City and Los Angeles, California.

Challenge Question 2 page 45

Ronald Reagan was the only President born in Illinois. (Lincoln was born in Kentucky. Ulysses S. Grant was born in Ohio.)

Just for Fun page 45

Neither, they both burn shorter.

Illinois or Someplace Else? page 47

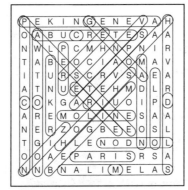

Unused letters: CHICAGO BEARS

Indiana

Underground page 49

Limestone Caves—1. Vincennes, 2. Mesker Park Zoo, 3. Wabash, 4. National

Challenge Question 1 page 49

Clement and John Studebaker

Just for Fun page 49

Jelly beans

Indiana or Someplace Else? page 51

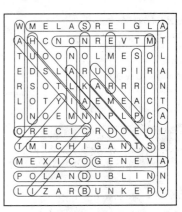

Unused letters: COLE PORTER

Iowa

Iowa Tic-Tac-Toe page 53

1. Hans Christian Andersen, 2. corn, 3. clear and plow, 4. hogs, 5. water (moisture), 6. river of the mounds, 7. Chief Black Hawk, 8. Ioway, 9 Sioux City

Challenge Question 1 page 53

Partial answer The Amana Colonies were founded by the Community of True Inspiration, a German Protestant sect. Until 1932 the villages had a communal form of government. Work was shared by members of the community, and all property was owned by the community.

Challenge Question 2 page 53

Herbert Hoover

Just for Fun page 53

Oinkment

Build by Number page 54

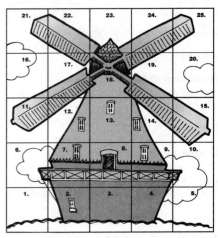

Kansas

Matchmaker page 56

1. K.; 2. T.; 3. C., J., O. and R.; 4. N.; 5. G.; 6. H.; 7. P.; 8. A. and S.; 9. Q.; 10. S.; 11. D.; 12. E.

Challenge Question 1 page 56

The words to "Home on the Range" were written by Brewster Higley.

Challenge Question 2 page 56

Amelia Earhart was the first woman to make a solo flight across the Atlantic Ocean in 1932. She disappeared while attempting to fly around the world.

TLC10029 Copyright © Teaching & Learning Company, Carthage, IL 62321

Just for Fun page 56

Its shadow.

The Wind Blew page 57

1. Overland Park
2. Hutchinson
3. Kansas City
4. Leavenworth
5. Manhattan
6. Dodge City
7. Topeka
8. Wichita
9. Olathe
10. Salina
11. Abilene
12. Lawrence

Kentucky

My Old Kentucky Home page 59

Stephen Foster—1. green, 2. bluish-purple, 3. Fort Knox, 4. Mammoth Cave

Challenge Question 1 page 59

Cumberland Falls is the only place in America where a moonbow can be seen. A moonbow is like a rainbow, but occurs on clear nights when the moon is full.

Just for Fun page 59

The mane part

Would You Like to Visit Monkeys Eyebrow? page 60

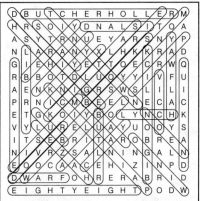

Louisiana

Louisiana Question Game page 62

1. Eastern brown pelican, 2. bayous, 3. agate, 4. Baton Rouge, 5. state songs, 6. Battle of New Orleans, 7. honeybee, 8. levees, 9. bald cypress, 10. Let the good times roll! 11. magnolia, 12. Cajuns

Challenge Question 1 page 62

The original site of New Orleans planned for a crescent-shaped piece of land between Lake Pontchartrain and a curve in the Mississippi River. Although the city soon out-grew its original boundaries, it is still referred to as the Crescent City.

Challenge Question 2 page 62

Parishes

Just for Fun page 62

By its bill.

Louisiana Wildlife page 63

Plants and Trees

JASMINE
ORCHIDS
CYPRESS
PALMETTO
MAGNOLIA
HIBISCUS
SPANISH MOSS
PITCHER PLANTS

Four-Legged Creatures

MINK
FOXES
NUTRIA
OTTERS
BOBCATS
WEASELS
BEAVERS
RACCOONS
OPOSSUMS
MUSKRATS
SQUIRRELS
BULLFROGS
ALLIGATORS
WHITE-TAILED DEER

Off the Coast

TARPON
SHRIMP
POMPANO
OYSTERS
DOLPHINS
FLOUNDER
MACKEREL
SEA TURTLES

In the Air

OWLS
GEESE
DUCKS
QUAIL
DOVES
CROWS
HAWKS
SWANS
HERONS
EGRETS
STORKS
CRANES
PELICANS
BALD EAGLES

Maine

Let There Be Light page 65

Portland Head Light—1. doughnuts, 2. capital, 3. York Tea Party, 4. wigwam

Challenge Question 1 page 65

Henry Wadsworth Longfellow

Just for Fun page 65

Very large holes in the baseboard.

What Rhymes with *Maine*? page 66

ABSTAIN	ENTERTAIN	PANE
AGAIN	EXPLAIN	PERTAIN
AIRPLANE	FANE	PLAIN
ARRAIGN	FEIGN	PLANE
ASCERTAIN	GAIN	POLYURETHANE
ATTAIN	GRAIN	PROPANE
BANE	HUMANE	RAIN
BIPLANE	HURRICANE	REGAIN
BRAIN	HYDROPLANE	REIGN
BRISBANE	INGRAIN	REMAIN
BUTANE	INSANE	RESTRAIN
CAMPAIGN	JANE	RETAIN
CANE	LAIN	SANE
CELLOPHANE	LANE	SLAIN
CHAIN	LORRAINE	SPAIN
CHAMPAIGN	MAIN	SPOKANE
COMPLAIN	MAINTAIN	STAIN

CONTAIN	MANE	STRAIN
CRANE	MEMBRANE	SWAIN
DEIGN	METHANE	TOULANE
DETAIN	MIGRAINE	TRAIN
DISDAIN	MONOPLANE	URBANE
DOMAIN	NOVOCAINE	VAIN
DRAIN	OBTAIN	VANE
DUANE	OCTANE	WAIN
DWAYNE	ORDAIN	WAYNE
ELAINE	PAIN	

Maryland

Matchmaker page 68

1. K. and S., 2. O., 3. L., 4. D., 5. B., 6. C., 7. I., 8. P., 9. U., 10. V., 11. E., 12. H., 13. Y., 14. M., 15. A., 16. Q. and/or A.

Challenge Question 1 page 68

During the Revolutionary War, George Washington praised Maryland's "troops of the line" for their bravery and courage. Maryland became known as the Old Line State.

Challenge Question 2 page 68

Barbara Fritchie

Just for Fun page 68

Look at its bill.

Massachusetts

Where in Massachusetts? page 71

1. Springfield, 2. Lexington, 3. Concord, 4. Boston, 5. Cambridge, 6. Gloucester, 7. Salem, 8. Plymouth (Plimoth), 9. Cape Cod, 10. New Bedford

Challenge Question 1 page 71

She voted.

Challenge Question 2 page 71

Paul Revere road to Lexington to warn Samuel Adams and John Hancock that British troops were on the way.

Just for Fun page 71

Nothing. Pickles can't talk, not even in Massachusetts.

What Can You Find in *Massachusetts?* page 72

ACE	MAT
ACHE	MATCH
CAUSE	MATE
AMASS	MATH
AMUSE	MEAT
ASH	MESA
ASSET	MESH
ASTHMA	MESS
ATE	MET
CAME	MUCH
CASH	MUSE
CAST	MUSH
CASTE	MUSS
CHASE	MUTE
CHASM	MUTT
CHASTE	SACHET
CHAT	SAM
CHEAT	SAME
CHEAT	SASH
CHEST	SAT
CHUM	SATE
CUE	SEAM
EACH	SEAT
EAST	SET
EAT	SHAM

HAM	SHAME
HASTE	STASH
HAT	STEAM
HATCH	STEM
HATE	SUCH
HEAT	SUE
HEM	SUET
HUM	SUM
HUT	TAM
HUTCH	TAME
MAC	TEA
MACE	TEAM
MACH	TESS
MASH	THAT
MASS	THEM

Michigan

Not Henry Ford page 74
Ransom Eli Olds—1. Detroit, 2. great lake, 3. Stephen Mason, 4. Sault Sainte Marie

Challenge Question 1 page 74
Detroit became the automobile center of the United States for many reasons. The industry's pioneers, Henry Ford and Ransom Olds were both from Michigan. Detroit had factories that could be converted to making automobiles and experienced workers able to learn the new industries. Michigan was rich in many natural resources needed to build factories and automobiles. As a port city, other supplies, like iron ore, could easily be shipped through the Great Lakes. Many people in Michigan were willing to invest money to finance the factories and equipment needed to begin a new industry.

Challenge Question 2 page 74
Sojourner Truth (Isabella Baumfree) was an African American preacher, abolitionist and feminist born in slavery in 1797. After escaping to New York City, she traveled through the United States preaching on behalf of the abolition of slavery and for women's rights. After the Civil War, she helped freed slaves find new homes.

Just for Fun page 74
They get wet.

"C" These Sites in Michigan page 75

Unused letters: Tulip Festival

Minnesota

Go, Vikings, Go! page 77
Purple People Eaters—1. calumets, 2. gophers, 3. Lake Superior, 4. Lake Itasca

Challenge Question 1 page 77
Duluth

Challenge Question 2 page 77
As a result of glacial activity, most of Minnesota is nearly flat or contains gentle rolling hills. The glaciers also were responsible for many of the over 15,000 lakes in Minnesota.

Just for Fun page 77
Run fast in the opposite direction.

What Can You Find in *Minnesota*? page 78

AMEN	MIST	SET
ANN	MITE	SIN
ANNE	MOAN	SINE
ANNIE	MOAT	SMITE
ANT	MOST	SOME
ANTE	NAME	SON
ATE	NAT	SONNET
EAST	NATE	STAIN
EAT	NEAT	STAN
INANE	NEST	STEM
INMATE	NET	STEIN
INN	NINE	STONE
INNATE	NIT	TAME
INTO	NOME	TAN
MAIN	NOSE	TEA
MAINE	NOT	TEAM
MAN	NOTE	TEN
MANE	OATS	TENNIS
MAST	ONE	TIM
MAT	SAINT	TIME
MATE	SAME	TIN
MEAN	SANE	TINE
MEANT	SAT	TOE
MEAT	SATE	TOM
MEN	SATIN	TON
MET	SEAM	TONE
MINE	SEAT	
MINT	SENT	

M Is for Minnesota page 79

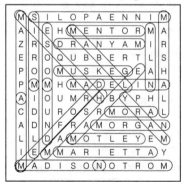

Unused letters: HUBERT HUMPHREY

Mississippi

Buried Treasure? page 81
Deer Island—1. Natchez, 2. Elvis Presley, 3. Pascagoula, 4. Hernando de Soto

Challenge Question 1 page 81
Nashville

Just for Fun page 81
A river

Mississippi Counties page 82

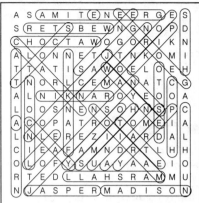

Missouri

Life on the Mississippi page 84
Peculiar—1. Big Muddy, 2. fiddle, 3. Pony Express, 4. Gateway Arch

Challenge Question 2 page 84
Three earthquakes occurred.

Just for Fun page 84
Unhoppy

Montana

Montana Question Game page 87
1. tyrannosaurus rex, 2. Pictograph Cave State Historical Site, 3. Eureka, 4. Montana, 5. Treasure State, 6. Chief Joseph, 7. Little Big Horn, 8. Iceberg Lake (Glacier National Park), 9. glaciers, 10. Paddlefish

Challenge Question 1 page 87
Last Chance Gulch

Challenge Question 2 page 87
Meriwether Lewis and William Clark were guided by Sacagawea.

Just for Fun page 87
10 grizzly bears

Treasures of Montana page 88

Unused letters: TUNGSTEN
 MANGANESE

Nebraska

Matchmaker page 90
1. B., 2. L., 3. J., 4. E., 5. W., 6. C., 7. U., 8. M, 9. G. and V., 10. H., 11. S., 12. T., 13. A.

Challenge Question 2 page 90
Nebraska was part of the land bought from France in the Louisiana Purchase of 1802.

Just for Fun page 90

Move to Oklahoma.

Nevada

Where in Nevada? page 93

1. Lake Tahoe, 2. Virginia City, 3. Lake Meade, 4. Reno, 5. Carson City, 6. Las Vegas, 7. Valley of Fire State Park, 8. Lunar Crater, 9. Berlin-Ichthyosaur State Park, 10. Pyramid Lake

Just for Fun page 93

The book was better.

New Hampshire

Legendary Chief page 96

Chief Passaconaway—1. Indian Stream, 2. Mount Washington, 3. Mystery, 4. purple finch

Challenge Question 1 page 96

Manchester, originally called Derryfield, was settled in 1722. Concord, founded in 1727, was first named Pennycook.

Challenge Question 2 page 96

The first warship to fly to American flag was the *Ranger*, commanded by John Paul Jones.

Just for Fun page 96

They were leap years.

Where in New Hampshire? page 97

1. AMHERST
2. BERLIN
3. CHARLESTON
4. CHESTERFIELD
5. CLAREMONT
6. CONCORD
7. CORNISH
8. DOVER
9. EXETER
10. FITZWILLIAM
11. FRANCONIA
12. FRANKLIN
13. JEFFERSON
14. KEENE
15. LONDONDERRY
16. MANCHESTER
17. NASHUA
18. NEWPORT
19. PETERSBOROUGH
20. PITTSBURG
21. PLYMOUTH
22. PORTSMOUTH
23. SALEM
24. SALISBURY
25. SANDWICH
26. SQUAM LAKE

A Sign of the Times page 97

1. h. PICNIC SITE, 2. a. STOP, 3. g. YIELD, 4. b. MERGE, 5. d. PEDESTRIAN CROSSING, 6. e. CROSSROAD, 7. c. CURVE, 8. f. NO BICYCLES

New Jersey

New Jersey Tic-Tac-Toe page 99

1. *The Great Train Robbery*, 2. New Jersey does not have a state song. 3. 66%–⅔, 4. Meadowlands Sports Complex, 5. Monopoly™, 6. Trenton, 7. hadrasaurus (duck-billed dinosaur), 8. Judy Blume, 9. 995

Matchmaker page 100

1. J.; 2. D. and G.; 3. R.; 4. K.; 5. O.; 6. T.; 7. B. and Q.; 8. E.; 9. H.; 10. L.; 11. I.; 12. N.; 13. A., C., P., U. and V.

Challenge Question 1 page 100

The phonograph, electric lights, transistors, weather satellites, Colt revolvers, steamboats and steam engines are some of the items.

Challenge Question 2 page 100

The building known as Lucy the Elephant is shaped like a giant elephant.

Just for Fun page 100

A smelly pincushion

New Mexico

Matchmaker page 102

1. R., 2. J., 3. I., 4. V., 5. O., 6. Q., 7. E., 8. T., 9. H., 10. F. and P., 11. D., 12. U., 13. G., 14. M., 15. L.

Challenge Question 2 page 102

Smoky Bear has become a national symbol for preventing forest fires. He lived at the National Zoo in Washington, D.C.

Just for Fun page 102

Because they have two left feet.

Break the Code page 103

New Mexico is home to many prairie dog towns. The towns contain many underground connecting burrows. Although they make a sound like a high-pitched bark, prairie dogs are not dogs. They are members of the squirrel family.

Welcome to New Mexico page 104

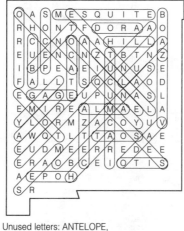

Unused letters: ANTELOPE,
MULE DEER and BEAR

New York

The Peacemaker page 106

Hiawatha—1. Ever Upward, 2. mammoths, 3. Manhattan, 4. New York City

Challenge Question 1 page 106

France, Liberty Island, Frederic Auguste Barttholdi

Challenge Question 2 page 106

A. Washington Irving, B. (Lyman) Frank Baum, C. Herman Melville, D. Maurice Sendak

Just for Fun page 106

With a "tuba" toothpaste.

New York Lakes page 108

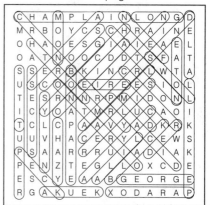

North Carolina

Tea Party Time page 110

Edenton Tea Party—1. Lost Colony, 2. Cape Hatteras, 3. Switzerland, 4. Kitty Hawk

Challenge Question 1 page 110

Blackbeard, Stede Bonnet, Anne Bonney and Mary Read were some famous pirates.

Challenge Question 2 page 110

The plane was named *Flyer I* but often called *Kitty Hawk*.

Just for Fun page 110

When there's two of them.

Who's Who? page 111

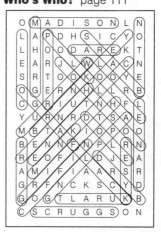

Unused letters: "OLD HICKORY"
JACKSON

North Dakota

Tales of the Wild West page 113

Louis L'Amour—1. Salt, 2. International Peace Garden, 3. Buffalo, 4. Minot

Just for Fun page 113

They don't have thumbs to ring the little bells.

North Dakota Wildlife page 114

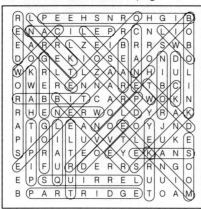

Ohio

Ohio, the State with Many Nicknames page 116

Annie Oakley—1. Buckeye, 2. *Philanthropist*, 3. tomato juice, 4. Oberlin

Challenge Question 1 page 116

Ulysses S. Grant, Rutherford B. Hayes, James A. Garfield, Benjamin Harrison, William McKinley, William H. Taft and Warren G. Harding

Just for Fun page 116

Because the tomato was in a can.

From A to Z page 118

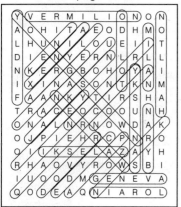

Oklahoma

Matchmaker page 120

1. D. and T., 2. L., 3. I., 4. S., 5. G. and O., 6. A., 7. E. and K., 8. U., 9. H., 10. C., 11. P., 12. N., 13. O., 14. R., 15. Q., 16. J.

Challenge Question 2 page 120

James Francis (Jim) Thorpe. Stockholm, Sweden

Just for Fun page 120

A mouse, because it squeaks.

Oklahoma Wildlife page 121

3. Armadillo, 1. Bison, 4. Scissor-tailed flycatcher, 2. Opossum

Oregon

The Deepest Gorge page 123

Hell's Canyon—1. Chinook, 2. Portland, 3. swallowtail butterfly, 4. Astoria

Challenge Question 1 page 123

John McLoughlin

Challenge Question 2 page 123

Warm, moist winds from the Pacific Ocean travel eastward across Oregon until they reach the Cascade Mountains. As the warm air rises over the mountains, it cools, causing quite a bit of rain to fall on the western side of the mountains. The heavy wet air also protects the area from extreme temperature changes. It rarely gets extremely hot in summer or extremely cold in winter along the coast. East of the Cascades, the land is much drier and temperature variations are much wider.

Matchmaker page 124

1. Y., 2. D., 3. E., 4. V., 5. L., 6. J. and U., 7. W., 8. B. and Z., 9. M., 10. T.,11. C., 12. R., 13. H., 14. G., 15. X.

What Can You Find in the Columbia River? page 124

ABE	COMB	MICE
ACE	CORE	MIRE
AIL	COVE	MOB
AIR	COVER	MOIL
ALE	CRAB	MOLAR
AMBER	CRAM	MOLE
ARIA	CRAVE	MOVE
AVE	CREAM	MOVER
AVER	CRIB	MULE
BAM	CRUMB	OIL
BAR	CUE	OVER
BARE	EAR	RACE
BEAM	ERA	RACER
BEAR	ERR	RAIL
BLAME	IRE	RAM
BLARE	LACE	RAVE
BLUE	LAIR	REAL
BOAR	LAM	REAM
BOIL	LAMB	REAR
BORE	LAME	RECOIL
BRAVE	LAVE	RIB
BRAVER	LIAR	RICE
BRIAR	LICE	ROAM
BROIL	LIMB	ROAR
BUM	LIMBER	ROB
CAME	LIME	ROLE
CAR	LIVE	ROVE
CARE	LIVER	ROVER
CAUL	LORE	RUM
CAVE	LOVE	UMBER
CLAIM	LOVER	VAIL
CLAM	LUMBER	VEAL
CLEAR	MACE	VEIL
CLIMB	MAIL	VIA
CLOVE	MAILER	VIAL
CLOVER	MALE	VICE
COAL	MAR	VIE
COB	MAUL	VOLE
COIL	MEAL	

Pennsylvania

Where in Pennsylvania? page 126

1. Philadelphia, 2. Harrisburg, 3. Punxsutawney, 4. Hershey, 5. Philadelphia, 6. New York, 7. Williamsport, 8. Pittsburgh

Just for Fun page 126

The outside

What Can You Find in *Pennsylvania*? page 127

AIL	LENNY	PIE	SPIN
AISLE	LINE	PILE	SPINE
ALIVE	LIP	PIN	SPLAY
ANN	LISP	PINE	SPY
ANNA	LIVE	PLAIN	SYLVAN
ANNE	LIVEN	PLAN	SYLVIA
ANNIE	LYNN	PLANE	VAIL
ANVIL	NAIL	PLAY	VAIN
ANY	NAP	SAIL	VALE
APE	NAPE	SAL	VALISE
ASP	NAVE	SALE	VAN
AVAIL	NAY	SALIVA	VASE
AVE	NIL	SANE	VEAL
EASY	NILE	SAVE	VENIAL
ELSA	NINE	SAY	VIA
ELVIS	NIP	SEAL	VIAL
EVIL	PAIL	SIN	VIE
INN	PAIN	SINE	VIENNA
ISLE	PAL	SLAIN	VILE
LAIN	PALE	SLAP	VINE
LANA	PAN	SLAVE	VINNY
LANE	PANE	SLIP	VISE
LAP	PAVE	SLY	YALE
LAVE	PAY	SNAIL	YAP
LAY	PEAL	SNAP	YELP
LEAN	PEN	SNIP	YEN
LEAP	PENNY	SPAIN	YES

cookies; Amish buggy; 76ers jersey; groundhog; baseball, glove, bat; basketball; mushrooms; miner; can of paint; cow; cannon; sheep; Liberty Bell; trout; firefly; loaf of bread; cap; hockey stick; chocolate Kiss®

Rhode Island

Rhode Island Tic-Tac-Toe page 129

1. Norsemen, 2. Ocean State and Little Rhody, 3. Hope, 4. Roger Williams, 5. religious freedom, 6. Arcade, 7. Rhode Island Red chicken, 8. Rhode Island and Providence Plantations, 9. Esek Hopkins

What Can You Find in *Rhode Island*? page 130

ADD	HIDDEN	ONE
ADE	HIDE	ORE
ADORE	HIE	RAID
ADORN	HIED	RAIDED
AID	HIND	RAIL
AIDE	HOD	RAIN
AIDED	HOE	RAINED
AIR	HOLD	RASH
ALE	HOLDER	READ
ALINE	HOLE	REAL
ALSO	HONE	REDIAL
AND	HONED	REIN
ARE	HOSE	RELOAD
ASH	IDEA	REND
ASHEN	IODINE	RID
DALE	IRE	RIDE
DANE	ISLE	RILE
DARE	LAD	RIND
DARED	LADDER	ROD
DASH	LAIR	RODE
DASHED	LAND	ROIL
DEAD	LANDED	ROSE
DEAL	LANE	SAID
DEAN	LARD	SAIL
DEAR	LASH	SAILED

DEN	LEAD	SAILOR
DIAL	LEAN	SAL
DIALED	LEARN	SALE
DID	LED	SALON
DIE	LEND	SAND
DIED	LEON	SANDED
DINE	LIAR	SANDER
DINER	LID	SANE
DISH	LIE	SEAL
DOE	LIEN	SEND
DOES	LINE	SHAD
DOLE	LINED	SHADE
DON	LINER	SHADED
DONE	LION	SHALE
DRAIN	LIRE	SHARE
DRAINED	LOAD	SHARED
EGO	LOADED	SHEAR
END	LOADER	SHED
HAD	LOAN	SHIED
HAIL	LOANED	SHIELD
HAILED	LOANER	SHINE
HAIR	LOIN	SHOAL
HALE	LONE	SHOD
HALED	LORE	SHORE
HALO	LOSE	SID
HAND	NAIL	SIDE
HANDED	NAILED	SLAIN
HARD	NEAR	SLID
HARDEN	NILE	SLIDE
HARE	NOD	SOAR
HAS	NODE	SOARED
HEAD	NOSE	SOIL
HEAL	OAR	SOILED
HEAR	ODD	SOL
HEARD	ODDER	SOLAR
HELD	ODE	SOLD
HEN	OIL	SOLE
HERD	OILED	SOLID
HID	OLD	

Number, Please page 130
1. E., 2. A., 3. B., 4. J., 5. G., 6. D., 7. H., 8. F., 9. I., 10. C.

Challenge Question 1 page 130
Aquidneck Island

Challenge Question 2 page 130
Rivers

Just for Fun page 130
He wanted to get to the other side of the state.

South Carolina

Number, Please page 132
1. 8, 2. 11, 3. I, 4. 1862, 5. 1984, 6. 1521, 7. 40, 8. 25, 9. 43, 10. 1670

Challenge Question 1 page 132
Indigo

Challenge Question 2 page 132
Charleston

Just for Fun page 132
Because nobody else would wag it for him.

A Visit to South Carolina page 133

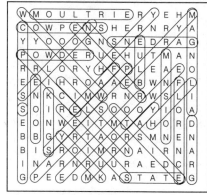

South Dakota

Mount Rushmore page 135
Abraham Lincoln—1. Gutzon Borglum, 2. four, 3. Lincoln, 4. Black Hills

South Dakota Question Game page 136
1. coyote, 2. Sturgis, 3. Lemmon, 4. Chief Sitting Bull, 5. cemetery at Deadwood, 6. ring-necked pheasant, 7. Dakota, 8. honeybee

Challenge Question 1 page 136
The monument to Crazy Horse was started in 1948 by Korczak Ziolkowski.

Just for Fun page 136
When they don't have cash.

Tennessee

The State of What? page 138
Franklin—1. water, 2. Cherokee, 3. Nashville, 4. five

Matchmaker page 139
1. C. and Y.; 2. B.; 3. T.; 4. G.; 5. O.; 6. X.; 7. K.; 8. P.; 9. U.; 10. A. and I.; 11. L., R. and W.; 12. V.; 13. E. and H.; 14. N.

Challenge Question 1 page 139
Reelfoot Lake was formed when an earthquake and its aftershocks rumbled through the state between December 1811 and March 1812. The quakes caused the land to sink in some places. Water from the Mississippi River rushed into one sunken area forming a shallow lake where a forest had once stood.

Just for Fun page 139
There are two *T*s in THAT.

Texas

Texas Tic-Tac-Toe page 141
1. chili, 2. Rio Grande, 3. Houston, 4. Mission San Antonio de Valero, 5. true, 6. true, 7. Stephen Austin, 8. Arkansas, 9. between 13,000 and 10,000 B.C.

Just for Fun page 141
A Texas mouse

Blooming Texas page 142

1. ASTER	14. JUNIPER
2. AZALEA	15. MAGNOLIA
3. BLUEBONNET	16. MESQUITE
4. CEDAR	17. OAK
5. CHAPARRAL	18. OLIVE
6. COTTONWOOD	19. PECAN
7. CYPRESS	20. PHLOX
8. DOGWOOD	21. PINE
9. GOLDENROD	22. PURPLE SAGE
10. GREASEWOOD	23. SAGEBRUSH
11. GUM	24. SUNFLOWER
12. HICKORY	25. WALNUT
13. INDIAN PAINTBRUSH	26. YUCCA

Utah

Utah Question Game page 144
1. "Utah, We Love Thee"; 2. Butch Cassidy; 3. Brigham Young; 4. Great Salt Lake; 5. Provo, Utah; 6. Joseph Smith; 7. beehive; 8. Dinosaur National Monument; 9. coal; 10. Deseret

Challenge Question 1 page 144
Promontory, Utah

Just for Fun page 144
A bee with a cold

Fun in Utah page 145
1. BIKING, 2. BOATING, 3. CAMPING, 4. CANOEING, 5. COOKOUTS, 6. EXPLORE, 7. HIKING, 8. JOGGING, 9. KAYAKING, 10. MOUNTAIN CLIMBING, 11. PICNICS, 12. RAFTING, 13. ROWING, 14. SAILING, 15. SKIING, 16. SWIMMING, 17. TAKE PHOTOS, 18. VACATION, 19. WATCH BIRDS, 20. WATER SKI

1. NATURAL BRIDGES
2. HOVENKEEP
3. BRYCE CANYON
4. ARCHES
5. CAPITOL REEF
6. CANYONLANDS
7. LITTLE SAHARA
8. ZION
9. DINOSAUR
10. GLEN CANYON

Vermont

How Cold Was It? page 147
The Year Without a Summer—1. Hermit thrush, 2. Wyoming, 3. maple syrup, 4. honeybee

Challenge Question 1 page 147
Our country's first Boy Scout troop began in Barre, Vermont, in 1909.

Just for Fun page 147
It quacks up.

What Can You Find in Vermont? page 148
maple tree, apple, log, covered bridge, maple leaf, monarch butterfly, silo, milk carton, tractor, pair of skis, eggs

Snowbody's Business page 149

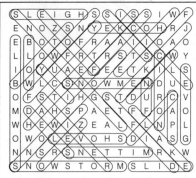

Virginia

Medical Marvel page 151
Walter Reed—1. eight, 2. William Harrison, 3. Richmond, 4. Jamestown

Challenge Question 2 page 151
Thomas Jefferson

Just for Fun page 151
Big holes in the ground

Washington

Washington Question Game page 154
1. Mount Olympus, 2. Evergreen State, 3. Ellensburg Blue, 4. Mount St. Helens, 5. Tacoma, 6. square dance, 7. Peach Arch, 8. mud slide, 9. totem poles, 10. Olympia

Challenge Question 1 page 154
Expo '74

Challenge Question 2 page 154
The exact boundary between the United States and Canada became an issue during James Polk's presidential campaign of 1844. He and his followers demanded that the British give up claim to all land south of latitude 54°40', a boundary that lies near present-day Alaska. Eventually a compromise was reached in 1846, and the 49th parallel became the boundary line between Washington and Canada.

Washington Lakes page 155

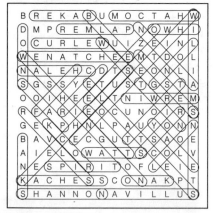

The unused letters spell the names of three other Washington lakes: Bumping, Young and Pacific.

West Virginia

The Nation's Capital in West Virginia? page 157
Shepherdstown—1. Switzerland, 2. panhandles, 3. Salt, 4. coal

Challenge Question 1 page 157
George Washington's youngest brother, Charles, founded Charles Town.

Challenge Question 2 page 157
New industries like lumbering, glassmaking, production of chemicals, sand and gravel, tourism, salt mining and the discovery of petroleum and natural gas have made West Virginia less dependent on King Coal.

Just for Fun page 157
A yardstick

Take Me Home to West Virginia page 158
1. "The West Virginia Hills," 2. Panhandle State, 3. Charleston, 4. brook trout, 5. Virginia, 6. Mountain State, 7. sugar maple, 8. blue and gold, 9. cardinal, 10. rhododendron, 11. Wheeling, 12. black bear

What Can You Find in West Virginia? page 158

AGE	RAGE	SING	VAT
AIR	RAIN	SINGER	VEST
ANT	RAT	SIRE	VET
ASTER	RATE	SIT	VIA
AVE	RATING	STAG	VIEW
AVER	RAVE	STAGE	VINE
GAIN	RAVING	STAIN	VIRGIN
GAINER	REIN	STAIR	VISA
GATE	REST	STEIN	WAG
GAVE	RESTING	STEW	WAIN
GENT	RISE	STING	WAIT
GET	RIVET	STINGER	WAITER
GIN	SAG	STIR	WAITING
GINA	SAGE	STRAIN	WAN
GIVE	SANE	STRAW	WANT
GIVEN	SANER	SWEAT	WASTE
GNAW	SANG	SWIG	WASTING
GREW	SAT	TAG	WAVE
GRIN	SATE	TAN	WAVING
IRE	SATE	TANG	WENT
NAG	SAVE	TIN	WEST
NAT	SAVER	TINA	WET
NATE	SAVING	TRIVIA	WIN
NEST	SAW	TWIN	WINE
NESTING	SENT	TWINE	WING
NET	SET	VAIN	WIRE
NEW	SEW	VAN	WIT
NEWT	SIN	VANE	WRIST
NIT	SINE	VAST	

Wisconsin

Matchmaker page 160
1. O., 2. L., 3. U., 4. T., 5. B., 6. M., 7. W., 8. P., 9. F., 10. K., 11. H., 12. G., 13. R., 14. N., 15. S., 16. E., 17. I., 18. A. and C.

Challenge Question 1 page 160
Baraboo

Challenge Question 2 page 160
Lead miners of the 1830s lived in dugouts like badgers. Like badgers, they burrowed into hillsides, looking for deposits of ore.

Just for Fun page 160
An "udder" failure

X Marks the Spot page 161
Fond du Lac

Words of Wisdom page 161
The world is your cow, but you have to do the milking.

Wyoming

Not So Inviting page 163
Hell's Half Acre—1. Hole-in-the-Wall, 2. National Elk Refuge, 3. Cheyenne, 4. glaciers

Challenge Question 1 page 163
William Frederick Cody's traveling show was called "Buffalo Bill's Wild West and Congress of Rough Riders of the World."

Challenge Question 2 page 163
The 19th Amendment passed in 1920.

Old Faithful page 164

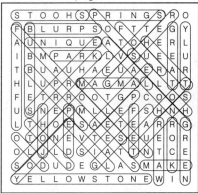

Washington, D.C.

The Nation's Attic page 166
National Air and Space Museum—1. Abigail Adams, 2. Jenkin's Hill, 3. District of Columbia, 4. Maryland, 5. Philadelphia

Challenge Question 1 page 166
The winged statue of "Freedom" was designed by sculptor Thomas Crawford.

Challenge Question 2 page 166
Washington Monument

United States

Her Real Name page 170
Liberty Enlightening the World—1. bald eagle, 2. Sears Tower, 3. Yellowstone, 4. Louisiana, 5. O'Hare

Challenge Question 1 page 170
France gave the Statue of Liberty to the American people in honor of the centennial celebration of 1876. The 150.9-foot (46m) high statue which stands in New York Harbor, was designed by Frederic Auguste Bartholdi. The statue was paid for by donations from the people of France. The people of the United States donated the money to pay for the base. The poem on the base of the statue was written by Emma Lazarus.

U.S. Tic-Tac-Toe page 171
1. Beringia, 2. "The Star-Spangled Banner," 3. 3.9 million and 248.7 million, 4. 25 cents an hour, 5. Mount McKinley and Death Valley, 6. bristlecone pines, 7. turkey, 8. $290, 9. 1800

TLC10029 Copyright © Teaching & Learning Company, Carthage, IL 62321